Financial Investigation and Financial Intelligence

This book critically analyses the conceptual understanding of financial investigation and financial intelligence among UK law enforcement authorities and their commentators. The work provides a critical review of financial investigation, including international standards, and how it is perceived and applied by law enforcement agencies. It adopts the position that financial investigation is an evidence-gathering process and not simply related to asset recovery. Here, the concept of "following the money" is superseded by the wider approach of "following the financial footprint" by generalist and specialist investigators and analysts. The book focuses on identifying the financial footprint as a skill set for routine investigation application inclusive of the emerging threat posed by the digital environment, including cryptocurrencies. It assesses the terminology, typologies and structures associated with the subject area at the national and international levels. It also examines the historical trajectory of financial investigation to understand current perceptions of it within law enforcement, among government ministers and policy makers. The book will be of interest to students, academics and policy makers internationally working in the areas of criminal law, criminology and finance.

Craig Hughes is former Head of Policing at the School of Law and Social Sciences, College of Business, Law and Social Sciences, University of Derby, UK.

David Hicks is Programme Leader MSc Financial Investigation and Digital Intelligence at the College of Business, Law and Social Sciences, University of Derby, UK.

The Law of Financial Crime

Series Editors:

Nicholas Ryder *Professor of Law, Cardiff University, School of Law and Politics, UK.*

Dr. Lachmi Singh *Associate Lecturer, Bristol Law School, University of the West of England, UK.*

Sam Bourton *Lecturer in Law, the University of the West of England, UK.*

While a growing number of high-profile financial crime cases have hit the headlines recently the topic of financial crime is also generating much attention amongst academics and practitioners. This series will be the first to be dedicated to the law of financial, or economic, crime and offers a platform for important and original research in this area.

Books in the series will cover traditional subjects of financial crime including money laundering, terrorist financing, fraud, market abuse, insider dealing, market manipulation, tax evasion, bribery and corruption. But broader legal and regulatory issues will also be covered as well as emerging areas of concern such as the risks to stability of the financial system posed by financial crime. Emphasis will be placed on comparative approaches to the subject considering legislation across a number of jurisdictions as well as international regulations where appropriate, giving the series a truly global outlook.

The titles in the series are primarily aimed at an audience of researchers, scholars and practitioners in the area but should also be of interest to policy makers, law enforcement agencies, financial regulatory agencies, as well as people employed within the financial services sector.

Available titles in this series include:

Countering Economic Crime
A Comparative Analysis
Axel Palmer

The Global Anti-Corruption Regime
The Case of Papua New Guinea
Hannah Harris

Financial Crime and Corporate Misconduct
A Critical Evaluation of Fraud Legislation
Edited by Chris Monaghan and Nicola Monaghan

For more information about this series, please visit: www.routledge.com/The-Law-of-Financial-Crime/book-series/FINCRIME

Financial Investigation and Financial Intelligence

A Critical Analysis

Craig Hughes and David Hicks

Routledge
Taylor & Francis Group
LONDON AND NEW YORK

First published 2025
by Routledge
4 Park Square, Milton Park, Abingdon, Oxon OX14 4RN

and by Routledge
605 Third Avenue, New York, NY 10158

Routledge is an imprint of the Taylor & Francis Group, an informa business

British Library Cataloguing-in-Publication Data
A catalogue record for this book is available from the British Library

Library of Congress Cataloging-in-Publication Data
Names: Hughes, Craig, author. | Hicks, David, author.
Title: Financial investigation and financial intelligence: a critical analysis / Craig Hughes and David Hicks.
Description: Abingdon, Oxon [UK]; New York, NY: Routledge, 2025. | Series: The law of financial crime | Includes bibliographical references and index. Identifiers: LCCN 2024041238 (print) | LCCN 2024041239 (ebook) | ISBN 9781032572710 (hardback) | ISBN 9781032572727 (paperback) | ISBN 9781003438649 (ebook)
Subjects: LCSH: Commercial crimes–Law and legislation--Great Britain. | Financial institutions–Law and legislation–Great Britain. | Financial institutions–Law and legislation–Great Britain–Criminal provisions. | Finance–Law and legislation–Great Britain–Criminal provisions. | Criminal law–Great Britain. | Criminology–Great Britain.
Classification: LCC KD7990 .H84 2025 (print) | LCC KD7990 (ebook) | DDC 345.41/0268--dc23/eng/20240905
LC record available at https://lccn.loc.gov/2024041238
LC ebook record available at https://lccn.loc.gov/20240412

ISBN: 978-1-032-57271-0 (hbk)
ISBN: 978-1-032-57272-7 (pbk)
ISBN: 978-1-003-43864-9 (ebk)

DOI: 10.4324/9781003438649

Typeset in Galliard
by Deanta Global Publishing Services, Chennai, India

Contents

1 **Introduction** 1

2 **Terminology and its effect upon perceptions of financial investigation** 7

Introduction 7
Terminology 9
Phraseology 9
Organised crime 10
Economic crime 15
Financial crime 17
White-collar crime (fraud) 19
Cybercrime 21

3 **Financial investigation and typologies associated with its application** 27

Financial investigation 27
Policy 28
Perceptions and research 33
Data gaps and limitations 37
Confiscation 50
Law Commission recommendations 52
Enforcement of confiscation orders 53
Drug trafficking 55
Money laundering 57
Cash detention 62
Conclusion 65

4 **Historical trajectory, government reports and financial investigation research** 68

Political hinterland to the proceeds of Crime Act 2002 68
Government reports and research concerning asset recovery and financial investigation 71
Conclusion 76

5 International standards and independent commentators 77
International standards 77
The Vienna Convention 1988 79
The Financial Action Task Force (FATF) 80
The United Nations Convention against Transnational Organised Crime 2000 83
Independent influences on UK acquisitive crime policy and strategy 84

6 Financial intelligence and the National Intelligence Model 90
What is Intelligence? 90
The National Intelligence Model 92
Suspicious activity reports (SARs) 93
Theoretical considerations: the "culture of control" 99
Conclusion 101
Proposed definition of (practical) financial investigation 103
Proposed definition of (usable) financial intelligence 103

7 Financial intelligence footprint and digital investigation and intelligence 106
The internet is a global phenomenon 106
The digital (cyber) environment 108
Policing the internet 110
Internet jurisdiction 112
Conclusion 113

8 Conclusion 115
Introduction 115
Contribution to the literature and the field of practice 116
Financial investigation (and strategy) and financial intelligence 122

References 127
Appendix 1: Table of proceeds of Crime Court Orders 157
Appendix 2: "Culture of control" (Garland, 1996, 2001) considerations 159
Index 163

1 Introduction

Financial investigation as a concept remains elusive, often perceived at all levels of law enforcement (strategic, tactical and practice) as a tool to be used in the tracing and sequestering of criminal assets (Home Office, 2007, 2011b; Levi, 2013). It is a term ubiquitous to policy makers and law enforcement, but which is not defined in law. Direct literature conceptually exploring financial investigation seems limited nationally and internationally with focus remaining primarily upon asset recovery (Bullock, 2010; HM Government, 2013) or the investigation of complex money laundering (Home Office and Her Majesty's Treasury, 2016; Madinger, 2012; Robinson, 1998). Available empirical research concerning the role financial investigation can play in the fight against crime appears to focus primarily upon serious and organised criminality (Brown et al., 2012; Wood, 2017). Accredited financial investigators (AFIs) have been the primary source of data (Brown et al., 2012; Howell, Horton and Gill, 2013). There appears to be limited research available which utilises general investigators as a data source although Gale and Kelly (2018) used 15 participants of which 3 were non-financial investigation trained. Nor does any published research appear to substantively compare the perceptions of specialist AFIs and non-specialists (general investigators and supervisors) to identify clear working practices for the widespread use of financial investigation. Characteristics which may be considered as constituting effective financial investigation appear to remain undetermined although government policy remains ardent that it is a skill set the potential of which remains only partially realised (House of Commons, 2016).

This book is written against a background of continuing calls from policy makers and the strategic layer of law enforcement for additional powers and increasingly draconian legislation for proceeds of crime and what is perceived to be financial investigation (Criminal Finances Act, 2017; Law Commission, 2018; Serious Crime Act, 2015). Focus will be upon areas within law enforcement where financial investigation is currently applied and whether perceptions of it at all levels (strategic, tactical and practice) affect its trajectory as a general technique to be utilised by all investigators and to support most investigations. The apparent juxtaposition of governmental ambition for general and integrated financial investigation and an acknowledged problem in its (and law

DOI: 10.4324/9781003438649-1

enforcement's) ability to deliver on this objective will be examined (House of Commons, 2016; Levi and Maguire, 2004). Chapters seek to review the understanding and impact of financial intelligence on investigations, how it is perceived and the level to which it integrates with the National Intelligence Model (NIM) beyond the traditional theatre of asset recovery. To conclude, new definitions of financial investigation and financial intelligence will be offered to accommodate a model of following the financial footprint together with recommendations to inform policy and practice stemming from it. This work, in part, is essentially a comparison between two groups: (1) accredited financial investigators (AFIs) who are trained as specialist investigators; and (2) the generalists who are all law enforcement personnel with access to powers within the Proceeds of Crime Act (2002) (POCA) and associated legislation. The purpose of this chapter is to introduce the reader to the subject area and the context in which the subject matter is approached, affording the opportunity to set out hypotheses concerning financial investigation, perceptions of it, the potential for its wider application and its role within intelligence.

Although it does not seem at any point to have been overtly declared within POCA, there appears to be a clear distinction by legislators between: (1) specialist confiscation powers (asset recovery) reserved for AFIs only; and (2) broad powers (money laundering, cash detention and use of investigative orders) available to all generalist law enforcement personnel as well as specialist AFIs. Notwithstanding the apparent intention within POCA for all police and customs officers to utilise broader financial investigation powers (excluding the specialism of confiscation), there appears to have been little re-organisation of resources across law enforcement to support the concept (Levi and Maguire, 2011). The calls for additional powers, particularly in relation to extended asset recovery have continued since POCA (2002) to the present, most notably perhaps in the Serious Crime Act (2015) and the Criminal Finances Act (2017) (see Appendix 1 for a list of associated legislation). The 2017 Act introduced far reaching powers to attack money invested in the United Kingdom (UK) by foreign nationals, to seize certain property from criminals including certain precious metals and jewellery and to enable more robust action to be taken regarding information supplied on suspicious activity reports (SARs). SARs are mandatorily required from financial institutions and other regulated sectors under UK money laundering regulations (Home Office, 2018b, 2018d).

Government and strategic thinking concerning financial investigation continues to recognise the mainstream potential of financial investigation (House of Commons, 2016), but asset recovery still appears to take precedence in the legislation being passed. The theme continues in publicly available governmental consultation regarding money laundering (Law Commission, 2019). It is against this national strategic outlook that the aim of this book will be to systematically examine the influence of proceeds of crime policy, terminology and legislation. Specifically, the focus will be the influence upon mainstream law enforcement, the identification of potentially effective financial investigation practice and the possibility of better integration across investigations.

The general aim of this examination is to identify, process map and critically analyse the existing nature of financial investigation across law enforcement within the UK. The specific aim of the study is to draw together the different strands (of thought, policy and action) to assess the prospects for a general and practically applicable philosophy of financial investigation. It is anticipated that by identifying the characteristics of financial investigation, the resulting model(s) may be capable of being transferable and applicable to a wide range of public and private sector investigative structures in the UK.

In seeking to explore continued governmental and strategic level ambition for general and integrated financial investigation and to investigate the partial delivery of their long-standing objective (Levi and Maguire, 2011) this book consistently examines the following themes to assist the reader in interpreting this work:

- Law enforcement officers at all levels perceive financial investigation as a specialist area of investigation which can only be applied to financial (acquisitive) criminality, primarily asset recovery; financial investigation is confused with the specialist confiscation area of proceeds of crime investigations.
- Fiinancial investigation is not an initial consideration as an investigative method and financial investigative strategy is mainly utilised to investigate asset recovery, acquisitive or serious and organised criminality.
- The term financial intelligence is not generally understood across law enforcement and is perceived as primarily relating to bank account information and asset identification.
- Law enforcement officers (including AFIs) engage with the NIM on a limited basis for financial intelligence and SARs are rarely utilised for general investigations.

There is a need for a broad-based synthesis across a diversity of parallel literature. This work seeks to develop and refine the concepts of financial investigation (and a new focus on the concept of the financial footprint) and financial intelligence. It will situate these concepts in a theoretical context and elaborate models for the integration of enhanced conceptual understanding, policy development and practice.

Conceptual clarity will be offered to the reader by developing and refining the subject area of financial investigation using a clear epistemological approach and ontological understanding. The historical trajectory of financial investigation will be explored to understand current perceptions towards it at all levels of law enforcement and among external commentators including government ministers, policy makers and academics. Consideration will be given to the theoretical context of the research within the broader pattern of the "culture of control" (Garland, 2001) and the extent to which the financial investigation skill set has been accepted into general investigation strategy. Throughout the chapters, the authors will repeatedly draw the distinction between financial investigation in its generalist sense (potential application to all investigations) and its specialist sense with respect to confiscation (asset recovery). This study will advocate the principle that the two are distinct and separate concepts and consider whether the idea of general financial investigation has been supressed by the leviathan of asset recovery. As advocated by Burrell and Morgan (1979), the methodology of this work provides a framework through which the reality of financial investigation can be understood, and the meaning of the research conveyed.

This work will include and explicitly focus on legislation, policy, regulation, literature and other secondary data. The project will focus on the UK to orient the research to a fixed reference point in which the authors have the capacity to guide the reader, but it will also include component elements involving international issues and entities. It will attempt to address the central question above as to whether a general practically applied philosophy of financial investigation, spearheaded by the concept of the financial footprint, is feasible. The authors will first undertake a comprehensive review of the English-language literature relevant to the central issue of asset recovery versus evidential application of the financial investigation skill base beyond the confiscation framework. That is, the secondary data available in academic journals and books, professional and government publications, grey literature, domestic and international legislation and case law.

Given that the literature on financial investigation as its own subject is not in abundance or its use is focused upon serious organised crime investigations (Brown et al., 2012; Wood, 2016), conjoined with the sparse availability of published primary research, the authors have elaborated a critical analysis of the existing sources for policing. This work is divided into eight chapters.

Chapter 2 focuses upon terminology used within the subject area of financial investigation. It examines the "grey" literature produced by policy makers and external to law enforcement commentators and academics. It will examine the perceptions of financial investigation from those sources, the potential link between asset recovery and/or organised crime focus at the expense of routine application and the effect upon the perceptions of routine investigators.

Beginning with an assessment of several commonly used phrases by law enforcement investigators, the public, government policy makers and research academics, it examines the extent to which they are perceived as, or associated with, financial investigation. In order to retain clarity for the reader, each of the terms is explored within its own subsection. The terms considered are organised crime, economic crime, financial crime, white collar crime (fraud) and cybercrime. The reader is offered an introductory exploration of accepted terminology within law enforcement relevant to this project which examines its effect upon the wider use of financial investigation skills separate to asset recovery. The chapter also examines whether terminological vagueness and confusing financial investigation with confiscation in the literature (alongside policy and practice) may have conspired to precipitate and perpetuate a myth of financial investigation as a specialist silo. Some consideration is given to the training available for specialists and generalists and whether it can support continuing government intentions of wider financial investigation application.

Chapter 3 explores typologies commonly associated with asset recovery and thereby financial investigation. It begins by considering the definitional problems of financial investigation and continues from the perspective of five inter-related areas of law enforcement. Those areas are confiscation and asset recovery, drug trafficking, money laundering and cash detention. The concept of financial investigation is discussed and whether it is intended as a generalised or specialised approach. Consideration is given to potential inhibitors within and between the strategic, tactical and practice levels of law enforcement and comments upon the national UK financial investigation strategy.

Chapter 4 considers financial investigation from a historical perspective on a national level. Research studies conducted regarding financial investigation and its strong connection with specialist investigators and asset recovery are explored to provide context for current policy and use. Recognition that financial investigation can offer potential beyond the role of asset recovery is explained against a backdrop of potential inhibitors which may not have been previously considered.

Chapter 5 examines international standards in the role of independent bodies and commentators within the UK and globally who aspire to affect the pathways of financial investigation. Insights are offered as to the influence of bodies outside of the UK upon domestic proceeds of crime legislation and their effect upon the trajectory of financial investigation outside the confiscation regime.

Chapter 6 examines what the term financial intelligence might mean as it appears to remain undefined. It considers the relationship between financial intelligence and the National Intelligence Model (NIM) and the understanding of the concept from the perspectives of specialists and general investigators at all levels (strategic, tactical and practice). In doing so, some insight is provided as to how suspicious activity reports (SARs) mandatorily supplied by the financial sector can be used in policing. Discussion also considers whether the UK anti-money laundering structure integrates at any level with financial intelligence or financial investigation and considers themes arising from it against the theoretical framework of the "culture of control" (Garland, 2001). At the end of the chapter the authors offer alternative definitional possibilities for financial investigation and financial intelligence.

The chapter offers insights as to why non-specialist investigators may perceive financial investigation to be the same as asset recovery (confiscation) and emerging themes are identified relevant to essential financial investigation characteristics and a wider generic philosophy among routine investigators. The seemingly disparate nature of the topics may provide some indicative insights as to the (lack of) integration of financial investigation. It may also provide insights into the areas of study and issues that are necessary to develop answers as to why the long-standing intention of policy makers has so far not translated into practice at routine level. This is one of the important areas where this book can make a significant and original contribution to the field of financial investigation and general criminal investigation.

The general goal is to analytically process map, cross-reference and validate understanding and investigative philosophies, at the same time, identifying the central issues, current trends, faults or fragmented approaches and potential good practice. The specific goal is to establish a baseline of empirical data to theorise, synthesise and elaborate answers to explain potential inhibitors to practice of wider financial investigation at strategic, tactical and practice levels across law enforcement.

Chapter 7 offers a critical discussion on the parallels between the financial footprint and the digital footprint in supporting investigation and intelligence. Digital investigation (much like financial investigation) is typically considered as a specialist area and there appears to be a lack of recognition of its potential across generalist as well as specialist investigation and intelligence. This chapter will argue for more co-operation and mutual support between digital and financial investigation and intelligence.

The conclusion in Chapter 8 will address key thematic issues and findings that are hypothesised throughout the book while the authors were undertaking the task of writing it, as well as any potential recommendations for future practice or research. It is anticipated that these empirically grounded recommendations should offer focused insights for improvement and good practice in the field of financial investigation. It is intended that the generic model will thereby offer a substantive and original contribution to the literature and the field by establishing the key tenets and principles of an effective philosophy of financial investigation.

Overall, this book offers a genuinely new and comprehensive approach to financial investigation and intelligence and how they can be practically applied in any type of investigation or enquiry at routine as well as specialist levels. This is achieved by extensive critical analysis of the conceptual understanding of financial investigation and intelligence within UK law enforcement at strategic, mid management and practice levels.

2 Terminology and its effect upon perceptions of financial investigation

Introduction

In this chapter, the authors critically examine the concept of financial investigation within the general arena of criminal and some civil investigation. The phrase is widely used throughout UK law enforcement and government at all levels (Cabinet Office, 2000; College of Policing, 2018, 2018a; House of Commons, 2016). It is also widely used throughout global law enforcement, governments at all levels and by international bodies (European Commission, 2018; Financial Action Task Force, 2012). Other phrases seem similarly used. The concepts of organised crime, economic crime, financial crime, white-collar crime, drug trafficking and money laundering often appear utilised in a wide term without clear and transferable identification of their meaning (Gold and Levi, 1994; Lilley, 2003). A more recent phrase, cybercrime, seems to have become the latest addition to policy and strategic vernacular (HM Government, 2013, 2016; Home Office, 2018; National Crime Agency, 2016). Financial investigation seems to have become associated with all seven of the above concepts as a specialist aspect of investigation (Cabinet Office, 2000; Van Duyne and Levi, 1999; Wood, 2017). Successive UK Parliaments have continued to pass legislation based upon a clear conviction that they understand the term and how it synchronises within overarching investigation frameworks such as the Proceeds of Crime Act 2002, the Serious Crime Act 2007, the Serious Crime Act 2015 and the Criminal Finances Act 2017.

The concept of financial investigation appears to possess a simplicity that may render it easily misunderstood in generalist usage and amongst a broad range of specialists. It is a topic seldom subject to critical scrutiny either from within the law enforcement community or government and rarely from the outside or external observers (Bullock, 2010). Financial investigation is typically presented as a specialised silo in the form of asset recovery according to Her Majesty's Inspectorate of Constabulary (HMIC et al., 2004).

The authors would advance the argument that the seemingly universal assumption of the conceptual simplicity of financial investigation, combined with the confidence of commentators on their apparent understanding of the

DOI: 10.4324/9781003438649-2

phrase, may be at the root of both the lack of critical scrutiny and the silo effect.

Financial investigation is a contested concept, remaining undefined in British law and, as such, it is subject to varying interpretations and applications by commentators, law enforcement and policy makers (House of Commons, 2016; Wood, 2017). Such variations in interpretation may be one of the reasons that financial investigation techniques are not widely used by generalists within law enforcement. Howell, Horton and Gill (2013: 4) observed that: "Despite the Government aspiration to mainstream the use of financial investigation, it appears to remain an underutilised tool". Brown et al. (2012) concluded that although financial investigation is now utilised more frequently in organised crime group inquiries (regarded as a specialist theatre of operation) it is still rarely utilised as a proactive tool in the first instance, to identify organised criminality and launch investigations.

Literature examining asset recovery and proceeds of crime legislation within the UK seems readily available, both in the form of government reports such as Her Majesty's (HM) Crown Prosecution Service Inspectorate (HMCPSI et al., 2010) and research by independent commentators such as the National Audit Office (NAO, 2013, 2016). Although mentioned in the literature, financial investigation does not appear to have been considered as a central theme. Where it has been considered in more detail, it appears to be dependent on the depth of study into specific criminal typologies such as money laundering or organised crime (Brown et al., 2012; Howell, Horton and Gill, 2013; van Duyne et al., 2003).

Historically, it seems there has been a disproportionate volume of research that focuses upon the laws, policies and particular issues within the United States, and little attention towards the international domain let alone the needs and issues of jurisdictions beyond America (Madinger, 2012; Reuter and Truman, 2004; Robinson, 1998). The literature that delves substantively into the UK – though always with significant reference to the United States – focuses explicitly on legislative and policy issues relating to money laundering, drug trafficking and asset recovery rather than financial investigation as the central topic (Gold and Levi, 1994; Hicks, 2010; Hicks and Graycar, 2019; Levi and Reuter, 2006).

If financial investigation is capable of being examined as a central theme, consideration should also be given to financial intelligence, and whether it integrates with the National Intelligence Model (NIM). Since 2000, the NIM has become the standard intelligence framework utilised by UK law enforcement (Association of Chief Police Officers, 2005; College of Policing, 2018; Richards, 2010). Having been productively applied to a wide range of enforcement and intelligence issues (Kirby and McPherson, 2004; Smith, 2009), it has been internationally recognised for its potential and utility to assimilate, sanitise and dispense information and provide for organisational efficiencies (Ratcliffe, 2009). The NIM is discussed in more detail below, examining its current level of integration with financial intelligence.

Terminology

There appears to be a minimal concentration of direct literature which examines financial investigation as a central topic. The Financial Action Task Force (FATF, 2012) and others (HM Government, 2013; Levi et al., 2015; Wood, 2016) commonly refer to financial investigation while focusing upon broader areas of criminality which are assigned labels such as organised crime, economic crime, financial crime, white collar crime (fraud) and so-called cybercrime (the emerging threat from the digital environment of the internet). An examination of these more commonly used phrases will be discussed with the objective of attempting to assess the current integration of financial investigation from a policy aspect and across all levels of law enforcement (strategic, tactical and practice).

References to financial investigation can also be found in literature concerning criminality such as money laundering (Madinger, 2012; Platt, 2015), drug trafficking (Levi, 2013; Lilley, 2003) and the confiscation regime (Cabinet Office, 2000; Council of Europe, 2014; HMIC et al., 2004), the process by way of which assets are sequestered by law enforcement using proceeds of crime legislation (Bullock, 2010; House of Commons, 2016). Such typologies involve a degree of benefit or acquisition for or by an offender, usually described in the vernacular as acquisitive crime (the offender gains a material benefit) (Crown Prosecution Service, 2018).

The phrases, financial investigation, asset recovery and the crime typologies of money laundering and drug trafficking will be considered in greater detail. Close association of financial investigation with asset recovery (Levi et al., 2015) will be explored and whether terminology has affected the integration of financial investigation as a wider law enforcement skill set.

The authors acknowledge that each of the areas discussed within this review are themselves subject to continuing academic and political debate. It is not the intention (nor is there enough room within this book) to engage in the minutiae of each topic area. Discussion will necessarily be confined to presenting a synopsis of each subject followed by an assessment of its potential influence (positive or otherwise) upon financial investigation in the UK.

Phraseology

Misleading terminology may be an endemic problem across government, strategic, tactical and practice levels, the legal profession and some commentators (Hodgson, 1984; Naylor, 2003; Ryder, 2013). Terminology can influence how individuals and groups perceive a particular issue (Levi et al., 2015) and some (if not all) of the terms considered herein, may have had impact upon financial investigation.

It is difficult to dislodge misleading terminology once it has entered routine use (Gold and Levi, 1994). This appears to be an unfortunate truism. Generic phrases seem ubiquitous, for example, financial crime, acquisitive crime, organised crime, profit driven crime, white collar crime, cybercrime, economic crime, corporate crime, business crime, dark economy, money laundering, terrorist financing and, of course, financial investigation (Croall, 2001; HM Government, 2013, 2016). It is important to remember that these terms are now part of a global vocabulary, not simply confined to any one nation, just as the criminality and typologies they attempt to describe may often be international and complex (Levi and Reuter, 2006; Wright, 2013). They are phrases used to describe similar problems in different countries, legal systems and law enforcement and their definitions vary within and across jurisdictions (Council of Europe, 2014; United Nations, 2004). The problem of broad terminology is that much more exacerbated and that much more difficult to positively address. The subsections below will concentrate on the effect such phraseology may have on the current use and perception of financial investigation within the UK.

Organised crime

What is organised crime? The term is problematic. Schelling (1984) asserted that organised crime is not simply crime that is organised. A definition is still elusive (Von Lampe, 2012). On the one hand, policy makers and investigators seek a consensus upon which operations can be based and risks identified and managed (HM Government, 2013; United States White House, 2011). On the other hand, definitions are sought by criminologists to provide a deeper conceptual basis for their analysis (Edwards and Gill, 2004; van Duyne and Van Dijck, 2007; Wright, 2013). Wright (2013: 2) observes that, "Unfortunately, the official documentation and the critical literature set out almost as many definitions as there are people with an interest in the subject".

The problem of definition is exacerbated when policy makers consider it in its international dimension, often described as transnational organised crime (Allum and Gilmour, 2012). The effects of national and international political policies upon organised crime does not appear to have been assessed. It may not be possible to do so, although an argument has been made that global politics has shaped the imagination of the public on the issue (Fernandez-Steinko, 2008; Pascual, 2017; Woodiwiss and Hobbs, 2008). In addition to political policies, media coverage and television features may also be responsible for shaping popular public perception regarding the concept of organised crime (Chamblis and Williams, 2011; Naylor, 2004; Woodiwiss, 2003). Contestation of the phrase organised crime seems set to continue. Although outside of the scope of this book, further reading can be found in van Duyne and Nelemans (2012) and Finckenauer (2005).

A good example of how broad terminology can be used is HM Government (2013: 7) which describes organised crime as including, "drug trafficking, human trafficking and organised illegal immigration, high value fraud and other financial crimes, counterfeiting, organised acquisitive crime and cyber-crime". The strategy, in the same paragraph, also deals with serious crime which demands a national coordinated response, notably, other fraud and child exploitation. The single paragraph uses no less than 12 general descriptions of criminality. There appears to be an inherent assumption within the document that the reader is familiar with the terminology used and, at the same time, fully understands the various meanings. The document does go on to offer some explanation of what is meant under each of the headings, particularly relevant statistics in each of the areas mentioned and provides references for further reading about organised crime. Government commitment to an array of serious crimes is explained at some length but the continued use of general epithets such as those quoted in this paragraph demonstrates a salient point for this review. Generalised terminology can be misleading in its use in strategic documents in order to make political points that may disguise problems in defining what is being described. A good example is the term cybercrime often used to describe criminality using the internet, such as cyber fraud and ransomware attacks (where criminals take control of computer systems remotely and a fee has to be paid by the user to unlock them). Government and media use of such terms may lead the public to perceive that offences are being described when it is not clear that they exist as mutually exclusive categories. It may be argued that ransomware is simply blackmail using electronic means and cyber fraud is simply fraud committed using the internet as a means to an end.

The document acknowledges that the main aim of much of organised crime is to make money but is candid in admitting, "it is difficult to assess the scale of the money laundered in and through this country" (HM Government, 2013: 19). It was originally estimated by government sources to be more than £100 billion per year (House of Commons, 2016), a figure which does not seem to have altered in the last 8 years. Conflicting slightly with the government figures, another source suggests that up to £90 billion GBP is laundered annually through the UK, its calculation based upon the International Monetary Fund's (IMF) estimate (Quirk, 1997) that money laundering globally represents between 2% and 5% of global domestic product (NCA, 2016a). Having identified the moneymaking aspect of criminality, financial investigation may well therefore be expected to be a primary focus of government attention. Although POCA is mentioned in the document, the focus seems to be more about POCA facing, "sustained legal challenge from criminals who are constantly seeking new ways to avoid its reach and frustrate asset recovery" (HM Government, 2013: 34). Asset recovery and the government intentions to amend POCA powers (see Appendix 2) remain the central issues and little mention appears to be made of the strategic and tactical uses of proceeds of crime legislation in uncovering evidence to underpin criminal prosecutions.

Not only are there definitional problems with the concept of organised crime. The extent of its political and social influence (cost) are difficult to establish (Berdal and Serrano, 2002; Levi et al., 2013). A Home Office study (Mills, Skodbo and Blyth, 2013) estimated that the cost of UK organised crime, social and economic, was at least £24 billion. A recent estimate by the NCA (2019d) is £37 billion. The United Nations Office for Drugs and Crime

(UNODC, 2011) previously estimated that globally organised groups had a turnover of $870 billion. The Federal Bureau of Investigation (FBI) maintains that global organised crime reaps over $1 trillion USD per year (FBI, 2015). Most sources accept that these are conservative estimates, and the reader should bear in mind that these figures only pertain to organised criminal groups (NCA, 2014a, 2016a, 2019d; Royal United Services Institute, 2019). Inclusion of other acquisitive criminality would result in a much greater global total.

There is currently no single international and standard definition of organised crime and Interpol accepts that definitions of what constitutes organised crime vary widely from country to country (Interpol, 2015). The United Nations (UN) maintains that the international omission of a definition for organised crime was intentionally decided upon at what became known as the Palermo Convention. The Convention agreed: "This lack of definition was intended to allow for a broader applicability of the (Transnational) Organized Crime Convention (2000) to new types of crime that emerge constantly as global, regional and local conditions change over time" (United Nations Office on Drugs and Crime, 2018).

The UK government acknowledges there is no legal definition but clearly states its understanding of it: "For the purposes of this strategy, organised crime is serious crime planned, co-ordinated and conducted by people working together on a continuing basis. Their motivation is often, but not always, financial gain" (HM Government, 2013: 14). The same definition is promulgated by the National Crime Agency as the leading law enforcement agency tasked with implementing the government's Serious and Organised Strategy (NCA, 2014, 2017b, 2017c).

In the United States, the Federal Bureau of Investigation (FBI, 2015: 1) defines organised crime as any group, having some manner of a formalised structure and whose primary objective is to obtain money through illegal activities. The common factor is that within both definitions, the primary motivation for it is identified as financial gain (money).

The FBI definition is very specific regarding Organised Crime Group (OCG) motivation (to obtain money) and does not appear to take into consideration those organised groups whereby the gain to offenders is within their own environment using what might be termed their own social currency. An example would be a group of paedophiles (national or international) whereby gain is sexual gratification rather than monetary remuneration (Europol, 2014), a point acknowledged by the NCA (2016a, 2017b, 2019d). The difference in definitional scope may reflect that US law enforcement indicts offenders from a prescribed list of offence types under the Racketeer Influenced and Corrupt Organisations Act 1970 (RICO) (Morris, 1982). RICO was enacted as part of President Nixon's war on organised crime (Levi and Reuter, 2006; Woodiwiss, 2001). It incorporated 24 types of federal crimes and 8 types of state felonies (Atkinson, 1978). Committing any two of the prescribed offence types could lead to a charge of racketeering (continued [organised] criminal activity) (Mecone et al., 2006). The RICO legislation is acknowledged as providing US law enforcement with broad and unprecedented powers, in particular the authorisation of asset forfeiture as a criminal penalty (Atkinson, 1978; Goldsmith and Linderman, 1989; Malani, 1999; Woodiwiss and Hobbs, 2008).

RICO powers were consolidated and enhanced by the introduction of the first money laundering legislation (Money Laundering Control Act, 1986), by the US Congress, "responding to the spiralling growth and pervasiveness of money laundering in the United States and the nexus between money laundering and organised crime" (Gurule, 1995: 824). In doing so, the United States became the first country to legislate against the profits of (organised) crime (Ngai, 2012). In part a component of the US Government's reaction against a well-publicised drug trafficking problem (Levi and Reuter, 2006; Lilley, 2003), federal offences criminalising money laundering of proceeds from "specified unlawful activity" were introduced (MCLA, 1986: 18; USC 1956, 1957). "Specified unlawful activity" related to the predicate offences (criminality underlying the charges from which the money laundering originated) indicted against an offender (Madinger, 2012). These could be any one of an extensive variety of offences defined by US statute.

The extent of American influence as the well-spring of legislation against organised crime and the shaping of it as an international problem is difficult to quantify, though it is alluded to by commentators (Levi and Reuter, 2006; Robinson, 1998). It is perhaps confounded by the task of separating populist fictional images of organised crime (Al Capone, the Mafia) from real criminality (Albanese, 2010; Fijnaut and Paoli, 2004). De-mythologising organised crime presents a difficult prospect. There appear to be two singular dangers, the extent to which international policy responses may have been affected and whether political (strategic) conceptualisation of the problem has been undermined in some way (Rawlinson, 2016; Shore, 2015).

The UK government makes a distinction between OCGs and urban street gangs, citing differences in levels of criminality, organisation, planning and control (HM Government, 2013: 14). Whether the distinction is a necessary one in practical terms or is due to anticipated resourcing issues is not made clear in their strategy. Recent UK legislation offers a legal definition of an OCG (but not organised crime) whereby an OCG is one that: "has as its purpose, or as one of its purposes, the carrying on of criminal activities" (Serious Crime Act, 2015: s45:6). It must have at least three people involved in the criminal activity (Jarvis and Earis, 2015).

The current legislated UK definition of an OCG seems based upon a definition proposed during the Palermo Convention in 2000 which was fully entered into force internationally by 117 of its signatory states on 29th September 2003 (UNODC, 2018). Article 2 (a) of that Convention reads, "Organised criminal group shall mean a structured group of three or more persons, existing for a period of time and acting in concert with the aim of committing one or more serious crimes or offences established in accordance with this convention, in order to obtain, directly or indirectly, a financial or other material benefit" (UNODOC, 2004a: 5). The Convention also criminalised the laundering of the proceeds of crime, considered an essential ingredient to any OCG longevity.

Since the ratification of the Palermo Convention Protocols, organised crime in the UK seems to be perceived at all levels (strategic, tactical and practice) as a specialist area of law enforcement activity (Brown et al., 2012; Home Office, 2011; NCA, 2017b, 2019d). Investigation of organised crime is viewed by many general law enforcement practitioners (and some AFIs) (Howell, Horton and Gill, 2013; Davidson, Walker and Dayman, 2014) as a specialist function. Such a viewpoint may be compounded by UK law enforcement agencies establishing dedicated localised OCG units (HMIC, 2016a, 2017, 2017a). High profile regional investigation units have also been formed to focus upon tackling organised crime (HMIC, 2015; East Midlands Police Collaboration, 2016). There are presently nine Regional Organised Crime Units (ROCUs) within the UK, each one drawing from several law enforcement agencies in addition to police forces. These units may further serve to reinforce the general perception of OCG work as a specialist area.

Financial investigation has become increasingly linked at strategic, tactical and practice levels to OCG investigations as a specialist feature, emphasis frequently upon the tracing and seizure of criminal assets (Home Office, 2004; HM Government, 2013). Literature examining organised criminality often refers to the financial elements of OCG networks including the complexities of money laundering trails and asset tracing faced by AFIs (Madinger, 2012; NCA, 2017b, 2019d; Platt, 2015; Robinson, 1998). From the perspective of financial investigation, already regarded as a specialist area by the Association of Chief Police Officers (ACPO, 2006) and the Cabinet Office (2000), its isolation from general investigation may be reinforced. International agreements and increased political rhetoric (BBC, 2013; Mason and Travis, 2013) and some academics all emphasise attacking the financial networks of OCGs (Golobinek, 2006; Levi, 2013). Embedding financial investigation within the perceived complexities of OCG investigation may contribute to the implicit or explicit assumptions of general investigators that it is a specialist tool. As observed by van Duyne et al. (2003: 92) financial investigation at its basic level needs to be integrated in the behavioural routine of generalist investigators, "as an integral part of information gathering". The question is to what degree the link between organised crime investigation and financial investigation may have affected the trajectory of the latter as a general law enforcement skill set.

A process known as Organised Crime Group Mapping has been previously applied to estimate that there were 5,500 active OCGs in the UK comprising some 37,000 individuals (NCA, 2014a). By 2015, the number of active OCGs had increased to over 6,000 (NCA, 2016a). As a result, OCG investigation has become the one area of law enforcement (other than confiscation) in which financial investigation is now used on a frequent basis and across most aspects of OCG cases (Brown et al., 2012). Financial investigation techniques were recognised as contributing to investigations in several key areas:

- Identifying organised criminality in the first instance.
- Identifying the extent of an organised crime group.
- Locating assets owned or used by organised crime group members.
- Identifying ownership and use of properties.
- Uncovering evidence of the lifestyle led by those targeted.
- Tracking the movements of individuals.
- Placing people at particular times, thereby linking them to criminality or particular criminal groups.
- Identifying additional offences and offenders (Brown et al., 2012: iii).

Extrapolating the first two points from the list, the other areas in which financial investigation was deemed to offer a positive contribution to OCG investigations seem just as relevant to all investigations as well as jurisdictions outside the UK (Hughes and Brown, 2022).

The problem is that OCG investigation appears to be perceived as a specialised area of law enforcement and necessarily secretive (covert) in nature (Kirby, Northey and Snow, 2015). Embedding financial investigation within the complex area of OCG investigation may contribute to implicit or explicit assumptions at all levels that financial investigation is a specialist area rather than an inclusive investigative tool.

Economic crime

Economic crime is a phrase embedded in governmental and law enforcement vocabulary (HM Government, 2018; Institute of Chartered Secretaries and Administrators, 2018; NCA, 2017, 2019c). It is a term often used in literature and it is at times synonymous with commercial crime or at other times with white-collar crime (fraud):

> Economic crime is one of the worst examples. The frequency with which it is used contrasts starkly with the infrequency with which it is defined... There are even on occasion, efforts to assimilate the term 'organised crime' (notoriously resistant to definition) with 'economic crime' on the apparent assumption that it requires an exceptional degree of organisation to commit complex business-related offences. Even the alternative term, 'business crime' is of little help – for it leaves unstated whether the problem is crimes against business, crimes by business or simply crime using business structures.
>
> (Naylor, 2003: 82)

Traditional economic crime according to Jeremie (2015: 230), "includes well-recognised forms of criminal conduct such as money laundering, the financing of terrorism, tax evasion and the facilitation by banks and financial actors of tax evasion and of course other well-recognised forms of corporate misconduct involving insider trading and self-dealing". It may be debatable (although outside the parameters of this project), as to whether financing terrorism, tax evasion or money laundering can any longer be described as economic crime (HM Treasury, 2007; Milosevic, 2016; Parliament UK, 2018; Ryder, 2018).

Prior to 2003 in the UK, the offence of money laundering could only be indicted to accompany a predicate offence. Predicate offence means an offence producing proceeds which may be subsequently laundered such as theft or drug trafficking (*Montila* [2004] UKHL 50; [2005] 1 Cr. App. R. 26; UNODOC, 2004). If an offender indicted for drug trafficking was not convicted, the money laundering charge could not stand. Legislation which passed into use in 2003 (Proceeds of Crime Act, 2002) introduced new money laundering offences which could be utilised as standalone indictments (Bell, 2002). Money laundering no longer required a predicate offence to which it had to be associated to be used.

Whether tax evasion should be construed as economic crime is also the subject of continuing debate. Tax evasion is usually described as the illegal practice of not paying taxes, a fraud against government fiscal protection (the tax system) (Cowell, 1990; McBarnet, 1992). Positive action of some sort is taken by the perpetrator not to pay tax, perhaps not reporting income or inflating expense claims (Kirchler, Maciejovsky and Schneider, 2003). Evasion of taxes is often confused with tax avoidance, the latter activity is not illegal, in effect the minimising of tax liability by utilising the existing tax framework (Gunn, 1978; Kirchler, Maciejovsky and Schneider, 2003). Public perception of tax evasion and tax avoidance perhaps makes little distinction between them (Christians, 2017), both seen as part of the shadow economy that defrauds the government and the public purse (Cowell, 1990; Schneider and Enste, 2013).

Powers to prosecute tax offences rest mainly with His Majesty's Revenue and Customs (HMRC), criminal tax investigations being conducted by the Criminal Taxes Unit. Prosecutions for income tax evasion are not widespread and a preferred method of negotiated settlements with transgressors is regarded as confidential tax matters (Minkes, 2017). Perceptions of tax offending linked to financial investigation across general law enforcement are therefore difficult to appraise.

Since the 1990s, UK AFIs have been generally ensconced within specialist financial investigation units (FIUs) (van Duyne and Levi, 1999), usually forming part of economic crime units (ECUs) (Cabinet Office, 2000). The Scottish government (2009) reached similar conclusions that FIUs were situated away from general investigators. That position seemed to reflect the peripheral position of financial investigation and POCA in general terms throughout UK law enforcement (Levi, 2013). This section reveals that general law enforcement practitioners may have had limited access to AFIs. Access issues may have resulted in inconsistencies and a lack of broader impact against criminality. As Levi (2013: 1) has observed: "Financial investigators – whether police, civilian or trained accountants – need to be embedded with operational and intelligence units, so that they are brought in early enough to help the investigation as well as to take away proceeds of crime".

Economic crime seems as open to interpretation as any other terminology discussed within this chapter. Internationally, the UN has previously recognised that economic crime is difficult to define, and rapidly advancing technology only serves to make its conceptualisation that much more complicated and challenging. Within the private sector, economic crime is described as, "becoming a more complex issue for organisations and economies" and local law enforcement is, "not necessarily perceived as able to make a material difference" (Price Waterhouse Cooper, 2016: 13). In terms of UK law enforcement, the Economic Crime Command of the NCA (2017: 1) suggests that, "Economic crime poses a major and growing, threat to the wellbeing of the UK and its people". It describes economic crime as including a range of crimes such as money laundering, international corruption, fraud and counterfeit currency. The subject area is complicated further by labelling certain internet enabled frauds, economic cybercrime, cyber-dependent economic crimes and cyber-enabled economic crimes (Fafinski, 2011; Gordon and Ford, 2006). A singular problem is that almost none of the terms used to describe economic crime is defined by legislation (excepting money laundering). Whether terminology evolves or is created to describe a particular aspect of offending or research (Gibson, 1984; Sutherland, 1940) it is often accepted into popular vernacular by various and common means such as government speeches, the press and television reporting, (Greer, 2007; International Monetary Fund, 2001; Kirby, Northey and Snow, 2015; Zavrsnik, 2014).

Financial investigation units seem largely ensconced in specialist ECUs (City of London Police, 2018b; Leicestershire Police, 2018; Nottinghamshire Police, 2018; Thames Valley Police, 2018). The extent to which placing financial investigation units away from general investigators (and use of the associated terminology, specialist, financial crime and economic crime) may have affected the perception of financial investigation at all levels (strategic, tactical and practice) is unmeasured. As acknowledged by Wood (2017), there has so far been little research into the area of financial investigation. The research that has been conducted has concerned itself with the viewpoint of AFIs or concentrated on how financial investigation can be useful in attacking serious and organised crime (Brown et al., 2012; Howell, Horton and Gill, 2013; Wood, 2017). There appears to be a gap in the literature concerning the views and experiences of general investigators. How financial investigation is perceived by them and the level at which it is used or not is something which may be one of the inhibitors to more general application of the skill set at routine levels.

Financial crime

The term financial crime is different to the others discussed within this section of the literature review in as much as it has been ascribed a definition by the UK Parliament:

"any offence involving

(a) fraud or dishonesty or
(b) misconduct in, or misuse of information relating to a financial market or
(c) handling the proceeds of crime (Financial Services and Markets Act, 2000: (section 6 (3) a) (FSMA)".

The FSMA also created the Financial Services Authority (FSA) which, since 2012, was succeeded by the Financial Conduct Authority (FCA) with respect to issues relevant to this thesis. The specific remit of the FSMA was to protect the financial and regulatory systems of the UK. Police and other law enforcement agencies do not prosecute offences defined under the FSMA.

The definition was amended in 2012 (FSMA, 2012 section 1H: 3) to include the financing of terrorism but still retains its all-inclusive breadth, particularly in its parts (a) and (c). Almost all acquisitive offences (where an offender derives benefit from crimes committed) could therefore be construed as financial crime. Additionally, the Fraud Act (2006) provides for seemingly limitless criminalisation of all dishonest conduct irrespective of victim losses or offender gains (Tolkovsky, 2018). Thus, all dishonest conduct could be viewed as financial crime inclusive of attempted offences. In that regard, the definition is perhaps unhelpful in debating the constituent parts of financial crime but the phrase (if not the definition itself) has become synonymous in the minds of the majority of law enforcement practitioners with financial investigation and fraud (Howell, Horton and Gill, 2013). It perhaps seems remarkable that although the FSMA and its amendments were (and still are) intended to combat financial sector criminality, the FCA only accessed POCA powers in 2009 under secondary legislation in the form of Statutory Instrument (SI 975/2009). A nine-year delay is apparent between the definition of financial crime relating to markets and the capability of the FCA to apply POCA powers.

Notwithstanding the UK definition, each law enforcement agency (nationally and internationally) appears to interpret financial crime in a different manner (perhaps according to its own objectives and budget limitations). The FCA (2016) now classifies financial crime into the five areas of bribery and corruption, data security, fraud, financial sanctions and money laundering. Interpol (2017) maintains that financial crime includes a wide range of criminal offences which are often closely connected to cybercrime. Its main initiatives to combat financial crime focus upon payment cards, money laundering, counterfeit currency and social engineering fraud (Interpol, 2017). The FBI (2017: 1) historically concentrates, "its financial crimes investigations on such criminal activities as corporate fraud, securities and commodities fraud, health care fraud, financial institution fraud, mortgage fraud, insurance fraud, mass marketing fraud, and money laundering". Other commentators focus on more complex criminality such as fund management abuse, insider share dealing and letters of credit (Platt, 2015). Rider (2009) divides financial crime into two different but related areas of conduct, the criminality which dishonestly and unfairly generates wealth and the criminality which facilitates the placing of such dishonestly gained wealth beyond the reach of the law (money laundering).

The legal definition of financial crime serves as a catch all for criminality affecting the UK financial system notwithstanding that each part of it is represented in other Acts of Parliament where specific offences such as fraud and money laundering are separately defined. The expectation of general investigators appears to be that financial crime is something which belongs within ECUs where financial investigation specialists are already ensconced and who will be able to deal with (perceived) specialist investigations (Davidson, Walker and Dayman, 2014; Howell, Horton and Gill, 2013). The general expectation appears to be that AFIs can be deployed from ECUs to assist other types of (complex) investigations when expertise is required (Brown et al., 2012).

White-collar crime (fraud)

White-collar crime also remains the subject of definitional debate. The original attempt to define the nature of it was by the American criminologist Sutherland (1940) as a crime committed by a person of respectability and high social status in the course of his occupation (Croall, 2001). The FBI website (2024) still alludes to the historic definition and states: "The term—reportedly coined in 1939—is now synonymous with the full range of frauds committed by business and government professionals".

The question is whether the perceived occupational nature of the criminal activities undertaken, or the social characteristics of the offenders should be the major defining features (Croall, 2001). White-collar crime continues to be the subject of academic discussion and it remains problematic. It was argued in the 1970s that the term should include all crimes committed in the course of occupations and be labelled accordingly (Quinney, 1964). A later approach suggested it should be based upon occupational abuses of trust (Shapiro, 1990). Abuse of trust is a criminal offence as defined in the Fraud Act (2006). White-collar crime has become interchangeable to some extent with corporate crime (Gottschalk and Rundmo, 2014) creating complex sub-arguments regarding the mind of the company (Croall, 1989). Two lines of argument have been marked between those who see the corporation as unable to commit crimes separately from those of its executives and those who identify a distinct and corporate *men's rea* (Mokhiber, 1988; O'Nwafor, 2013; Suleh-Yusuf, 2017).

The varying descriptions of fraud may well be necessary in academic attempts to understand the subject matter and to posit theories (Naylor, 2003). Whether the continued attempts at defining fraud in all its forms has any effect upon the clarity of national policy seems unmeasured. The dichotomy appears to be that academic and political environments continue to subdivide areas of criminality such as fraud whereas law enforcement agencies are observed to adopt a discrete approach to crime types (Nevitt, 2013; Tett, 2016). Skill bases seem to receive umbrella titles for them to be assimilated into policing structures and working vernacular (Sutherland, 1940; Croall, 1989). Recognising the suggested terminological dichotomy (and its possible effects) may be a fundamental point when attempting to theorise an answer to why financial investigation remains unembedded into routine investigative practice.

In the ever-expanding technological society of the 21st century, what were rightly or wrongly regarded as once clearly defined lines seem to have become blurred. White-collar crime can be described as economic or financial crime, commercial crime or business crime, computer crime (the emerging cybercrime) or serious fraud (Naylor, 2003). How so-called white-collar crime should be described in the modern technological world of business, social networking and cyberspace is not within the scope of this project. The problem seems to be acknowledged at government level, recognition that technology is utilised by criminals in different ways to commit fraud (Ministry of Housing, Communities and Local Government, 2016; National Fraud Authority, 2011). However, the investigation of such issues remains the same as, largely, do the offences charged when offenders are prosecuted. In terms of investigation, whether it be white-collar crime, corporate crime or economic crime, the criminal justice system will tend to address such issues under the umbrella of the Fraud Act (2006). Despite the seemingly expansive potential application of the dishonest conduct offences in that Act, there appears to be persistent traditional perceptions among specialists and laypersons as to what is criminal fraud versus what is a civil matter or not addressed at all (Tolkovsky, 2018). Notwithstanding the continuing academic debate concerning terminology, white collar fraud and corporate fraud are terms which (like cybercrime) cannot be charged as offences. The emergence of counter-fraud specialists and attempts to provide baseline training in that regard (Button et al, 2007) seem intrinsically linked to financial investigation. It remains to be seen whether fraud and financial investigation are sufficiently integrated to foster good practice and impact.

Police Fraud Squads (sitting within ECUs) typically deal with fraud offences. Largely ignored until the past few years, criminality involving digital communication is becoming part of an emerging cybercrime remit. It seems that AFIs are not currently integrated into the cybercrime arena and the two spheres work largely independently of each other (siloed) (Levi et al., 2015). By building so-called "Chinese walls" or sterile corridors between specialist practices, intelligence flow and dissemination may suffer as a result (Richards, 2010). Similarly, fraud investigators are not AFIs and though there is some overlap in basic tools and techniques used (such as credit searches and bank checks), they are traditionally two very distinct areas of practice. To demonstrate this point, the readers' attention is drawn to the City of London Police (2018) fraud courses where delegates learn the early phases of a criminal investigation, learn how to develop strategy when dealing with fraud enquiries as well as topics covering the Bribery Act (2010), cyber-enabled fraud, media strategies and international enquiries. The syllabus mentions financial investigation on one occasion and only in connection with cybercrime. Financial investigation seems to be isolated from areas of shared interest, and AFIs often appear isolated in law enforcement financial investigation units (FIUs) in which also sits a money laundering team.

A basic finding in Brown et al. (2012: 16) echoes this observation, concluding that "there may be a benefit in closer working between asset recovery enforcement teams and wider investigation teams, and that in some cases co-location might be appropriate". No suggestions were made as to how the components of financial investigation could be properly integrated into those wider investigations or at what levels. This appears to be a key evidence gap in the literature and strategic thinking.

Cybercrime

This section should not conclude without briefly examining the so-called emerging threat of cybercrime (Cabinet Office, 2011) and how (if at all) it is perceived by government, law enforcement and commentators to integrate with financial investigation. What is perhaps significant is that the NCA has recognised that cybercrime is financially motivated (NCA, 2016b). The term cybercrime appears to have been first used in science fiction (Gibson, 1984). Cybercrime has rapidly become synonymous with cyberspace, the general term for the internet (environment). Although cybercrime is used as a descriptive term to identify internet crime at policy level (HM Government, 2010, 2016) it is arguable that not many people would be able to precisely explain the term (Gordon and Ford, 2006). Defining the term becomes, "a key analytical problem" (Fafinski, Dutton and Margetts, 2010: 4). Without context (like the other terminology discussed thus far) the term appears meaningless. A more apt description might be to refer to internet-based criminality as digital crime.

The potential criminal threat posed by the Internet was recognised at least 20 years ago (Lilley, 2003; Robinson, 1998), but the growth of the phenomenon appears to have taken global authorities by surprise (HM Government, 2013; Office for National Statistics, 2015). Cybercrime or cyber-enabled crime does not simply refer to a single distinctive type of criminal activity. It is a broad description of a diverse range of illegal and illicit activities, the majority of which are simply the migration of real-world crimes into an electronic environment (Brenner, 2001; Gordon and Ford, 2006). The common factor is cyberspace (the unique electronic environment) by way of which they take place (Yar, 2013). Brenner (2001) predicted early in the debate that cybercrimes would exponentially exceed real world crimes (Jewkes, 2007). Robinson (1998) had already postulated that cash originating from internet offending (cyber-cash) could potentially undermine not only the global banking system but also the administration of justice.

It does not yet appear possible to determine the actual scale of the alleged cybercrime problem (HM Government, 2013; NCA, 2018c; ONS, 2016). For the year ending March 2015, 6.8 million criminal incidents were recorded against households or resident adults (16 and over) (ONS, 2015). This was a 7% decrease in 2014. Police recorded crime, however, rose by 3% with 3.8 million offences being allocated a crime number according to the Office for National Statistics (ONS, 2015). The ONS website stresses the point that the Crime Survey 2015 excluded cybercrime (and fraud). An accurate estimate of the scale and cost of cybercrime may never be established and the limited evidence available suggests it is already costing the UK several billions (sterling) per year (Action Fraud, 2016; HM Government, 2011). Despite the lack of data, the UK government is investing £1.9 billion pounds in cyber security between 2016 and 2021 (HM Government, 2016). There appears to be no available data as to how many cybercrime investigations utilise proceeds of crime powers or engage with financial investigation. Instances of financial investigation leading to conviction or asset recovery for cyber offences seem uncategorised. The identified gap in available information may be a consideration relevant in any attempt to transcend silo mentalities and theorise a more holistic approach as to how financial investigation might better integrate across specialisms (as well as in the broader sense of general investigations).

The authors are interested in any current (or foreseeable) investigation relationship between cybercrime and financial investigation. This is of interest as the NCA (2016a, 2019d) identifies cybercrime, high-end money laundering, organised immigration crime and online child sexual exploitation as four of the top five threats to the UK. The current law enforcement environment appears to separate cybercrime investigators and AFIs into separate investigation units.

The latest research to attempt to identify and establish the general value of financial investigation (regarding digital offending) suggests there is little in the way of it across general law enforcement (a survey completed by 2,500 investigators whose role involved financial investigation). Perhaps surprisingly, in a list of 24 areas of criminality including money laundering, fraud, drugs and terrorism there is no mention at all of crimes committed via the internet (Howell, Horton and Gill, 2013). It would seem to suggest either that AFIs do not investigate internet enabled crimes or that the recording of internet crime (and its investigation) is in some way different from traditional police recording systems (McGuire and Dowling, 2013). There seems to be no current correlation in the literature, strategically or otherwise, between cybercrime and the value that may be added by financial investigation. From the perspective of financial investigation, the underlying mechanism of an offence seems (to some extent) irrelevant. What matters is evidence of the crime committed, the evidence of proceeds of crime and whether that evidence is detectable and usable, irrespective of any medium used to obscure it. As Hicks, Tolkovsky and Hughes (2017) maintain, "Integrated investigative strategies and tactics that focus on the proceeds of/for (cyber) crime offers investigators a powerful and flexible toolbox to achieve real-world impact on what is (currently) perceived as a virtual-world problem".

Evidence of siloed strategic thinking appears to be present in the Serious and Organised Crime Strategy (2013) under the heading, "Develop our capabilities to detect, investigate, prosecute and disrupt serious and organised crime" (HM Government, 2013: 32). The section identified that cybercrime investigations require continuous improvement in digital forensic techniques to trace criminal identities. No mention is made of integrating financial investigation techniques or following the money trail through cyberspace (or tracing criminal identities). There also seems to be an assumption (then) that all police forces had set up so-called cybercrime units to begin to combat the digital problem. It took until 2019 before all 43 UK police forces had formed a cybercrime unit and until that milestone, only 31% of police forces had created a dedicated cybercrime facility (National Police Chief's Council, 2019). Until 2019, it seems that no extra funding had been centrally allocated for police forces to specifically combat digital criminality in any of its forms.

The strategy also explained that the National Intelligence Model (NIM) will be used consistently for the first time to inform priorities and deploy resources, notwithstanding the NIM was then 15 years old (Flood and Gaspar, 2009). Integrating the NIM with financial information is not mentioned in the document, possibly due to the assumption within law enforcement that the intelligence aspect of the NIM is fully integrated with working practices (HMIC, 2015; Kirby and McPherson, 2004; NCA 2015b). In terms of investigating financial crime, the same section referred the reader to a later section entitled, "Attack criminal finances by making it harder to move, hide and use the proceeds of crime" (HM Government, 2013: 34). Unfortunately, that section simply explains the NCA and government intention to further strengthen POCA with a view to asset recovery. There is no outline provided for an intended financial strategy whereby financial investigation techniques could enhance general investigation capabilities. This appears to have identified a potential dichotomy between a government intention to tackle criminal finances and the need for an effective implementation structure in order to do so. The situation appears to remain the same in the strategy of 2018 and for 2023 to 2028. There is, however, lengthy explanation concerning the plans of the government to charge businesses under the anti-money laundering framework (called the Economic Crime (Anti-Money Laundering) Levy, plans for a national fraud unit, extending international liaison officer numbers for the NCA and several other policy or legislative ambitions including creating 475 additional financial investigators "dedicated to tackling money laundering and asset recovery". The Labour government in 2002/2003 took similar steps and created 83 new financial investigation posts to underpin the new POCA (2002). The problem, as discussed above is that creating new financial investigator posts does nothing to embed the skill set across the wider routine law enforcement landscape, a problem continually identified by successive reports and commentators (HMIC et al., 2004, 2010; House of Commons, 2016).

The various Serious and Organised Crime Strategies are examples of how terminology can affect the perception of particular subject matter (Brown et al., 2012: 7). AFIs who were interviewed identified that financial investigation works better in closer alignment with other parts of an investigation, each element supporting the other. Yet, cybercrime and financial investigation seem to continue largely unlinked except for asset recovery, a process that can only take place after the conviction of an offender. The attention of the National Cyber Security Strategy (Gov.UK, 2011) to financial investigation is not detailed, with only some mention of criminal infrastructure and financial pathways. There is comment upon its intention to reduce cybercrime upstream by dismantling criminal infrastructure and financial networks (HM Government, 2016). What exactly is meant by upstream is not explained. The traditional view of financial investigation as a specialist skill set (Cabinet Office, 2000; City of London Police, 2018; House of Commons, 2016) appears to hamper policy makers and strategic thinking in moving forwards to effectively combat the emerging threat. Levi et al. (2015: 9) observe that cybercrime investigations, "need to be mainstreamed into criminal investigation and proceeds of crime prevention". The title of cybercrime appears to be allowed to mutually exclude the concept of financial investigation. The use of the title (cybercrime) may not prove to be the appropriate description of internet crime and should perhaps be used more judiciously because, "wrong terminology encourages us to adopt unsuccessful strategies" (Levi et al., 2015: 9). The current National Cyber Security Strategy sets out the requirements seen as essential until the year 2030 admitting that the workforce as it develops "continues to lack the diversity it needs" (HM Government, 2022: 61). Whether the diversity includes removing the apparent siloed work streams of financial investigation and cyber investigation remains undetermined and unmentioned. The focus appears to remain upon cyber security, not on how to investigate cybercrime.

Cybercrime (extrapolating dedicated denial of service (DDOS) and malware attacks for the moment) might be construed to be acquisitive crime, involving a material benefit to the offender (Cabinet Office, 2011; National Audit Office, 2017). Currently in the UK there are no specific cyber offences which can be indicted against an offender. This is indirectly acknowledged by the NCA (2018c: 46) while attempting to explain why convictions under the Computer Misuse Act (CMA, 1990) offences may appear weak to the public, "as many convictions are under the Fraud Act rather than the CMA, this compounds the problem and furthers the perception of cybercrime without consequence".

Cyber fraud is indicted as fraud and using digital means to interact with the proceeds of/for crime (cyber laundering) should be indicted as money laundering. The fact that a traditional burglar utilises a crowbar to pry open doors and windows did not result in crowbar crime. Although crude, the analogies seem sound. Offenders are now utilising the digital environment (the internet) by way of computers, smartphones (mobile phones with internet access) and other electronic devices to commit fraud and other acquisitive crimes (Alpna, 2016; Price Waterhouse Cooper, 2018).

The outcome (in real world terms) is the same as any other type of fraud. Vulnerable victims still lose money to criminals. The immediate problem is that there is very little data to accurately understand the scope of the problem and the way that law enforcement records crime numbers (and offence types) may well be outdated and somewhat misleading (United Nations Office on Drugs and Crime, 2012). In fact, it is recognised that up to one fifth of crimes reported to police are not recorded (HMIC, 2014). Under-reporting of digital offending (although outside the scope of this study) may prove to be an ongoing problem, one which requires resolving if a more accurate understanding of the cybercrime phenomenon is to be achieved (McGuire and Dowling, 2013). Better recorded crime figures may provide scope for financial investigation to contribute. If that contribution generates increased reporting, it may also offer scope for better understanding of the problem.

Fraud offences were not included in the Crime Survey for England and Wales (CSEW) (ONS, 2015), nor were money laundering offences (seen as a consequence of crime) or cybercrimes. They were (for the first time) included in a similar survey for 2016 with two million computer misuse offences reported but a further year was required to afford comparable data for publication in 2019 (ONS, 2016a). In the five years up until and including 2023, the ONS CSEW (June 2023) estimated that fewer than 1 in 20 computer misuse offences were reported to either Police or Action Fraud with 850,000 offences being reported. The National Fraud Investigation Bureau (NFIB) reported a 10% decrease in computer offences referred from Action Fraud to police forces to investigate (ONS, 2023a). In the face of most evidence to the contrary, figures appear to show decreases in computer crime (misuse). Similarly, where fraud is concerned, Action Fraud recorded a 9% decrease in fraud offences. It is beyond the scope of this chapter, but these figures seem difficult to believe although the authors note with caution that they represent a best estimate (ONS, 2023a)

To date, there still appears to be no available data to demonstrate how many cyber investigations (particularly into Computer Misuse Act 1990 offences) have directly utilised POCA powers (requiring careful consideration towards formulating an answer to what the essential financial investigation characteristics may look like). Nor does there appear to be any reliable and comprehensive data concerning the number of successful prosecutions involving digital criminality or how widespread POCA powers were used in any primary investigations. This potentially highlights a distinct gap as to the extent (or otherwise) of the integration of financial investigation techniques in law enforcement cybercrime units and to what extent financial intelligence may be used in cyber investigations (including the use of suspicious activity reports). The lack of empirical data within the available literature indicates that more research in the area is required.

The section above identifies a number of key themes in relation to questions regarding what essential financial investigation characteristics might be. First, there appear to be gaps within and between the strategic, tactical and practice levels, which are underpinned by the apparent lack of a comprehensive national UK financial investigation strategy or any concerted effort to go beyond the traditional focus on confiscation and asset recovery. This is not mitigated by the partial coverage of financial investigation in the national UK Organised Crime Strategy, and the generalised disconnect between financial investigation and the National Intelligence Model (NIM). Second, there seems little or no mention of financial investigation and related techniques in the literature that may offer an integrative theme (to substantially enhance NIM application) that could be used for general law enforcement across a wide range of investigation and intelligence processes. Notwithstanding all this potential, terminological confusion in the literature (alongside policy and practice) appears to have maintained a myth of financial investigation as a specialist silo. Third, no definite and collective training strategy appears to have been devised which will underpin the implementation of financial investigation techniques into mainstream law enforcement practice. Available literature provides little or no data upon which a general training requirement can be based. Empirical data seems required regarding the extent to which dysfunctions might exist, measuring these, and identifying what might be done to attempt to rectify the situation.

3 Financial investigation and typologies associated with its application

Financial investigation

This section will consider the definitional problems of financial investigation and how commentators advocate it should be applied, the close association of the term with asset recovery (confiscation) and how strategic intention advocates financial investigation as a wider investigation skill set. The effect of target driven asset recovery will be examined and whether training issues (specialist and non-specialist) may have had an impact upon the use of financial investigation. Accessibility of POCA powers to general investigators such as production orders and money laundering powers are debated, and some thought is given to what may be regarded as good financial investigation (Hall, 2012). A production order is a document issued by a Crown Court Judge empowering the applicant to serve the order on the relevant financial institution and breach normal client confidentiality. The application is subject to the Human Rights Articles, Article 8 (the right to privacy).

Between the first (asset-based and drug trafficking related) proceeds of crime legislation in the UK (Drug Trafficking Offences Act, 1986) and POCA (2002), the role of an AFI was to identify and sequester criminal assets (Cabinet Office, 2000). The link which has developed between financial investigation and asset recovery is a strong one. The two terms are often used together, and the focus is usually on asset recovery (Bullock, 2010).

Legislation was initially targeted towards confiscating assets (the ill-gotten gains) from drug trafficking criminals (Drug Trafficking Offences Act, 1986; Ryder, 2013). Media focus concentrated on why criminals should be allowed to enjoy spoils generated by their criminality. The problem was that in reacting to a well-publicised drug problem (R v Cuthbertson, 1981; Hodgson, 1984), politicians and legislators focused on that specific type of offending in modelling the response. Although financial investigation is one of the main means by way of which assets can be identified and confiscated, commentators have already suggested it need not be exclusive to expert AFIs (van Duyne et al., 2003). Confiscation (asset recovery) was initially the remit of detectives assigned to police drug squads, the origin of present-day financial investigation units (Cabinet Office, 2000; Ryder, 2013). Even the title of the first AFIs,

DOI: 10.4324/9781003438649-3

that of Drug Profit Confiscation Officers (Metropolitan Police, 1988), seems to allow no conclusion other than financial investigation was a specialist function and concerned only with asset recovery from drug traffickers. Financial investigation became associated with drug trafficking and with the confiscation of assets (Levi, 2013; Madinger, 2012; Wood, 2017).

Any distinctions between using financial investigation as a general investigation tool and the more specialist work of a trained confiscator seem to have been obfuscated from the outset. So too was the opportunity to embed investigation of criminal finances as an integral part of standard operating procedures. Confiscation (in its fledgling state) was not well publicised in the late 1980s or the 1990s and for those investigators who may have been aware of the new legislation (outside of the drug squad environment) it became regarded as a specialist area. The perception that it was a specialist function and that it could therefore not be anything to do with general policing issues engendered a long-lasting legacy and is still a mainstream viewpoint in present law enforcement mentality (Brown et al., 2012).

The problem continued to be exacerbated by successive legislation, almost exclusively concerned with asset recovery until the advent of the money laundering section of POCA (2002). It has become perceived to be the remit of AFIs and something which is only of real use after a conviction has been obtained at Court (confiscation) as a tool primarily for locating assets (Levi, 2013). Effectively, it has become an afterthought in the minds of investigators and prosecutors alike (House of Commons, 2014). The perception by UK general law enforcement practitioners that financial investigation and confiscation is the same thing (and treated as separate to criminal investigation) remains one of the overriding and determining beliefs which may hamper effective financial investigation at all levels (Davidson, Walker and Dayman, 2014).

Except for Regional Organised Crime Units (ROCUs) within law enforcement agencies (2014 onwards), strategic considerations still tend to focus on asset recovery after the conviction of an offender (Levi, 2013). It (financial investigation leading to confiscation) is a process which is seen as secondary to the primary investigation (Brown et al., 2012). Recovery of criminal benefit is not a high priority at the start of an investigation, and it is argued that a culture shift is necessary (House of Commons, 2016). The perception among general investigators that financial investigation is predominantly an asset recovery tool may be difficult to alter (Howell, Horton and Gill, 2013; Davidson, Walker and Dayman, 2014).

Policy

Focus on all levels (policy, strategic, tactical and practical) has generally remained upon the area of asset recovery ensuring financial investigation skills have remained largely within specialist units (Howell, Horton and Gill, 2013; Levi, 2013). The advantages of financial investigation were extolled to non-specialists in a practice advice booklet from the Association of Chief Police Officers (ACPO, 2006: 12): "Financial investigations may provide material of use in all types of investigations, including those with no obvious link to money or assets". This organisation was superseded by the National Police Chiefs' Council (NPCC) in 2015. A review of the available literature does not provide evidence of any recent or continued follow up by the NPCC to attempt to implement their intention to better utilise financial investigation in non-specialist environments. Since the Cabinet Office (2000) the precursor report to the Proceeds of Crime Act (2002), government reports and independent commentators have continued to advocate more general use of financial investigation (ECORYS, 2015; House of Commons, 2016; NCA, 2014; Wood, 2017). Effective implementation of financial investigation across all investigation and intelligence procedures seems to remain problematic (Hall, 2012; NAO, 2013; Wood, 2017). Understanding the continuing problem of implementing financial investigation techniques into the general investigators' skill set may be one of the central factors in formulating an answer to a more generic philosophy of financial investigation.

On behalf of ACPO, the National Police Improvement Agency (NPIA, 2008) – which was superseded by the College of Policing in 2012 – produced an advice booklet concerning the management and use of proceeds of crime legislation. It extolled the potential of proceeds of crime legislation if used in general investigations. The booklet appears to have been aimed at the strategic layer of policing in its assertions that: "To successfully embed POCA and realise its provisions, strong leadership from the top down is required" (NPIA, 2008: 8). The document included a flow chart of the criminal investigation process reproduced for the reader in Figure 3.1.

Based on a template produced on behalf of ACPO by the National Centre for Policing Excellence (2005: 48), the above figure is identical save the addition of the last box "Potential Further Investigation" (e.g., financial investigation). This addition offers clear acknowledgement that the criminal investigation process does not necessarily end with prosecution and conviction. What is not clear from the chart or from the advice booklet is whether it is simply referring to confiscation procedures which can only take place after a conviction. Ten separate recommendations were made in the NPIA (2008) practice advice regarding proceeds of crime but all of them concentrated on asset recovery rather than general investigation. This leads the authors to conclude that, notwithstanding comments about POCA's suitability for general investigators in certain investigations (money laundering), focus appears to have remained upon financial investigation as a tool for asset recovery. It may have been wiser to reference it earlier in the flow chart at the stage of initial investigation and to map financial investigation alongside each step of the criminal investigation process inclusive of, following a conviction, the use of confiscation (asset recovery). Whether the advice was widely circulated or read by those members of the strategic layer for whom it appears to be intended remains unknown.

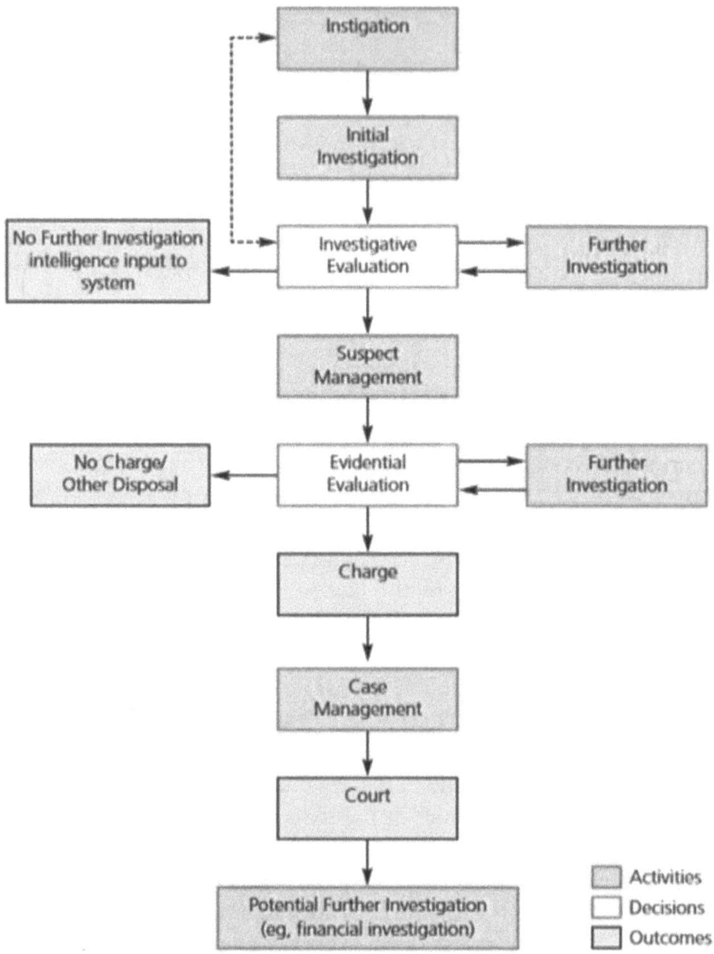

Figure 3.1 The criminal investigation process.

Source: NPIA (2008:15).

The chart provides insight that after POCA (2002) was enacted into law, some attempt was being made to understand that its potential was wider than the asset recovery (confiscation) regime and that it required the support of the strategic layer as one of the pillars of success. Whether it affected the trajectory of financial investigation or confiscation awareness remains undetermined.

It appears to be the only pictorial reference to financial investigation in terms of criminal investigation which the authors have been able to identify in published literature. What seems clear is that in subsequent explanations of the criminal investigation structure which are publicly available, financial

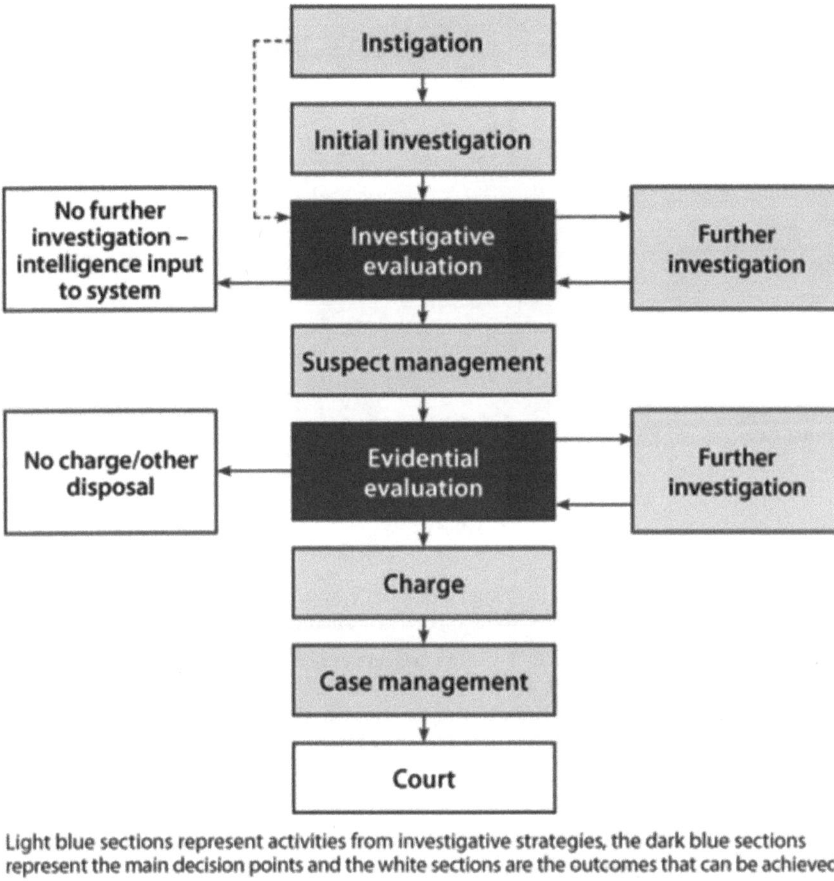

Figure 3.2 The stages of criminal investigation. Source: College of Policing (2018b: 1). Reproduced with permission from the College of Policing Ltd.

https://www.app.college.police.uk/app-content/investigations/investigation-process/

investigation is not mentioned or reproduced in the same manner again. Police training flowcharts from the College of Policing (2018b: 1) depicting the criminal investigation process had reverted to the original template of the National Centre for Policing Excellence (2005) as contained in Figure 3.2.

Financial investigation at this point appears to have been dispensed with as a possibility across the criminal investigation process, and this will tend to reinforce prevailing views that it is a parallel and specialist area associated with confiscation. The irony is perhaps that the first section of NPIA (2008: 8) stated: "The benefits of embedding POC [proceeds of crime] legislation into routine investigations will help us to ensure that the police are able to fully

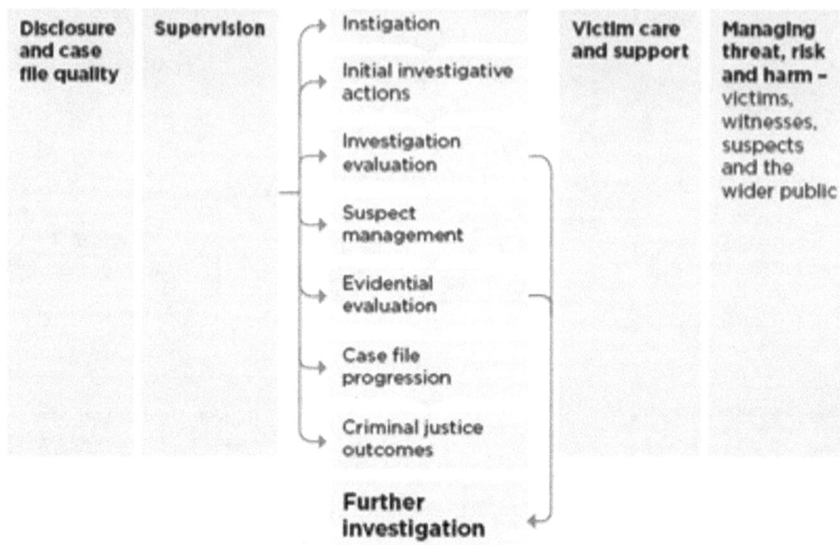

Figure 3.3 Updated stages of investigation (College of Policing, 2024). Reproduced with permission from the College of Policing Ltd.

https://www.college.police.uk/app/investigation/investigation-process

exploit the financial investigation techniques as a preventive measure to deter criminals".

The accepted and perhaps rigid depiction of the investigation process seems to have recently changed, presumably to allow decision makers some flexibility within the current arena of investigative enterprise. The latest diagram of the investigation process appears to have been created with some flexibility in what it deems necessary in any investigation. It can be seen from Figure 3.3 that the diagram no longer appears prescriptive as to the phases and within each step offers flexibility of approach and application of resources and skill-bases.

Financial investigation appears to remain entwined with confiscation investigations (asset recovery), a specific factor that may limit its effectiveness in terms of the general field of investigation. This point is well demonstrated in the explanation of financial investigation in a document commissioned by the Council of Europe (Golobinek, 2006) as a training manual for law enforcement and the judiciary in member states:

> The financial investigation is a part which is conducted in parallel with the criminal investigation and is aimed at discovering the proceeds of crime, identifying the property that can be confiscated and temporary securing (seizing) this property to allow future final confiscation. While the goal of the criminal investigation is to detect a criminal offence and

> the perpetrator and to collect the evidence for the criminal procedure, the goal of the parallel financial investigation is to confiscate proceeds from crime.
>
> (Golobinek, 2006)

The focus of the explanation seems a narrow one and, if adhered to, could result in opportunities to combat all criminality (not just acquisitive criminality) being lost (Hall, 2012). Current available literature, including government documents and law enforcement manuals advocate the conduct of more effective confiscation investigations and that asset recovery opportunities should be recognised from the outset of criminal investigations (European Commission, 2018; HMCPSI et al., 2010; HMIC et al., 2004; House of Commons, 2016). None of the available literature seems to focus upon how that is to be accomplished, nor does it generally make a distinction between financial investigation and confiscation. Where the distinction is made, commentators usually begin by applauding the possibilities of financial investigation outside of the confiscation environment but continue to link it directly with serious and organised crime (Brown et al., 2012; Wood, 2017).

Perceptions and research

Howell, Horton and Gill (2013) did conduct research into the wider implications of financial investigation and what it may offer to non-specialist investigators. They acknowledge that the only participants in their survey were AFIs, perhaps the most likely to understand and advocate the wider benefits of financial investigation. There is an implicit risk that its conclusions may be biased as only the specialist point of view is represented. Their research does confirm the points made in previous appraisals of the asset recovery environment, the tendency for financial investigation to be regarded as a specialism by general investigators and a lack of awareness of it within the command structure (Brown et al., 2012; House of Commons, 2016). Having identified that general investigators regard financial investigation as a specialist area of investigation, it is interesting to note that only four in ten participants believed that some financial investigation tasks could be undertaken by non-specialists. This may suggest that although AFIs understand their skill set is not integrated into general law enforcement and suspect some of the reasons for it, a majority may feel it is not an area where non-specialists are capable.

Research appears currently limited regarding the perceptions and understanding of financial investigation by non-specialist investigators. Gale and Kelly (2018) interviewed 4 non-AFIs and 15 AFIs. A key gap is still evident in the literature as to what constitutes the financial investigation skill set (separate to asset recovery), how it may be used across investigations and how to embed it across general law enforcement. The possible options to address this situation (including suggesting a possible definition of financial investigation within this book will be a key facet for consideration not only in attempting to create a transferable generic philosophy to embed into routine investigations but in attempting to define the core essential characteristics of it.

The Financial Action Task Force (FATF), the international body created in 1989 to safeguard against money laundering, and a perceived threat to the international financial system, describes the term financial investigation as an "enquiry into the financial affairs related to criminal conduct. The major goal of a financial investigation is to identify and document the movement of money during the course of criminal activity" (FATF, 2012: 3). Perhaps unhelpfully, the FATF also advocates what it terms a parallel investigation (in other words the financial investigation) so that the predicate offence (the underlying offending) and any money laundering offence can be investigated simultaneously. The rationale is that "The concept of having parallel investigations brings together expertise from both investigative backgrounds and ensures offences are fully investigated" (FATF, 2012: 9).

This appears to be suggesting that two investigations should run parallel, the criminal investigation and what the FATF terms the financial investigation; the former to be conducted by general criminal investigators and the latter by specialist AFIs with a clear division between the two. It continued a theme of parallel investigations mentioned in an earlier document presenting amendments and revisions of the FATF's original forty recommendations against money laundering compiled in 1990 (FATF, 2010). In a more recent document, which again revises the forty recommendations against money laundering, parallel investigations continue to be advocated: "At least in all cases related to major proceeds-generating offences, these designated law enforcement authorities should develop a pro-active parallel financial investigation when pursuing money laundering, associated predicate offences and terrorist financing" (FATF, 2018: 1).

Such reasoning possibly detracts from financial investigation as a general investigative practice and the logic of a parallel investigation seems to invite a potential jeopardy. If a financial investigation is considered a separate investigation to what the FATF refers to as the predicate investigation (money laundering or major proceeds generating offence) certain risk factors may require consideration. First, it would seem necessary that the investigation team and the AFI(s) communicate effectively notwithstanding they may work in different locations. Second, a risk may arise that disclosure of documents from two investigations may become confused. Documentary disclosure of case papers from the state prosecutor to the defending legal representatives in an investigation is a vital part of the court process. The prosecution must disclose anything to the defence which may assist their case, or which may undermine the prosecution per the requirements of the Criminal Procedure and Investigations Act (1996). If financial investigation is an integral part of investigations, rather than separate from them, disclosure problems and lack of communication should generally not present problems.

Financial investigation should be an integral consideration for all investigations and the basic aspects of it should be a requirement across law enforcement (College of Policing, 2024a). In the UK, this tenet is reflected in the way POCA powers were drawn up by legislators and made available in money laundering investigations to all police and HMRC officers and not just to proceeds of crime specialists (POCA, 2002). The FATF is one of the bodies which informs UK government policy and although well intentioned, recommendation 30 (FATF, 2012a) may well be the wellspring of confusion for policy makers in understanding how to separate financial investigation techniques and the specialist area of confiscation.

Research commissioned by the UK Home Office appeared to have settled upon a broad definition of financial investigation:

> The term financial investigation refers here to the collection, analysis and use of 'financial' information (in its broadest sense) by law enforcement organisations… A financial investigator is someone who has been accredited to undertake financial investigation by the National Police Improvement Agency (NPIA), following a course of study.
>
> (Brown et al., 2012: 2)

The logic of the two descriptions may, at first glance, seem appropriate and correct. Where the first one may appear acceptable, the second raises certain questions. It appears to imply two things. First, that a financial investigation is something which can be conducted and second, that only an AFI can undertake such investigation. Both implied points seem erroneous. Unlike money laundering (POCA, 2002: s327) or a confiscation investigation (POCA, 2002: s341), financial investigation has no legal definition and is thus not something an investigator can approach a court with and claim to be investigating, either statutorily or by common law. The NPIA description may mistakenly lead the reader to conclude that only an AFI can investigate a person or entity financially. Such statements do little to alter the perceptions of general investigators that financial investigation, like asset recovery, is only to be conducted by trained specialists. Confiscation investigations are the only proceeds of crime investigation which must be conducted by an AFI although all general investigators within the police and HMRC are able to legally conduct money laundering investigations and financial enquiries.

A third point arises from the quoted section. There seems to be little ambiguity in legislative intent by the UK government that financial investigation should be practised in the broadest sense by all law enforcement agencies (HMIC et al., 2004; House of Commons, 2016). Various examples of that intention are evident throughout this literature review. Yet it seems the practical translation of that consistent intention to embed financial investigation into law enforcement practice remains problematic. Whether financial investigation is discussed regularly enough (and separate to asset recovery) at the appropriate levels seems questionable. As Hicks (2016) asserted, the implementation of POCA is not a standing item on the agendas of The House of Commons Justice Committee or the ACPO Crime Committee (the National Police Chief's Council since 1 April 2015).

The FATF (2012: 6) continues to assert that all countries, "should ensure that financial investigations become the cornerstone of ALL major proceeds generating cases". The same document also asserts that all criminal investigators should be trained on the value of financial evidence to support all criminal investigations. Indeed, "Basic financial investigative skills should be routinely included in training for entry level police officers and other competent investigators" (FATF, 2012: 29). Attempting to comply with those assertions, successive UK governments have continued to underline a desire to embed financial investigation into general law enforcement practices (Cabinet Office, 2000; HM Government, 20;11 2011a). That intention to embed financial investigation (politically, strategically and practically) into general policing strategies appears to remain unfulfilled (House of Commons, 2016; Wood, 2017).

Responsible for all UK law enforcement training content, the College of Policing (CoP, 2024a) advocates that AFIs should be integrated with all other operational support staff and financial investigation should be considered within each individual force policing plan and force strategy. "Financial investigation should be used alongside all other investigative methods. It is not just a tool for specialists or concerned only with POCA and asset recovery" (CoP, 2024a). One of the problems in translating that intent into practice may be that new police recruits seem to be provided a one-hour input about proceeds of crime (House of Commons, 2016). Financial investigation as a skill set does not appear to be taught, nor does it appear to be taught on detective training courses, although the City of London Police (2018a) allows one day of a six-week detective training course to deliver a module on money laundering.

The available literature concerning training suggests at least four basic issues which seem to be in need of redress. First, legislators and policy makers need to recognise that the focus of financial investigation should be wider than asset recovery. Second, law enforcement leadership and management need to recognise that financial investigation is a technique to be fully integrated into strategic and tactical planning and adequate training is required (House of Commons, 2016). Third, general practitioners should be taught to incorporate financial investigation techniques into their investigative skill set in at least two ways: To utilise the proceeds of crime toolbox to enhance general investigation and evidence gathering capabilities; and to be able to recognise the opportunity for asset recovery and pass that information to confiscation specialists. Fourth, prosecutors should be better equipped to deal with proceeds of crime legislation in all aspects, particularly money laundering and confiscation.

The problem of training general law enforcement practitioners (at all levels) has been recognised repeatedly (Hall, 2012; HMIC et al., 2004; HMCPSI et al, 2010). Even so, there does not appear to have been any substantial and objective academic research in this area of identified concern. There seems to be a clear gap in the literature concerning financial investigation and its integration into the various law enforcement training regimes. Potential deficiencies in the training of financial investigation techniques to general law enforcement practitioners are beginning to be recognised (House of Commons, 2016) but focus remains fixed on asset recovery linked to financial gain and acquisitive crime (Criminal Finances Act, 2017; Keen, 2017; National Audit Office, 2016).

Data gaps and limitations

It is significant that there is only limited available data to demonstrate whether financial investigation techniques are used in non-acquisitive investigations such as murder, rape, assaults and other examples. Howell, Horton and Gill (2013) provide some examples where financial investigation has been used in criminal investigations, not necessarily with the primary goal of identifying assets, although many examples they provide do involve financial gain such as money laundering, fraud or drugs offences. The study is unclear in terms of the depth of any financial investigation conducted in the various examples provided but identified that financial investigation had been relevant in:

> a range of other offences which are diverse, including for example, sex offences, murder and terrorism to name but a few, and for a variety of purposes including tracking offenders, determining whether an offence had taken place and in establishing offenders' motives.
>
> (Howell, Horton and Gill, 2013: 95)

Limitations of the research were acknowledged within the study such as "focusing solely on the views of financial investigators and being unable to test or balance criticisms made" (Howell, Horton and Gill, 2013: 96).

Brown et al. (2012) examined the contribution financial investigation could make in criminal investigations but only in terms of serious and organised crime operations. Research focused upon the views of AFIs, and a small number of cases (60) were examined. One of the conclusions reached was that,

> The contribution that financial investigation makes to tackling organised crime goes beyond simply a mechanism to recover assets. This investigative approach has the potential to be successfully applied across the full extent of criminal investigations. In particular it should be viewed as a tool that yields most value when it is used in collaboration with other investigative methods, rather than an approach that is used in isolation.
>
> (Brown et al., 2012: 15)

The point is an important one which underpins similar conclusions in the available literature (College of Policing, 2018a; HMCPSI et al., 2010; HMIC et al., 2004; House of Commons, 2016; Wood, 2017). A gap in the literature appears to be in two key areas. First, the apparent absence of any solution to the strategic problem of incorporating financial investigation across law enforcement as a general skill set. Second, a clear need for empirical data from the viewpoint of non-POCA practitioners which might begin to demonstrate why general investigators may not engage with financial investigation. Important questions (relevant to what may constitute essential financial investigation characteristics) will be whether general investigators understand what financial investigation offers to them in terms of investigative advantage and whether they understand how to access information which could be available to them such as credit checks and suspicious activity reports (SARs). SARs contain information from financial institutions concerning account holders and possible suspicious financial activity. There seems to be no available data in the literature to provide an accurate picture as to whether SARs (or credit checks) are routinely used by general investigators.

Having previously acknowledged that target driven confiscation is possibly detrimental to financial investigation (HMCPSI et al., 2010), later government reports do not appear to deviate from the asset recovery path (even after continuing to identify that it is inhibitive to the broader use of financial investigation techniques). A good example of this is contained within the House of Commons (2016) which concerned itself with several aspects within the proceeds of crime arena. One of those areas is training.

The Committee (after hearing evidence from a mix of law enforcement representatives, banking and business representatives and private individuals) acknowledged that the area of financial investigation training (to general practitioners) was problematic. One of the recommendations made by the Committee stated:

> We recommend that, upon entry into the service, all police officers receive at least one full day of financial investigative training, accredited by the National Crime Agency (NCA), so that all officers are equipped to secure recovery at a much earlier stage and have a good understanding of the impact of charges, offences and pleas on asset recovery. Secondly, all detective officers should receive advanced financial investigation training on at least an annual basis so that appropriate evidence is gathered about financial gain, as well as criminal conduct in every investigation into a serious crime offering financial gain. We recommend that NCA training and accreditation of specialised financial investigators emphasises the importance of initiating asset freezing at the earliest stages of an investigation. Performance against this objective should be measured for all the agencies involved by recording whether assets are frozen and ready to be recovered as soon as a confiscation order is made.
>
> (House of Commons, 2016: 10)

The paragraph highlights two clear issues that this literature review has begun to identify, reference to financial investigators as specialists and continued focus upon asset recovery (and therefore financial investigation as it is currently approached), measuring success by the amount of assets frozen (restrained) or confiscated (Bullock, 2010). Even though the problem of mainstream training is identified and discussed, the response seems misdirected. The Committee and its various advisors appear (as have previous reports and reviews) not to separate financial investigation from confiscation and asset recovery (FATF, 2012). The techniques may be the same, but the outcomes are very different. As Wood (2017) recognised, financial investigation techniques have potential when there is no clear acquisitive benefit. Confiscation is an investigation which has asset recovery as its objective. Until policy makers understand the difference between the two concepts and make recommendations accordingly, the apparent gaps between policy, training and implementation for best practice seem set to continue. Without a better training programme (House of Commons, 2016) and the complete integration of financial investigation techniques into all standard law enforcement courses (and thereby general practice) the government seems to have no way forward except to continue calling for better implementation and for more legislation such as the Criminal Finances Act of 2017 (Home Secretary, 2016).

POCA (2002) was the first clear attempt by legislators to attempt to translate strategic intention into effective practice. Although it was recognised that proceeds of crime legislation may have use in non-specialist areas of investigation, its initial implementation focused upon asset recovery (HMCPSI et al., 2010; HMIC et al., 2004; NAO, 2013). This, notwithstanding the assertion in the review that led to POCA (2002) that: "Financial investigation should be made central to UK law enforcement, to make it as routine to tackle criminals through their financial arrangements as to use techniques such as surveillance" (Cabinet Office, 2000: 56).

POCA was delivered with strong political support behind it, indeed the Assets Recovery Agency (ARA) 2003–2008 reported directly to the Home Secretary (David Blunkett) at the time of its inception. The remit of ARA was to reduce crime by recovering assets from criminals using civil and criminal processes introduced by POCA (2002). POCA (2002) was directly supported by Prime Minister Tony Blair (Cabinet Office, 2000). Police forces were provided with directives to embrace the new legislation and make it effective. Asset recovery and the proceeds of crime were mentioned in the first National Policing Plan to make Chief Constables take note of POCA directives and act upon them. The government laid out its intention for policing very clearly: "Chief Officers and Police Authorities should make clear in their plans how they will make maximum use of the new powers available in the Proceeds of Crime Act to attack the assets of local criminals – including those involved in drug dealing and supply" (National Policing Plan, 2003–2006: 8 (Hansard, 20 November 2002) (parliament.uk)).

As can be seen from the Policing Plan extract, focus (within government and law enforcement alike) continued to firmly remain upon the areas of asset recovery and drug trafficking. There is no mention of implementing financial investigation techniques into the general practitioner levels of law enforcement to be routinely used as an investigation skill set, a crucial element for consideration if an answer to embedding financial investigation into routine law enforcement is to be postulated. It is a matter of record that more AFIs were trained as a direct result of POCA (2002) (Hansard, HC Deb 30 Oct 2001, vol 373 c758) but there appears to an absence in the available literature of a systematic implementation strategy across police and HMRC regarding non-specialist investigators.

Conversely, the Cabinet Office (2000) had set out a clear timetable for the implementation of POCA (2002). Its focus was not upon how to integrate POCA powers into the skill set of general investigators. Government attention (pre POCA and subsequently) remained firmly upon monies confiscated from criminals using the new powers and targets were set accordingly (House of Commons, 2007). It is arguable that the drive to fill the government coffers (the "tin box") may have hindered any initial intentions to properly fuse POCA powers into the investigation environment (House of Commons, 2007; HMCPSI et al., 2010; Long, 2016). It is interesting to note that AFIs could undertake a variety of training courses after initial POCA accreditation, but no training was available for general investigators. By omitting any form of training for non-POCA specialists the government appears to have missed a prime opportunity to integrate financial investigation into mainstream areas of law enforcement.

In 2004, because of initial governmental support, the formation of the first Regional Assets Recovery Team (RART) in the West Midlands occurred. Four more such units quickly followed and increasing numbers of civilian AFIs began to be employed (HMIC et al., 2004).

The money laundering aspect of POCA was enthusiastically awaited and certain forces robustly embraced the new laws. Some police forces formed specialist Money Laundering Units within their ECUs and one East Midlands Force enforced a policy of arresting offenders living beyond their means and stripping them of any property they owned (City of London Police, 2018a; HMIC et al., 2004). The message was that offenders would no longer be able to enjoy the benefits of their criminality with impunity. The period of such law enforcement activity was short-lived, however. It presents an interesting question as to the quantity of property which had to be returned to arrested individuals who were not prosecuted. Although it may be an interesting question, it is outside the scope of this project and there appears to be no publicly available data to formulate an answer.

The so-called "Payback Review" appears to be the first assessment of asset recovery since the instigation of POCA (HMIC et al., 2004). It identified low levels of awareness of asset recovery issues among operational officers, at the same time stating that "It is vital that from initial training onwards they (the police) have sufficient knowledge of core POCA powers and the confidence to exercise these powers – there remains a mystique around the area of financial investigation that needs to be removed" (HMIC et al., 2004).

This appears to be a persistent and durable problem (House of Commons, 2016). Management of cases by the Crown Prosecution Service (CPS) and the lack of knowledge to deal with POCA legislation was also criticised by the Review although it recognised a few examples of partnership working. An underlying key message of the Review was simple enough in its concept: "The key message of this Review is that POCA represents a powerful opportunity to substantially disrupt and deter criminality but only if it is used as a routine process against a wide range of criminality" (HMIC et al., 2004: 10). This appears to encapsulate a continuing problem in the implementation of financial investigation techniques across general and specialist law enforcement practice and appears central to limiting the potential impact.

The reader is reminded that POCA introduced money laundering offences for all investigators to use within police and HMRC. Money laundering investigations and the accompanying powers, such as production orders, to obtain confidential details from financial institutions were not restricted to specialist AFIs. Money laundering powers appear to have been intended for general policing use. Reliable money laundering data is not easy to obtain and since 2012 published figures are scant. This may be due to inaccurate recording (Davidson, Walker and Dayman, 2014), a general perception that money laundering is perceived to be a consequence of other acquisitive criminality and the fact that money laundering crimes are not recorded by the ONS. In terms of the money laundering impact upon the UK, the NCA (2024: 1) can only state; "Although there are no exact figures there is a realistic possibility that the scale of money laundering impacting the UK annually is in the hundreds of billions of pounds".

It is interesting to note that money laundering is acknowledged to be a significant threat to the UK but in the latest crime survey for England and Wales, it does not feature on the list of the main crime types (although fraud registers at a figure of 3,526,000 offences) (Office for National Statistics, 2023).

An inspection of all 43 police forces concluded that "Victims of crime are being let down. The police are failing to record a large proportion of crimes reported to them. Over 800,000 crimes reported to the police have gone unrecorded each year" (HMIC, 2014: 18). Such under-reporting of crimes, particularly money laundering and other acquisitive crime only serves to undermine financial investigation across general law enforcement. Erroneous data belies the real extent of acquisitive crime. Whether it has any degree of detrimental effect upon financial investigation as a non-specialist tool, particularly in the case of money laundering offences is currently unknown.

HMIC et al. (2004) concluded there seemed little point to investing in training general law enforcement practitioners to engage with offences which neither the judiciary nor the CPS were likely to pursue. Money laundering training is no longer provided to police (and other agency) investigators including AFIs (College of Policing, 2018b). It was the only non-specialist training originally offered but courses were cancelled from 2008 onwards. Enhanced Financial Investigation Skills (EFIS) courses have also been discontinued which effectively ensures there is no additional planned training available for specialist confiscator AFIs either. Training is limited to AFIs and police officers alike (Chave, 2017). The initial inadequacies of, and the subsequent demise of POCA training (across the entire spectrum of judiciary, courts, prosecutors and law enforcement) cannot be seen as an acceptable situation and the point has been recently acknowledged at government level (House of Commons, 2016). Levi (2013) had made the same point three years earlier.

Change in the attitudes of law enforcement, prosecutors and the judiciary towards financial investigation and confiscation (in all countries) is necessary if routine mainstreaming is to be achieved. It seems that decisions need to be made as to how the concept of financial investigation is to be approached and where focus should lie. If it is to be more generalised, it seems prudent to attempt to define what would be included in that ethos and the limitations of it in order to be clear to non-specialists. It should also be decided as to the extent general investigators require financial investigation techniques as the risk from a broader approach may unintentionally lead to restricted use. An example would be the UK money laundering definitions which appear to empower all of law enforcement but which for varying reasons have been so far found to have limited application (Davidson, Walker and Dayman, 2014; Hicks and Graycar, 2019). If formal and structured plans to replace the lack of POCA training for general investigators and confiscation specialists are being considered at governmental or strategic levels, they have not been made public.

Commentators have little doubt that financial investigation remains an untapped resource for evidence gathering in general investigations (Brown et al., 2012; Gale and Kelly, 2018; HMIC et al., 2004) but focus tends to remain on its potential in the fight against serious and organised crime (Levi, 2013; Wood, 2017). Lack of training opportunities for non-specialist investigators cannot be advantageous (Chave, 2017). If most commentators agree that financial investigation can be beneficial across a breadth of general investigations (Chave, 2017; House of Commons, 2016; Wood, 2017) it is arguable that lack of financial investigation training opportunities for general investigators may be detrimental to its widespread use. Whether that is the case remains unknown. Recent research by Gilmour (2020) suggests that detectives who were questioned regarding their skills investigating financial crime stated they felt under-trained in financial investigation. Any impact caused by lack of training opportunities for general investigators in financial investigation and any detriment to criminal investigations appears to remain unmeasured.

It is not only law enforcement agencies which have resisted broader use of POCA powers. Initial opposition or indifference (and sometimes open hostility) of the judiciary to proceeds of crime legislation has not weakened with time. Recent government documents have contained testimony from leading prosecution and defence barristers admitting that "most judges do not enjoy or look forward to doing confiscation" (House of Commons, 2016: 14). Leading proceeds of crime barrister Kennedy Talbot QC reported to the same Committee that he had sent an e-mail to all of his colleagues working in confiscation and that "overwhelmingly, the response was unenthusiastic reception [of cases] at courts" (House of Commons, 2016: 14). Levi and Osofsky (1995: vii) recognised the same issue early in the ongoing proceeds of crime debate:

> The consensus among those police and lawyers interviewed is that though they take their role seriously, some counsel and Crown Court judges appear to view the rigorous implementation of confiscation procedures as a marginal or even dispensable adjunct to their core tasks of dealing with the case to the point of jury decision and imposing sentence (of which confiscation is not formally part).
>
> (Levi and Osofsky, 1995: vii)

The British Bankers' Association (BBA) in its written response to an invitation by the Committee to comment upon the effectiveness of proceeds of crime legislation, was also critical of the judiciary: "Some Crown Court Judges are openly critical of this piece of legislation [POCA] and consider it to be 'two bites' at the sentencing of criminal conduct" (BBA, 2016: 1). The response also commented that, "Recent publications show that very few Judges have attended training in this area of the law [POCA]. In addition, the relevant training, in what is a complex legislative area, has been scaled back" (BBA, 2016: 1). Judiciary training (or the identified lack of it), like that of specialist and non-specialist AFIs, is problematic if the asset recovery aspect of financial investigation (money laundering, confiscation and civil recovery) is to be adequately prosecuted. The CPS and the judiciary appear to have played their own role in limiting the implementation of proceeds of crime legislation and (directly by so doing) it is arguable they have played their part in ensuring financial investigation has not expanded beyond its current peripheral role. Both of these aspects of the criminal justice system and the way in which they have restricted use of proceeds of crime legislation are relevant to a wider acceptance and implementation of financial investigation and require integration into any potential solution.

After the initial impetus of POCA (2002), it seems accepted at all levels that financial investigation has remained on the periphery of law enforcement (Hall, 2012; HMIC et al., 2004; House of Commons, 2016; Wood, 2017). Proceeds of crime powers are retained mainly within the specialist environments of ECUs and generally misunderstood or ignored by ground officers (including the cash detention powers within POCA): "Most police forces currently lack an effective approach to cascade POCA activity into everyday policing" (HMIC et al., 2004: 87). The situation was compounded by senior officers who did not (and largely still do not) understand the nature of confiscation or financial investigation: "In the absence of direction from chief officers, BCU (basic command units) commanders are doing little to implement POCA" (HMIC et al., 2004: 87).

It has more recently been acknowledged that senior police officers still have not prioritised confiscation and financial investigation (Hall, 2012; NAO, 2013; Wood, 2017). Their training was (and continues to be) short and without any real depth: "There has been little if any training pitched at chief officers and this is reflected in their limited awareness of POCA" (HMIC et al., 2004: 94). Senior Appropriate Officer training, offered by the NCA Proceeds of Crime Centre, is a one-day course. The objective of the course is to equip managers equivalent in rank to a police superintendent on the points to check for when authorising POCA production and restraint orders (NCA, 2015a). The course does not offer training in confiscation, money laundering, cash detention or civil recovery aspects of the legislation. Nor does it offer training concerning the tactical potential of POCA powers and how financial investigation can enhance non-AFIs in general investigations.

In strategic terms lack of training and (therefore) understanding, appears to have resulted in either a reluctance or a general ignorance of supervisors at all levels (strategic, tactical and practical) to incorporate financial investigation (including confiscation possibilities) into their investigation strategy (House of Commons, 2016; NAO, 2013). It is a problem that senior staff seem generally unaware of the benefits of utilising financial investigation techniques to gain evidence or of methods which are available to be used in a wide spectrum of investigations (Hall, 2012; Davidson, Walker and Dayman, 2014; Wood, 2017). At the practice level there is insufficient data as to whether officers are regularly (or otherwise) provided with any kind of investigation strategy or ability to recognise and use financial intelligence on a day-to-day basis. Investigation strategy (financial or otherwise) will be a necessary consideration intrinsic to defining the answer to what constitutes essential financial investigation characteristics as they might be applied to investigations beyond asset recovery.

There appears to be a clear need for better education of law enforcement officers at all levels (House of Commons, 2016) and the formulation of methods whereby financial investigation can be assimilated into their training and thought processes without it being considered as a complicated specialist silo. Despite all the repeated calls for better integration of financial investigation into all aspects of law enforcement, a singular problem appears to have remained constant. An effective and practical training programme model for all levels of law enforcement investigations (strategic, tactical and practical) has not been theorised let alone implemented. As an important and emerging theme from the available literature, training (within and extraneous to law enforcement) appears to be a central element required for a broader understanding and routine application of financial investigation techniques.

What equivocates to good financial investigation is therefore open to question and there is a clear gap in the literature on the subject. Hall (2012: 17) suggests that financial investigation (confiscation) has been stifled for six main reasons:

- Too many agencies.
- Non-transparency of funding.
- Lack of awareness by senior staff.
- Unambitious targets.
- Limited career progression of financial investigators.
- Ineffective public/private interaction.

The comments seem typical of current commentators and appear broad and high level. Each one of his points may have a degree of bearing on the current state of confiscation (and proceeds of crime legislation generally) throughout the UK although there is no data available to suggest to what extent. The comments do not seem to recognise financial investigation as a skill set extraneous to confiscation (the complex area of asset recovery). As main reasons Hall (2012) neglects to identify why attempts to implement financial investigation techniques outside the remit of asset recovery have to date remained elusive (although he does allude to lack of awareness of senior staff). The six points do not address any CPS and judiciary issues and the expectations of specialist and non-specialist investigators (including supervisors). Adequate training for general investigators is not considered, or that additional courses for AFIs no longer exist. Although the six points may or may not each have a degree of validity, no attempt is made to at suggest possibilities for any type of systematised implementation process, something which this book will attempt to consider in understanding what a more generic philosophy of financial investigation might look like.

From the intelligence perspective of financial investigation, there is no evidence available in the literature to suggest to what degree the concept of it has integrated with the NIM model. Empirical data to establish levels of understanding at any level (strategic, tactical, or practice) does not appear available within current literature. As a general concept it therefore remains unclear as to the extent financial investigation or its intelligence aspect have permeated non-specialist areas of investigation. Nor is it clear from available data the extent to which it has achieved strategic and tactical integration into command structures or the decision-making process within the NIM. It might be anticipated that fuller financial investigation integration within the general investigation community would be reflected to some extent in case strategies at all levels of investigation. Data appears to be currently unavailable to support or contradict that expectation or any of the others. Similarly, it would be reasonable to expect a more robust approach to utilising financial investigation and financial intelligence in the prosecution of all offences rather than the type of specialist cases reported on by commentators to date (Brown et al., 2012; Howell, Horton and Gill, 2013; Wood, 2017). All these points need careful consideration if routinely embedding basic elements of the financial investigation skill set into routine policing is to be achieved.

Although financial investigations play an important role in assisting to identify and detect offences (not just financial ones) they are still not core to officers' thinking (Davidson, Walker and Dayman, 2014). Research has so far ascertained that although police officers and senior staff haphazardly perceived some benefits, they remained generally unaware of the advantages of using financial investigation as an investigatory technique (Howell, Horton, and Gill, 2013). It appears to be in thinking and practice an end of process bolt-on with a focus on confiscation and asset recovery (NAO, 2013). This identified gap in the use of financial investigation seems ubiquitous to all law enforcement agencies (House of Commons, 2014, 2016). The problem is that although the gap appears recognised at government level, no solution has yet been theorised or synthesised alongside consideration of the implementation challenges. Contributory factors to the ad hoc use of financial investigation seem to have been identified on a fragmented basis. Given the above issues, the prevailing government and strategic level response seems to be unanimous on the need to provide more legislation (Attorney General, 2016; Criminal Finances Act, 2017; Ryder, 2014; Serious Crime Act, 2015) described by the Home Secretary (2016: 1) as "tough new legal powers".

It is important to recognise that some of those contributory factors may be extraneous to law enforcement but injurious to its attempts to deal with the financial investigation enigma. There are 43 separate police forces within the UK, all of which have individual policies on innumerable matters, including financial investigation. Prior to the Police Reform and Social Responsibility Act (2011), oversight of UK police forces was the responsibility of police authorities in each constabulary area. Each authority usually consisted of 17 members comprised of magistrates, councillors and independent members (Home Office, 2003). They seem to have been phased out in 2012 after concerns about lack of accountability to the communities they represented (Police and Crime Commissioners' Treasurers' Society, 2012).

Since 2012, there are currently 47 individual Police and Crime Commissioners who have their own agendas (Association of Police and Crime Commissioners, 2018; Garland and Terry, 2012). Prosecutions and subsequent confiscation proceedings are the remit of the Crown Prosecution Service (CPS) over which the police have no control. There are numerous other authorities (NCA, Security Services, Trading Standards), all with the remit to utilise financial investigation within their own policy directives. Successive governments, the Cabinet Office and the Home Office, often respond to prevailing political climates, nationally and internationally (Cabinet Office, 2000; HM Government, 2011; Home Office, 2018c). There are also innumerable government and law enforcement committees and working groups. A practical and workable solution regarding broader and consistent law enforcement use of financial investigation seems to be made that much more difficult.

The private sector

The private sector is an additional complication to this mix and its limited integration with law enforcement and governmental policy drives is not helpful (Ellis and de Oliveira, 2015). In the current and so-called age of austerity the private sector is acknowledged as beginning to operate in areas previously the bastions of law enforcement and prosecuting authorities "the creeping privatisation of policing" (Johnston, 2014: 1). A private prosecution is a prosecution brought by a private individual or entity, for example the Royal Society for the Protection of Cruelty to Animals (RSPCA), who is not acting on behalf of any prosecuting authority (CPS, 2018a). In a private prosecution case where the Metropolitan Police assisted the Virgin Media company, with the former eligible for a percentage of any compensation achieved (R (Virgin Media Ltd) v Zinga [2014] EWCA Crim 52, [2014] All ER (D) 211 (Jan): para 57), the Appeal Court Judge on the issue of private prosecutions and asset recovery resulting from them commented:

> At a time when the retrenchment of the state is evident in many areas, including the funding of the Crown Prosecution Service and the Serious Fraud Office, it seems inevitable that the number of private prosecutions will increase, particularly in areas relating to the criminal misuse of intellectual property. In the overwhelming majority of such cases, a prosecution will serve the public interest in addressing such criminal conduct.

The Appeal Court decision confirmed that not only are private prosecutions assisted by the police lawful, any prosecutor can apply for confiscation proceedings at the Crown Court, not necessarily a state prosecuting authority (POCA 2002: s40(9)(b)). Although private prosecutors cannot be held to be (and cannot employ) an appropriate officer (an AFI) under POCA (2002: s378 (1)), it does not exclude them from participating as a prosecutor in confiscation proceedings or seeking assistance from an appropriate officer.

There seems to have been no impropriety in the police being properly remunerated for the assistance they provided (*R v Hounsham* [2005] EWCA Crim 1366, [2005] All ER (D) 406 (May)). The Police Act (1996, s93 (11)) allows a police authority to accept gifts or loans in the discharge of its duties. It also governs the extent of any such remuneration. The *R v Zinga* judgement opens the prospect for more private prosecutions assisted by police at a time when public funding faces continuing difficulties. The key driver appears to be the private sector choosing cases which allow for the possibility of financial remuneration to the law enforcement agency involved for engaging in cases they may otherwise have no interest in. There is a danger present, that law enforcement engages with such cases only when there is a potential financial reward for doing so. There is a danger that such cases would be corporate sector driven not necessarily in line with the best interests of the public.

The potential for the gradual merging of private sector cases and law enforcement resources upon the promise of an outcome from a private confiscation application seems to do nothing to simplify the perception of financial investigation as complex and specialist. It is an emerging area for both sectors, private and public, largely based upon case law decisions allowing any prosecutor to make a confiscation application (*R (on a prosecution by Mirchandani) v Somaia* [2017] EWCA Crim 741 [2017] All ER (D) 66 (Jun)). It changes the way in which a financial investigation is conducted in one significant manner, the POCA (2002) toolbox cannot be used but corporate sector investigators are quite at liberty to utilise open-source methods to construct benefit and realisable asset values to present to the court. The merging of two different sectors represents an interesting issue but as this thesis is delimited to criminal process and its immediate connections, the reader can find more information regarding private prosecutions in Edmonds and Jugnarain (2016) and Mujuzi (2015).

The overall disparate and thus far un-coordinated situation in which proceeds of crime legislation finds itself was perhaps best summed up by the Parliamentary Chair of the Public Accounts Committee, Margaret Hodge in January 2014 after scrutiny of the confiscation regime at that time. In addressing the attending Permanent Secretary of the Home Office and the NCA Director General, she candidly stated: "New strategies will not take you any further, it is the implementation that has failed. There has been a clear implementation failure and a failure to get co-ordination or a grip across government on it" (House of Commons, 2014: EV1).

The seemingly fragmented approach towards the implementation and use of financial investigation is not unique within policing. Similar fragmented approaches have recently been identified as endemic to policing in general terms. Her Majesty's Inspector of Constabulary (HMIC) annual reports (HMIC, 2016, 2017b) concerning the state of policing have identified several points of concern. Information technology remains problematic, and the inspection of all police forces found that there were too many instances where forces had failed to keep abreast of technical developments. This theme continues in HMIC (2017b), "The history of police use of ICT is not a distinguished story". In many cases police officers are less well equipped than the public they serve (HMIC, 2016: 22). Chief Officers need to work together more "effectively and efficiently" and adopt "consistent standards of leadership, behaviour and practice" (HMIC, 2016: 26). Concerns were raised by the report about the consistency of leadership and some forces disregarding what is required of them to comply with national standards. A report from the College of Policing (2015) underpins the call from the HMIC for leadership consistency and the development of a leadership model which is more collegiate in its approach.

The critical paragraph of the HMIC (2016) report in respect of this book appears to be:

> The fragmented and fragmentary nature of policing in England and Wales makes assessing policing and prosecuting measures for national best practice in efficiency and effectiveness in many respects very considerably more complex than is the case with the economic regulation of other safety-critical essential public services.
>
> (HMIC 2016: 30)

Financial investigation may be one of those fragments of policing, additionally handicapped by the lack of knowledge, understanding (and real interest) at all levels (political, strategic, tactical and practice) (Hall, 2012; House of Commons, 2016). National best practice may prove to be a problematic but important consideration when attempting to develop generic financial investigation techniques for routine investigators to understand and apply.

As financial investigation has largely been confined to asset recovery work since DTOA (1986) a myth has developed across general law enforcement (and one that is difficult to rebut) that POCA powers can only be used by AFIs (Howell, Horton and Gill, 2013). The myth is possibly enhanced by the AFIs having access to their own exclusive website, the Financial Investigation Support System (FISS). The FISS site is the national secure site administered by the College of Policing for all accredited financial investigators (AFIs) trained in the proceeds of crime. Approximately 2,500 AFIs in the UK have access to FISS but a parallel system to support general investigators does not appear to exist. FISS acts as a conduit for all ongoing AFI training and provides a secure and members only national chat room facility as a means of communication for AFIs nationwide. It also provides an electronic library of case law and articles of interest pertinent to proceeds of crime issues. Accreditation is gained through one or more of three available courses. A financial intelligence course is available for investigators working in intelligence roles or who need to contact financial institutions on a regular basis as part of their role (NCA, 2020b). It is a prerequisite of attending a financial investigation course. The financial investigation course delivers a foundation for investigators in a more permanent AFI role and the confiscation course for AFIs who will be involved in asset recovery (NCA, 2020b). Once an individual has been accredited as an AFI, access to FISS is automatic and applies to AFIs from all UK law enforcement agencies. All AFIs must contribute to a personal development portfolio regarding the work they do. Each month a mandatory assignment on FISS must be undertaken. If assignments are not completed within a certain time the accreditation of the individual is suspended.

POCA allows all police and HMRC officers to apply to the Crown Court for production orders and search warrants as and when required for a money laundering investigation (POCA, 2002: s378). The College of Policing (2024a np) is quite clear: "You do not need to be a financial investigator to make use of financial investigation tools". In pursuing a money laundering investigation (as defined within POCA), an investigator is perhaps not consciously conducting a financial investigation. Rather, the investigator is utilising powers to establish financial elements of a criminal offence by obtaining evidence of the laundering event or mechanism concerned. Any evidence gained in the money laundering investigation can be utilised later in any post-conviction confiscation case. Without being aware of the fact, in pursuing money laundering investigations (and some other offences) and gaining evidence to prosecute offenders, general investigators are (to some degree) utilising financial investigation skills. How to build upon this as yet unrecognised and rudimentary skill base remains elusive.

Complexities of an increasingly integrated technological environment with existing social pathways ensure it is difficult to avoid leaving traces of personal or business financial activity. Whether general investigators (or AFIs for that matter) are currently sufficiently capable and well trained enough to expose those traces remains an unanswered question.

Confiscation

Confiscation is a distinct specialism and is administered by AFIs who are trained in the relevant legislation. Confiscation should not be confused with financial investigation. The confiscation regime is the mechanism introduced and amended many times by various governments and courts since 1986 (the inception of the Drug Trafficking Offences Act (DTOA)) and by way of which proceeds of criminality can be lawfully recovered. Confiscation orders are made by a Crown Court, after a defendant is convicted of an offence, to recover the criminal proceeds to the value of the criminal benefit determined by the Judge in the proceedings. If the amount is not repaid within a set time period, the court can impose a default sentence that is issued at the time of the confiscation determination in case of non-compliance (Brown et al., 2012). A default sentence is a term of imprisonment if the confiscation order is not paid by the defendant in the time set by the court. The default sentence represents an incentive for the defendant to pay the order. If the order is not paid, not only will the defendant be liable to serve a term of imprisonment in addition to any other sentence or penalty, but the confiscation order debt is still enforceable after a default sentence has been served. It is essentially a debt for life and can include future assets for settlement. The current intention of the confiscation provisions is to deny criminals the use of their assets and to disrupt and deter further criminality (House of Commons Committee of Public Accounts, 2014). POCA (2002) itself states that the aim of the legislation is the reduction of crime. It is arguable that this original intention has been lost in some degree to the passage of time as well as being occluded by asset recovery. There also appears to be a paucity of research which examines whether POCA (2002) and subsequent proceeds of crime legislation have been successful to any extent in that regard.

If an offender cannot immediately pay the amount determined in the confiscation order, the order must be paid in full within six months of it being issued by the court (Serious Crime Act, 2015). In a confiscation hearing, the Crown Court must determine two things: the level of criminal benefit obtained by a defendant from his criminal activities and the available amount the offender is able to pay (which is calculated from the assets identified in the confiscation investigation). This is known as the realisable amount. A confiscation order only represents a value-based assessment of benefit accrued from criminality (Wood, 2016). Property cited within a confiscation statement (submitted by the confiscator in the case) is not automatically forfeited. A benefit determination by the court is essentially a debt to the state and can be discharged by any legal means available to the defendant. The benefit figure certified by the court remains until it is fully discharged by an offender. Benefit may be determined in excess of the value of the offences charged and has a far wider meaning than profit. Assets that a defendant has owned for years and not necessarily as a result of recent criminal activity may be used to satisfy the figure determined by the court (*R v Layode*, 1993; R v Vernon, 1993).

Primary responsibility for collection of confiscation orders lies with Her Majesty's Courts and Tribunals Service (HMCTS), the Serious Fraud Office (SFO) leads on its own and the CPS leads on some complex cases. It is interesting that there is an enforcement rate of almost 90% for orders under £1,000 but just under 18% for orders over £1 million. It seems that low value confiscation orders may be easier to enforce than high value ones. Notwithstanding any difficulties in enforcing higher value confiscation orders, politicians continue to articulate the power of POCA legislation in the face of poor enforcement results (House of Commons, 2016b; Woods, 2017).

In the financial year 2012–2013, £133 million was collected from outstanding confiscation orders (NAO, 2013). This represented an estimated 26 pence in every £100 generated by criminal activity. Debt from uncollected orders remained at an approximate figure of £1.5 billion (House of Commons, 2014) but increased to £1.61 billion in the two years to 2016 (NAO, 2016). Audit review of outstanding confiscation orders concluded that a large part of the debt relates to orders over five years old. Her Majesty's Courts and Tribunals Service (HMCTS, 2016) and Ministry of Justice (2016) both estimated that only £203 million of the outstanding 1.6 billion (17.5%) is collectable. There should be no surprise in learning that (due to continuing poor results in the eyes of the government and commentators) the Law Commission (2019) was engaged to consult on whether confiscation law should again be reviewed (Ministry of Justice, 2016). The Law Commission report (2022) makes 119 recommendations for change, a brief precis of which can be found at the end of this section.

The number of confiscation orders reduced in the two years from 2014 by 7% and are made in "only a tiny fraction of total crimes" (NAO, 2016: 12). Use of restraint orders to freeze assets fell by 12% in the same period but the reasons for the fall are not verified. Problems encountered by law enforcement (particularly police) are well documented in the results of court cases, case law, legal advice papers and reports from government sources which are mainly critical of the general application (or lack of it) of proceeds of crime powers (House of Commons, 2016; NAO, 2007, 2013, 2016). Proceeds of crime as a specialism became besieged by government targets practically from the onset of POCA (House of Commons, 2007; HMIC et al., 2004; NAO, 2007).

Figures from the most recent Asset Recovery Bulletin (Home Office, 2023) claim that in 2022–2023, £339.1 million has been recovered from criminals, although the amount still represents a fall of 5% from the previous year, although there is a general and continued rise over the previous six years. Confiscation was responsible for £179 million although in the five-year period reviewed, the overall number of confiscation orders has reduced (Home Office, 2023). Forfeiture orders amounted to £97.2 million over five years, determined to be a 50% fall between 2012 and 2022. Civil recovery orders accounted for the rest with a total of £62.9 million. On closer analysis, the apparent increase in total figures for civil recovery and for confiscation orders in 2022–2023 can be attributed to two separate case results. For civil recovery, an order achieved by the NCA of £53.9 million and for confiscation, an order achieved by the SFO for 93.5 million. Restrained assets decreased by 34%. All of these figures and results should be read in conjunction with the entire Asset Recovery Bulletin.

As stated previously, the legislative intent of POCA (2002: 2 (1)) was the "reduction of crime", an intention which is arguably juxtaposed with achieving monetary targets. How government asset recovery targets were arrived at is unknown and beyond the scope of this book. From 2011, the government appeared to recognise that financial targets for asset recovery were not working. Presumably to redefine that strategy failure, politicians became [publicly] committed to removing asset recovery targets (Home Office, 2011b). As Garland (1996: 458) observed when considering how governments alter criteria by which failure is determined: "performance indicators tend to measure 'outputs' rather than 'outcomes', what the organisation does rather than what, if anything it achieves". A relevant question is whether government targets had a detrimental effect on the wider use of financial investigation techniques within the broader investigation community. The question remains unanswered, but asset recovery totals continued to be measured (despite what officials said publicly) and used to justify organisational performance (Crown Prosecution Service, 2014; Home Office, 2017).

Law Commission recommendations

Essentially, the Law Commission was tasked with identifying issues with confiscation legislation and practice to 2018 and then to identify potential solutions to any issues found. Wherever possible, the task was to attempt to modernise and simplify confiscation law wherever possible (Home Office, 2023a). The Law Commission (2022) responded to the challenge with 119 recommendations including timetabling for service of statements and arranging court appearances, earlier consideration of confiscation matters, a variation to the period whereby a court may vary a confiscation order, defining and apportioning benefit and a host of other issues. Should the reader wish to know more about the proposed changes to the confiscation regime, reference should be made to the Law Commission (2022) and to the government response to it. The situation is mentioned briefly in this work as confiscation has long occluded the drive to embed some of its skill-base more widely among routine investigators. An in-depth consideration of changes to the confiscation regime is not the purpose of this book but the reader should be aware that alterations are constantly being recommended and have been so since the inception of POCA (2002).

Confiscation remains the main area for the application of financial investigation techniques and it appears to remain in the minds of general practitioners across law enforcement that it is a complicated specialist area removed from everyday policing activity (Davidson, Walker and Dayman, 2014). The perception that financial investigation and confiscation are the same does little to persuade non-specialist investigators of the potential benefit available to them if they were to apply and implement financial investigation techniques. These may be significant hurdles if wider use of financial investigation techniques is to be achieved.

Enforcement of confiscation orders

Enforcement of low-level confiscation orders appears to function efficiently whereas high-level orders remain problematic and attract a great deal of government criticism (NAO, 2013, 2016). This may be due to the more complicated measures available to courts in the case of high value non-payment cases. Legal arguments and litigation often take years and defendants can rely substantially on the Human Rights Act 1998 to challenge proceeds of crime legislation (Giles, 2013). The House of Commons Committee of Public Accounts (2014) might have missed the point regarding the enforcement process, assessing the problem to result from late introduction of AFIs in high value cases, a lack of collaboration and failure to freeze (restrain) assets early enough in investigations. The NAO (2016) repeats the same message that enforcement and prosecution agencies have not increased early intervention action (restraint orders) or early use of AFIs in investigations. The extent to which such factors may affect enforcement of confiscation orders appears to remain undetermined.

Enforcement of confiscation orders continued to be made difficult by two key elements. First, until recently it has remained the domain of Her Majesty's Courts and Tribunals Service and there is a clear lack of co-ordination and inter-agency working across the confiscation system which is not readily equipped to deal with pursuing assets subject to confiscation orders (Bullock, 2010; Wood, 2016). Second, once the confiscation determination was made there was no longer a live investigation. Production orders could not be utilised unless it was a clear matter of tracing original benefit from the original criminality. Such circumstances appear to be rare. The legislation in this regard, has therefore been very clearly limited and successive governments have been slow in reacting to the problem (although they have been consistently vociferous in condemning poor enforcement results). Amendments to POCA (Serious Crime Act, 2015: section 38) allowed production orders to be used post confiscation determination to investigate previously unidentified assets (Wood, 2016). However, the measure only became operational after the issue of amended POCA Codes of Practice were published in March 2016 (Home Office, 2016) and any effect of the new powers appears currently undetermined.

The enforcement aspect of the confiscation process is isolated from the rest of the confiscation process and presents a key information gap in the literature where there does appear to have been only limited research (Bullock et al., 2009; Wood, 2016). Until the establishment of several Asset Confiscation Enforcement (ACE) teams in 2015 to concentrate on unpaid confiscation orders, successive governments do not appear to have focused on the issue. Enforcement appears to have remained somewhat of an afterthought of the confiscation process (Wood, 2016). This links directly with a more generic philosophy of financial investigation and perhaps identifies what appear to be problems in government and strategic policing comprehension of what financial investigation entails and the associated challenge of increasing its effectiveness (Law Commission, 2022).

There does not appear to be a cohesive approach at any level (strategic, tactical or practice) which attempts to identify and integrate effective and generic financial investigation and proceeds of crime legislation across law enforcement, the prosecution and court system. The NAO (2013, 2016), government reports and available proceeds of crime literature generally do not focus upon the practicalities of embedding financial investigation and proceeds of crime legislation as an integrated process. Reports to date, perhaps even including Howell, Horton and Gill (2013) and Brown et al. (2012), invariably focus on identification of problems and poor results for asset recovery. This literature review acknowledges that the point is intermittently made that financial investigation presents a potential which may be of benefit to investigations other than confiscation (HMIC et al., 2004; House of Commons, 2016). Few commentators seem to distinguish financial investigation as a broader skill set and even where commentators recognise its potential to assist in criminal investigation, it is usually in conjunction with investigations involving serious and organised crime (Wood, 2017).

Commentators frequently use the term financial investigation, but available research appears to be devoid of an examination of what the essential characteristics of it might be. An integrated and systematised process does not seem to have been theorised. Although the (limited) research to date examines particular areas of the process, such as confiscation (NAO, 2013, 2016; Levi and Osofsky, 1995; Ryder, 2013) and enforcement (Wood, 2016), recommendations tend to be made at policy level rather than identifying and overcoming inhibiting factors at the tactical, practical and training levels across law enforcement (House of Commons, 2016). This may be a gap in the literature and this book identifies and addresses some of those inhibitors in order to move beyond policy recommendations and theorise an answer to the issue of wider routine use of parts of the financial investigation skill set.

The current confiscation process appears to remain problematic. A lack of incentive for anyone to deal vigorously with confiscation matters was identified by Levi and Osofsky (1995). It is unclear whether matters have significantly improved over time. It seems difficult to dispute the conclusion that, "Poor implementation of the confiscation order scheme has severely hampered its effectiveness" (House of Commons, 2014: 3). One of the Committee recommendations was that law enforcement and prosecution agencies should agree a common set of criteria to ensure consistent consideration across all acquisitive crimes with a view to the confiscation process. The current and long-standing perception among general law enforcement practitioners that financial investigation is only useful for confiscation and money laundering investigations remains, both regarded as complex specialist areas requiring AFIs (Brown et al., 2012; HMIC et al., 2004; House of Commons, 2016).

The perception that proceeds of crime legislation is for specialists does not appear helped by the introduction of new powers such as unexplained wealth orders (UWOs) under the Criminal Finances Act 2017. It has become apparent to the government and various money laundering commentators that funds used for foreign investment in the UK (particularly in London) may originate from criminality abroad (NCA, 2018c; Saviano, 2012; Transparency International UK, 2015a, 2017c). The NCA (2018c: 44) is explicit about the matter: "The UK is a prime destination for foreign corrupt politically exposed persons to launder the proceeds of corruption. Investment in UK property, particularly in London, continues to be an attractive mechanism to launder funds".

How to alter that perception and to prevent constant new legislation from re-enforcing it is an issue for consideration across the entire spectrums of routine evidential gathering as well as asset recovery.

Drug trafficking

It can be argued that the Drug Trafficking Offences Act (1986) and the trafficking offences therein is the initial wellspring of the confiscation process and the route along which financial investigation initially progressed. Drug trafficking can be defined as a group of actions, whether committed in England, Wales or elsewhere, each of which is an offence under the various statutes dealing with drug related crime (Bell, 2002). Trafficking of narcotics remains problematic for law enforcement at all levels, local, regional and international. Bean (2008) and Madinger (2012) stress that each distribution system is different and poses distinct problems, often requiring bespoke strategies on the part of the authorities. The introduction of an asset recovery regime (in the DTOA 1986) was a process that could be applied universally (though with differing degrees of success) to all drug trafficking offences in an attempt to curtail the financial threat they presented. In the long term, the strategy can now be assessed as short-sighted.

The initial thrust of financial investigation and asset recovery connected solely in the first instance to drug trafficking offences may have in large part been responsible for a disconnect at all levels (strategic, tactical and practice) with its broader use. It has remained disconnected from mainstream law enforcement (House of Commons, 2016; Levi, 1991). Levi and Osofsky (1995) observed that financial investigation had become regarded as a specialist area of some complexity largely as a direct result of its first 15 years associated with drug squads. It has proven a difficult route to re-negotiate (House of Commons, 2016; van Duyne and Levi, 1999). The House of Commons (2014: 3) concluded: "Each agency uses different criteria to determine when to use confiscation orders and there is a widespread lack of awareness among staff within these agencies of the relevant legislation". It seems a reasonable supposition that lack of awareness of relevant legislation at all levels (and therefore the powers available) has impacted upon the general use of investigative powers. The extent of that impact is difficult to assess. Research appears currently unavailable which might offer data to allow an empirical assessment of how use of POCA powers may have been affected. The point seems to relate directly to broader routine use in terms of strategic approach, availability and levels of training and any systemic issues which may inhibit financial investigation becoming ubiquitous across all law enforcement investigations.

This section has identified that the approach to financial investigation continues to be disparate and problematic (Brown et al., 2012; House of Commons, 2014; Howell, Horton and Gill, 2013; National Audit Office, 2013). The confused and fragmented situation outlined by the House of Commons (2014) is exacerbated by an apparent lack of objective and analytically based literature that might assist in understanding where financial investigation has faced problems, initially as a result of its umbilical attachment to the drugs arena and subsequently as a result of its ubiquitous relationship with asset recovery. Where drug trafficking is concerned, Levi (2013: 1) states clearly: "Financial investigation is often mistakenly seen only in the context of proceeds of confiscation rather than in revealing the financial relationships in drug networks".

There appears to be a clear evidence gap in available literature as to whether the correlation between drug squads and initial asset recovery powers under drug trafficking legislation had any detrimental effect on the general and effective use of financial investigation. The result has been a succession of legislative attempts to strengthen proceeds of crime powers (and thereby financial investigation techniques) without addressing the apparent problem of the perception that financial investigation has little benefit to offer the general investigative arena. Nor has the impact of confiscation on drug markets (or other areas of criminality) been properly assessed (Levi, 2013). The question is whether general investigators understand what tools are available to conduct basic financial investigation enquires and to attempt to provide some insight which may, in the long term, assist future practice to better align financial investigations with all law enforcement investigations.

Money laundering

It is perhaps worth pausing a moment to consider that money laundering is a relatively new legal concept both in the UK and internationally. Prior to 1989, hardly any anti-money laundering controls existed anywhere in the world (Levi and Reuter, 2006). Within the UK, the POCA concept of money laundering now seems simple enough. An offender illegally obtains property and either retains it or transfers it (for benefit or otherwise) on behalf of himself or another. Money laundering is now recognised in law as an act, or a stand-alone offence, separate to what was once termed the predicate (underlying) offence (examples such as theft, robbery and most commonly drug trafficking).

In that regard, money laundering may still be affected by its origins, firstly in drug trafficking legislation and then as a supporting offence to predicate criminality (the underlying criminal offence) created by the Criminal Justice Act (CJA, 1988). The proceeds of the criminality were required to be proven under the Act. By its own admission, the CPS prior to POCA (2002) had difficulty in charging, "under the appropriate Act, the source of the criminal proceeds" (Crown Prosecution Service, 2018b). A predicate offence, the crime committed to enable the indictment of an alleged offender with money laundering, was also essential to successfully attaining its conviction. If the offender was found not guilty of the predicate crime (underlying offences such as theft, burglary, robbery) or the charge was withdrawn for some reason, the money laundering indictment would automatically fall. Perceptions of money laundering among many police officers that it is relevant only to serious, high value and complex investigations, usually with an international aspect, are a major inhibiting factor to better use of POCA legislation and financial investigation techniques (Davidson, Walker and Dayman, 2014).

Such relative simplicity belies the difficulties faced by investigators in addressing what has become an endemic international problem at all levels of acquisitive criminality (HM Treasury and Home Office, 2015, 2017; House of Commons, 2016; NCA, 2014b). Due to its highly publicised history with gangsters such as Al Capone, Charles "Lucky" Luciano and Meyer Lansky (Madinger, 2012; Robinson, 1998) it may not be surprising that the United States of America (USA) was the first country to begin to enable investigators to attack the asset bases of criminals by establishing money laundering as a federal crime under the Money Laundering Control Act (1986). Since 1970, The Bank Secrecy Act had required banks and other financial institutions to maintain accurate transaction records as well as reporting cash transactions of over $10,000. The 1986 legislation introduced civil and criminal forfeiture procedures and subsequent legislation such as the Anti-Drug Abuse Act (1988) and the Annunzio-Wylie Anti-Money Laundering Act (1992) strengthened sanctions for Bank Secrecy Act violations according to the Financial Crimes Enforcement Network (FinCEN, 2016).

In an international context, any domestic USA legislation could only have limited impact and the primary focus for money laundering offences remained upon highly publicised drug trafficking criminality. Drug trafficking was already recognised in many countries as an area of criminality which rewarded criminal behaviour with vast profits, much of which was retained by offenders with impunity (Hodgson, 1984; UN, 1988). Two years after the first criminalisation of money laundering in the USA, the United Nations (1988) "Vienna Convention" enlisted 106 signatory states which committed to implement various measures based upon what were to become long-standing global definitions (in varying forms) of money laundering, initially to deal with property originating from drug trafficking:

1) The conversion or transfer of property, knowing that such property is derived from any offence or offences established in accordance with subparagraph a) of this paragraph, or from an act of participation in such offence or offences, for the purpose of concealing or disguising the illicit origin of the property or of assisting any person who is involved in the commission of such an offence or offences to evade the legal consequences of his actions.
2) The concealment or disguise of the true nature, source, location, disposition, movement, rights with respect to, or ownership of property, knowing that such property is derived from an offence or offences.
3) The acquisition, possession or use of property, knowing, at the time of receipt, that such property was derived from an offence or offences.

Article 4 of the United Nations (1988) went on to make the commission of drug trafficking offences and money laundering offences liable to various penalties, one of which was confiscation. Though it took nearly a decade and a half for domestic legislation, the UK offence definitions proved far-reaching and with very similar wording being recognisable in the money laundering sections of POCA (2002: 198).

Money laundering in the UK is currently attacked on two fronts, by a series of money laundering regulations and by a prosecution regime (Hopkins and Shelton, 2019). A contemporary core issue is that UK definitions of money laundering have now extended to potentially include most underlying offending as well as virtually any interaction with proceeds of crime (Hicks and Graycar, 2019; POCA, 2002). In summation, section 327 creates offences of concealing, disguising, converting, transferring or removing criminal property (from the UK), section 328 creates offences of committing any offence under s327 by or on behalf of a third person and section 329 creates offences for a person to acquire, use or possess criminal property. The very important consequence of these offences is that money laundering is no longer simply about cash. It is about all criminal property and concealing or disguising it includes its nature, source, location, disposition, movement or ownership of it (POCA, 2002 s327: 198). These offences seem intentionally far-reaching and are not just the remit of AFIs. The standard definition and understanding of money laundering in its pre-supposition of substantive criminal involvement linked to organised crime has now extended to all acquisitive criminal offences in the UK (and offences abroad but which could be prosecuted in the UK) (Hicks, 2010). It should be noted that the wording of the offences closely reflects that of the definitions created by the UN Convention of 1988 described above as well as the expanded scope in the UN Convention of 2000.

Two problems present themselves regarding how money laundering is perceived at strategic, tactical and practice levels. First is the term money laundering. Second is the traditional view of how money laundering is arranged by acquisitive criminals in the form of placement (inserting proceeds of crime into the financial system such as banks or financial instruments, layering (transferring property to disguise its origins as proceeds of crime) and integration (re-insertion of seemingly clean monies into legitimate commodities or assets). This tripartite sequence of money laundering is grounded in knowledge and experience around drug trafficking. The sequence and the nature of the offending from which it is derived may lead non-specialist investigators to perceive that some specialist knowledge is required to uncover evidence of it. Money laundering as an adjective has become so well used in recent times that it, "has become almost meaningless, as it does not adequately convey the method by which the vast amount of funds involved across the world have been generated" (Lilley, 2003: 6). At least one critic goes as far as stating that the label money laundering has acted to the detriment of the activity it seeks to describe (Platt, 2015: 25).

Money laundering continues to be a phrase which is conceptually elusive. Is it a separate activity (like handling stolen goods) or is it no more than an element of criminal offences such as robbery, theft or fraud? (Levi and Reuter, 2006). The UK Office for National Statistics does not include money laundering in its annual crime surveys of England and Wales as it is regarded as either the precursor to, or consequence of a crime (Levi et al., 2015). Use of the term is beginning to be challenged. The term gives rise to an assumption that money laundering involves some formal process which must be undertaken to clean criminal property, long held to be the three-stage process of placement, layering and integration (FinCEN, 2016; Platt, 2015, Robinson, 1998). It appears to be a prevailing misconception which leads to the majority of non-specialist investigators (and senior managers) failing to see money laundering as a priority as, according to the existing model, it is only identified when other offences are fully detected (Davidson, Walker and Dayman, 2014; Law Commission, 2019). Under current UK legislation, committing a money laundering offence no longer must involve money. The underlying practical issue (and outside the scope of this project) will be to critically assess prospects to alter the perception of money laundering towards it being accessible to the general investigative environment and everyday evidence gathering.

Where financial investigation is concerned, money laundering appears to be regarded as a financial enquiry and therefore considered to be the domain of AFIs rather than general investigators (Davidson, Walker and Dayman, 2014). In a survey of AFIs the common offence investigated was money laundering, closely followed by fraud and drugs offences (Howell, Horton and Gill, 2013) The conclusion seems to be that money laundering is generally perceived (at all levels) as part of the economic crime specialism. This is in no small part probably due to the offence being defined in proceeds of crime legislation and perceived as the complex domain of AFIs. An additional and integral problem appears to be how to combat the perception at all levels that financial investigation is not necessarily a specialist function and how to disassociate it with the traditional view of confiscation (which can only be a specialist role) in order to use it effectively elsewhere. This point will be important to the synthesis of any transferable philosophy for financial investigation as part of the wider research project undertaken.

Put simply, money laundering refers to the efforts of criminals to convert or conceal the proceeds of crime and to give them the appearance of legitimacy (Hicks, 2010). The general perception within the literature is that money laundering is the conversion of illegal (dirty) cash into apparently legitimate (clean) cash by way of the three-stage process of placement, layering and integration (Robinson, 1998; Madinger, 2012). It is a perceived process which perhaps can no longer be considered as accurate in terms of the definitions within UK law (and in the definitions promulgated by the Vienna Convention 1988) (Platt, 2015). As Hicks, (2010) points out, money laundering is no longer solely to do with cash.

Where then, should law enforcement focus its attention? Strategy and policy continue to direct their focus on what can perhaps be termed high level traditional money layering (Brown et al., 2012; Howell, Horton and Gill, 2013). At the same time (and perhaps confusingly) there is now an almost ubiquitous intonation within strategic documents that the tools available to investigate money laundering (and therefore financial investigation techniques) should be a capability of all law enforcement practitioners (HMCPSI et al., 2010; NAO, 2013; NCA, 2014, 2015).

It seems broadly accepted that financial gain is the principal motivation for most criminals whether acting alone or as part of organised groups (Home Office, 2016a; Kuhns, Blevins and Lee, 2012) and this applies with limited exceptions (NCA, 2014). The premise appears a simple one, but a series of influences seem to have transformed what appears to be a straightforward concept into one of complexity.

At face value, money laundering appears no longer concerned simply with the movement of actual cash but despite the increasing prevalence of non-cash payment methods in developed economies, somewhere between 46% and 82% of all transactions globally are still conducted in cash (Financial Action Task

Force and Middle East and North Africa Financial Action Task Force, 2015). If such is the case, then is money laundering really the complex area that investigators think it is? The extent of the UK money laundering problem remains unknown as assessments of it tend to rely on historical cases and recorded prosecutions. It is currently suggested that London alone is subjected to money laundering in excess of £100 billion per year (House of Commons, 2016). The NCA (2018c) acknowledges money laundering figures are estimates at best and have no reliable way of distinguishing between domestically or internationally invested criminal funds. Despite the threat from money laundering to financial systems, the UK does not have a dedicated national money laundering unit (NCA, 2019f).

One money laundering commentator makes a promise that if you were to walk one mile in any direction from any railway station in any major city in Europe or North America, you will pass within an elbow's distance of a property that is owned, managed or constructed by dirty money (Robinson, 1998: 2). With regard to what it terms high end money laundering the NCA (2016a, 2019d) candidly acknowledges that its knowledge is limited but improving. Keatinge (2023) acknowledges that the NCA may well lead the money laundering law enforcement portfolio within the UK, but is inhibited on its own by what is described as the current "fragmented response" to the problem.

The subject becomes more complicated when distinctions are made by reports of governmental or international commentators. For example, are money laundering and terrorist financing two different things? There is a more recent distinction made between organised crime (nationally in any country) and transnational organised crime which continues to be linked ever more closely to terrorism and the issue of national security (Berdal and Seranno et al., 2002). They may appear as interrelated topics but there is perhaps a distinction to be made. Money laundering is usually considered to be the process of making dirty money clean (proceeds of crime) whereas terrorist financing frequently involves clean money (proceeds for crime) being utilised for nefarious purposes (Financial Action Task Force, 2012). Platt (2015: 21) postulates that the two concepts are distinct: "to the extent that money laundering is concerned with the origin of the money, whilst terrorist financing is largely (though not exclusively) about the destination of the money". There appears a great deal of academic discussion for consideration around both points, but under POCA (2002) and the current terrorism provisions (2000 and 2001) both contexts appear to be money laundering. The first concept is about the proceeds *of* crime, the second is about the proceeds *for* crime, the latter not being often recognised particularly when applied to emerging criminal threats such as distributed denial of service attacks (DDOS), a common type of cybercrime activity.

This section has established that money laundering is well documented and discussed within the literature but that primary focus remains directed towards serious crime within the UK (OCGs) and the international threat to the financial system (UK and globally). The reality is that money laundering appears to remain the domain of AFIs ensconced in specialist units (ECUs). This seems to perpetuate the already widespread misunderstanding that money laundering (like confiscation) is a specialist area of investigation. There is little discussion in the literature regarding the different levels of money laundering and how they correlate to the effective use of financial investigation techniques particularly at the practical level.

The literature focuses attention on money laundering at the highest echelons of criminality, and largely ignores criminality at other levels. This appears to have resulted in a distinct disconnect between money laundering offences (and therefore financial investigation techniques) utilised by specialist units and those investigated as part of general policing. Financial investigation techniques appear routinely disregarded by general investigators (and supervisors) at the tactical and practical levels (Brown et al., 2012). Thus, the financial investigation techniques that could be applied broadly and deeply against the diversity of criminality are instead applied in a limited and fragmented fashion. This is a clear problem relating core financial investigation characteristics and needs to be carefully considered in considering how to apply them more broadly at routine level. To measure the extent of the identified disconnect, empirical data to help distinguish between specialised and non-specialist use of financial investigation techniques would be required. Such evidence-based data might also provide insight into conceptual differences of financial investigation that may exist between strategic, tactical and practical levels.

Cash detention

The cash detention regime engenders civil proceedings in a criminal court (Magistrates). For UK law enforcement and for the criminal courts it has meant a step change in dealing with cases. Cash detention proceedings are *in rem* (Hall, 2012), they are proceedings against the property (cash) itself. The question the court has to address is whether the property is guilty (not whether the person is). Available literature investigating or analysing the use and application of cash detention powers under POCA or previous legislation is very limited. There are several examples of case law and legal comment (*R v Fletcher*, 2013: *R v Iqbal*, 2010) but little in the way of academic research.

The power to detain cash over the amount of £10,000 was introduced as a tool for law enforcement (police and Her Majesty's Customs officers) by section 25 of the Criminal Justice (International Co-operation) Act (1990). It was limited to drug trafficking investigations, uplifted cash had to be estimated to be in excess of £10,000 and cash was defined as including notes and coins in any currency. The standard of proof in any cash detention proceedings would be determined on a balance of probabilities (the civil standard), a lower standard than in a criminal prosecution (beyond reasonable doubt). Aside from ports as the domain of Her Majesty's Customs and Excise (HMCE) the power was little used, particularly by police. A point of some significance is worth noting in relation to the POCA (2002) cash detention powers. They demonstrate the long-standing Parliamentary intention to establish seizure of cash at the grass roots level of law enforcement as an everyday practice. That intention and the previous limitation on the powers involving drug trafficking offences appear to have proven mutually exclusive.

Similar powers were included in section 42 of the Drug Trafficking Act (1994), but with the same limitations and at the expense of other acquisitive criminality. It was only with the passing of POCA (2002) that the cash detention regime was expanded to include cash originating from or intended for use in any criminality (POCA, 2002: s294). One point that had not altered was that cash seizure powers remained available to all constables and customs officers. The threshold for cash detention under POCA initially remained at £10,000 but quickly fell to £5,000 (2004) and then £1,000 (2006) at which level it has remained to the present (Statutory Instruments 420/2004; 1699/2006). Initial uptake and use of the powers (particularly by police officers) seemed promising and a total of £16.7 million was subject to cash detention provisions in the first year (HMIC et al., 2004). Since 2004 (except for 2006–2007 which was £47 million), the average national amount of cash seized under POCA provisions has been between £62 million and £65 million (Home Office 2010, 2023). In 2009 the powers were extended to other agencies (Legislation.gov.uk, 2009/2707). Logic may suggest that the extension of cash detention powers to other law enforcement agencies would result in an increase in cash seized. Such appears not to be the case and the average amount seized annually across all law enforcement, remains similar to pre 2009 (Home Office 2013, 2014a, 2015). Reasons for what in effect appears to be a gradual decline in the use of cash detention powers are not clear and more research (outside the scope of this study) is required. The latest figures to be released do not show any real increase in the amount of cash seized annually (Home Office, 2023).

What is clear is that cash detention powers were intended for use by general investigators across law enforcement. Like money laundering, use of the powers was clearly not envisioned as a specialist area by government legislators. Hence their availability to all police and HMRC officers in all three Acts where they have been described (CJICA, 1990; DTA, 1994; POCA, 2002). A singular problem has been that the only cash detention training originally available was provided for AFIs, most of whom were already specialist confiscators. General investigators were not given the opportunity to attend cash detention training courses. The apparent lack of foresight combined with lack of a national implementation strategy (relevant to a generic philosophy of financial investigation) resulted in piecemeal application across law enforcement and a limited trajectory of the powers. Basic detective training courses now provide a one-hour training session on cash detention (College of Policing, 2024a) but the chronic lack of training (including other areas of proceeds of crime training) is the subject of much political criticism (House of Commons, 2016). Usage of cash detention powers by general investigators and whether they are effective remains unmeasured.

References concerning the government and law enforcement intention to "take the cash out of crime" are to be found in various sources, even including the national newspaper for convicted offenders (Durham Constabulary, 2015; Insidetime, 2014; National Archives, 2011; Northumbria Police, 2009). There is little discussion in the literature as to whether cash seizure powers are effective, how they are used by law enforcement and whether their potential is understood. There appears to be a distinct disconnect (potentially due to lack of appropriate training) in the awareness of cash detention provisions among general investigators (*R v Iqbal*, 2011) and their tactical use particularly as an intervention opportunity in any investigation. Underpinning this supposition, are the latest Home Office (2023) figures which show a 37% fall in cash seizures made by police forces.

Evidence of the lack of use of cash detention powers as a tactic (and its lack of integration with the NIM) can be demonstrated. Powers exist within POCA (2002) whereby authority to search for cash can be obtained judicially (from at least a magistrate) or from a senior officer (POCA, 2002: s290). Obtaining such an authority only applies to planned investigations where the location of cash is suspected. For all other instances where cash is located as a result of other investigative practices there are two initial criteria: whether the uplifting officer (of the cash) is lawfully on premises and whether the amount seized is over £1,000 (or estimated so to be).

For those planned searches where cash is suspected to be located and where recovery of the cash is one of the primary reasons for the search there is an inherent implication that some type of intelligence is involved. Hence the authorisation required to search for it. With the quantity of intelligence received daily by law enforcement, particularly the number of SARs (380,000 in 2016) the expectation might be that searches for cash would by now have become a routine practice for law enforcement (particularly for police). Statistics produced by the Home Office (2010, 2011, 2012, 2013, 2014a, 2014b) which are submitted by each law enforcement agency annually, suggest that only 17 such searches for cash took place between 2003 and 2015. More recent figures are unclear.

From the very limited available data, three possibilities present themselves. First, law enforcement practitioners are unaware of the available powers regarding searches for cash. Second, intelligence received about the whereabouts of cash is a rarity. Third, the NIM (or its operators in intelligence units) is deficient in processing information to present intervention opportunities to seize cash. In view of the available evidence, the government intention that cash detention should be a non-specialist power across law enforcement appears to require further work. The powers are utilised in unplanned situations averaging £40.3 million annually (Home Office, 2017) but as a targeted intervention tactic (particularly useful for attacking organised criminality) the evidence suggests otherwise (Home Office, 2010, 2011, 2012, 2013, 2014a, 2014b). Addressing the issues identified in this section will be an intrinsic feature of establishing the characteristics of following the financial footprint as they apply to general law enforcement investigations and integration of financial intelligence within the NIM. Consideration of the seemingly piecemeal application of cash detention powers will also form part of the challenge for embedding wider routine use of financial investigation techniques at all levels (strategic, tactical and practical).

Conclusion

The reader is reminded that the first part of this chapter in relation to terminology as it applies to financial investigation identified key themes related to the essential characteristics of financial investigation and the broader application of it as a practicable philosophy across law enforcement for all investigations. First, the apparently continuing dysfunction within and between the strategic, tactical and practice levels, which is underpinned by the apparent lack of a comprehensive national UK financial investigation strategy or any concerted effort to go beyond the traditional focus on confiscation and asset recovery. This is not mitigated by the partial coverage of financial investigation in the national UK Organised Crime Strategy, and the generalised disconnect between financial investigation and the National Intelligence Model (NIM). Second, there seems little or no mention of financial investigation and related techniques in the literature that may offer an integrative theme (to substantially enhance NIM application) that could be used for general law enforcement across a wide range of investigation and intelligence processes. Notwithstanding all this potential, terminological confusion in the literature (alongside policy and practice) appears to have maintained a myth of financial investigation as a specialist silo. Third, no definite and collective training strategy appears to have been devised which will underpin the implementation of financial investigation techniques into mainstream law enforcement practice. Available literature provides little or no data upon which a general training requirement can be based. Empirical data seems required regarding the extent to which gaps might exist, measuring these, and identifying what can be done to attempt to rectify the situation .

The discussion in this section identifies additional key themes which can be integrated with the points already raised and which further inform the two central research questions. First is the lack of a legislative definition of financial investigation. As identified by Levi (2013) the term has an unlimited breadth of range from the simple to the complex. It is a factor that may be integral to the seeming inability of policy makers and practitioners to remove inhibitors preventing the effective implementation of the political and strategic desire to embed financial investigation within the standard investigation environment. A clear and legislated definition appears requisite. If financial investigation can be de-mythologised from being perceived as a specialist area only useful in asset recovery cases, general investigators might begin to be persuaded that financial investigation is something they can utilise. In this regard, the authors offer an alternative definition of financial investigation at the conclusion of Chapter 6.

Second, this chapter appears to have identified a clear gap in the literature regarding the lack of comprehensive identification and disparate discussion within the available literature concerning factors that constitute essential characteristics of effective financial investigation. Basic techniques of financial investigation need to be clearly separated from the specialist area of confiscation (for which NCA accreditation is required to practice). This is not facilitated by the apparent disconnect at the strategic and tactical levels where there appears to be little use of investigative strategy to better utilise financial investigation techniques across all criminal enquiries as an investigation skill set (House of Commons, 2016), a key element for consideration. Nor is it assisted by the apparent absence of a clear implementation strategy at government and management levels to standardise basic financial investigation techniques for use in general investigations. Effective financial investigation for non-specialists seems limited to sporadic use of proceeds of crime tools such as production orders, land registry and credit reference checks (Howell, Horton and Gill, 2013). The repeated source of information for researchers or government reports about financial investigations has mainly been AFIs themselves (Brown et al., 2012; Gale and Kelly, 2018; Howell, Horton and Gill, 2013; Wood, 2017). There is a clear need to establish a baseline of empirical data (an objective for this project) which may afford a clearer picture of financial investigation outside the specialist environment and any inhibitors to its wider application.

Third is the practical issue of proceeds of crime training not only within law enforcement at all levels, but involving the judiciary, the court service, the CPS and other prosecuting authorities. There appears to be a clear problem at all levels (political, strategic, tactical and practice) in recognising and understanding factors which might negatively influence the trajectory of financial investigation. Such factors may exacerbate the absence of a clear implementation process identified herein by way of which its techniques can be accessed and effectively used by investigators at all levels and regardless of specialisation or generalised application.

Where then, should law enforcement focus its attention? Strategy, policy and most literature continue to directly focus on what can perhaps be termed high level traditional money layering and asset recovery (Howell, Horton and Gill, 2013; Brown et al., 2012). That attention largely ignores criminality at other levels. This appears to have resulted in a disconnect between money laundering offences (and therefore financial investigation techniques) utilised by specialist units and those investigated as part of general policing. Financial investigation techniques are routinely disregarded by general investigators (and supervisors) at the tactical and practical levels (Brown et al., 2012; Hughes and Brown, 2022). Thus, the financial investigation techniques that could be applied broadly and deeply against a diversity of criminality are instead applied in a limited and fragmented fashion. This is a clear problem relating to the essential financial investigation characteristics which routine investigators could be taught (beyond the more complicated realm of asset recovery) and needs to be carefully considered in applying financial investigation more widely at all levels of law enforcement. To measure the extent of the identified disconnect the researcher intends to offer empirical data to help distinguish between specialised and non-specialist use of financial investigation techniques and identify the level of knowledge of them within a sample of the law enforcement environment. Inhibitors to better practice may lie in the lack of effective, broader training of investigators but also in potential conceptual differences of financial investigation that may exist between strategic, tactical and practical levels.

Fourth is the clear gap identified in this chapter concerning structured attempts to ascertain the value of financial investigation outside of the confiscation and civil asset recovery processes. More research seems required in addition to the specific areas already targeted involving organised crime groups where financial investigation is more frequently used (Howell, Horton and Gill, 2013; Wood, 2017). The apparent confusion between the disciplines of confiscation and financial investigation, coupled with attaining (confiscation) financial targets set by the government may have contributed to the perception that financial investigation is best left to experts in the minds of general investigators. The aim of this book has always been to understand what non-specialist tools are available for general investigators to conduct basic financial enquiries and to attempt to provide some insight which may, in the long term, assist future practice to better align financial investigation with law enforcement investigations.

The extent of the perception that financial investigation equates largely with confiscation within the general law enforcement community appears to remain currently unmeasured. This work attempts to understand how endemic that perception is. Financial investigation techniques seem generally unused by general investigators (and supervisors) at the tactical and practical levels (Brown et al., 2012). It is currently difficult to measure the extent of the identified disconnect between specialised and non-specialist use of financial investigation techniques and to identify the level of knowledge of them within all levels of the law enforcement environment. Any current conceptual differences of financial investigation that may exist between strategic, tactical and practical levels remain elusive at this point.

4 Historical trajectory, government reports and financial investigation research

Political hinterland to the proceeds of Crime Act 2002

This section considers two aspects which may have influenced continued efforts to successfully implement an effective UK asset recovery structure against a political backdrop focused largely on the amounts of money being confiscated from criminals. The first aspect is the continuing review process administered by successive governments (including any directly commissioned academic research) since the advent of POCA (2002). The second aspect concerns the various groups and agencies to which governments have given responsibility for driving the implementation of POCA forwards.

The focus of different governments concerning asset recovery since the Cabinet Office (2000) is an interesting one and seems to have remained contradictory. The key function for the Proceeds of Crime Act (2002: 2) is to contribute to the reduction of crime. That key objective has been considerably hindered by the almost immediate introduction (after the enactment of POCA) of an incentivisation scheme reimbursing law enforcement a portion of what it confiscated or forfeited under the Act (House of Commons, 2006; Leong, 2016). The Treasury Department takes the first 50% of all proceeds before any money is paid to law enforcement (Home Office, 2017). Prior to and particularly since the POCA legislation (2002), successive governments, the Home Office and the Treasury focused upon achieving monetary targets (Hansard, HC Deb 30 Oct 2001, vol 373 c759; Home Office, 2007). Law enforcement has been expected to achieve those targets. Contemporaneous with that expectation, law enforcement (particularly police and HMRC) have been expected to embed POCA as a general investigation tool within the criminal justice system (Home Office, 2018a).

The two ambitions do not seem to conjoin. Reduction of crime and the achievement of financial goals set by the Home Office appears to be an unresolved contradiction. Under the guise of asset recovery and meeting government targets, financial investigation implementation may have been negatively affected. Post POCA (2002) financial investigation may have been obscured from the outset by the asset recovery drive to fill the "tin box", the euphemism for the government Recovered Assets Incentivisation Fund (HMCPSI et al.,

DOI: 10.4324/9781003438649-4

2010). On that point, Levi (2013: 11) observes that: "The creation of the 'asset recovery' culture has had some negative effects on appreciation of the wider benefits of financial investigation. This culture is difficult to break even in the UK, where the financial targets have been abandoned as counter-productive".

The government set an asset recovery target of £60 million by 2004, one year after POCA became law (Hansard, HC Deb 30 Oct 2001, vol 373 c759). The baseline target for asset recovery was increased in 2006 with the figure of £125 million (Home Office, 2007). In October 2007, the target was doubled to £250 million and expected to be achieved by 2009/2010 from an annual criminal economy then estimated to be £15 billion (HMCPSI et al., 2010; Home Office, 2007). That target was not met, and it could be argued that the trajectory of confiscation was adversely affected (HMCPSI et al., 2010). The acquisitive crime problem was rapidly outstripping the solution (confiscation), and three years later in 2012–2013, the National Fraud Authority estimated that the annual total for fraud alone was £52 billion (NFA, 2013). That figure was then estimated to have risen to a minimum of £193 billion per year (University of Portsmouth, Experian and PKF Littlejohn, 2016). It is an interesting point that the Office for National Statistics (ONS) (September 2023) maintains that the number of fraud offences has fallen by 13%. Juxtaposed with this statistic in the same report, is the estimate that less than one in every seven fraud offences are reported to the police.

The point has been previously made in this book that the National Audit Office (NAO) (2013) stated confiscation represented 26 pence in every £100 of criminality. It is relevant at this juncture because the House of Commons Committee of Public Accounts (2014) used the figures in its own condemnation of the confiscation system. An important point was made in its conclusions and recommendations. There was an admission of limited understanding of the extent to which crime had been disrupted by confiscation orders (House of Commons Committee of Public Accounts, 2014: 3). The reduction of crime was the singular objective of proceeds of crime legislation (House of Commons, 2008; POCA, 2002: 2). There appears to be no available research to suggest that attempts to measure the effectiveness of the asset recovery regime or use of powers have been made (then or now), other than in the monetary terms above (paid into the "tin box"). POCA did not stipulate, define or otherwise explain how the reduction of crime was to be measured generally and still seems defined by how much money is restrained or confiscated (NAO, 2013, 2016). Neither the government or law enforcement agencies seem to have any reliable parameters within which POCA powers can be judged to be effective or not, either in terms of general investigations or impact upon criminality. Aside from attempts to identify the potential value of financial investigation to serious and organised crime investigations (Brown et al., 2012; Howell, Horton and Gill, 2013) the effectiveness of POCA powers remains difficult to measure.

Post Cabinet Office (2000) investment in government asset recovery strategy (confiscation) was considerable. In the year prior to POCA (2002), £45 million was set aside for the set-up of an Assets Recovery Agency (ARA) (Public Bill Committee, 2001), and the Home Office agreed funding for an additional 86 AFIs for police in England and Wales to last three years (Hansard, HC Deb 30 Oct 2001, vol 373 c758). The Crown Prosecution Service (CPS) received additional funding over three years totalling just over £18 million (House of Commons 2003, 2004, 2005). The government expectation was that ARA would be self-funding by the financial year 2005–2006 (House of Commons, 2007). That ambition was not realised. The NAO (2007: 11) concluded that: "The Agency has not met its objective of recovering assets to the value of its annual revenue budget by 2005-06. The Agency has now revised the date for achieving this self-financing position to 2009-10". In April 2008 the ARA was disbanded (Gov.UK, 2020) and its staff transferred into the Serious and Organised Crime Agency (SOCA) which had replaced the National Crime Squad in 2006. It is perhaps ironic that calls from politicians (and some law enforcement agencies) have begun to revisit the idea of a single point of responsibility for the confiscation regime (and thereby financial investigation). Such calls favour the NCA as the host, particularly regarding training issues (House of Commons, 2016) and of course, the National Economic Crime Centre has been established since 2018 (NCA, 2023). It seems that the issue of terminology persists, the question being what exactly is economic crime and is the NCA sufficiently equipped in one agency to fight the surge of acquisitive criminality in the guise of fraud and corruption offences alone (in addition to a myriad of other forms of crimes which might be termed "economic".

Aside from operating the Agency in accordance with its visions and values, the ARA had two primary strategic objectives:

1. To adopt and conduct confiscation, civil recovery and taxation investigations under the provisions of the Proceeds of Crime Act 2002, that lead to a reduction in criminal activity.
2. To promote and support the use of the powers conferred by the Proceeds of Crime Act 2002 through the successful training of financial investigators and to provide such support and expertise to the law enforcement community as may otherwise be required (Assets Recovery Agency, 2006: 6).

Reducing the effects of criminality by attacking criminal assets seems to have at its core the social impact which POCA might achieve if more consistently applied. The significant point seems to be that it is advocating asset recovery as part of a crime reduction objective, not to raise money for Treasury coffers (the "tin box").

Where policing was concerned, there was early clear indication of what it would mean to attempt to embed financial investigation as a general investigation technique as clearly stated by the HMIC et al. (2004: 26): "It was accepted from the outset that the successful implementation of POCA would require significant initial resourcing to ensure that the intended step-change approach to asset recovery registered on agencies' agendas. Policing received two forms of support, namely additional funded posts and performance incentives" [incentivisation].

The Home Office appears to have missed two essential points. First, it had identified that a step-change was required across law enforcement to actively embrace asset recovery rather than much needed and more widely apply financial investigation skills. Second, the government responsible for POCA (2002) had only assured investment in asset recovery. Funding for AFI positions and associated training is evident before and after POCA was introduced (Cabinet Office, 2000; HMIC et al., 2004). The authors have been unable to identify any available literature indicating that non-AFI POCA training was considered in the UK. None of this was perceived by general investigators at tactical or practitioner levels as any of their concern, a recurring problem to the present time (Brown et al., 2012). Financial investigation appears to have remained on the periphery of law enforcement as a specialist area of investigation that is automatically associated with and limited to, confiscation and asset recovery.

Government reports and research concerning asset recovery and financial investigation

Several reports reflect the continuing political attention upon asset recovery and meeting Home Office financial targets (HMCPSI et al., 2010; HMIC et al., 2004; House of Commons, 2016; NAO, 2007). Due to the lack of academic research directly focusing upon financial investigation (except in connection with serious organised crime) and its potential use in general investigations, it is these government reports which provide much of the information and detail which is publicly available. The authors' intention is to briefly consider the themes within the relevant documents in order to ascertain whether their content impacts upon the formulation of answers to why financial investigation techniques are only partially used in routine investigations and to identify any potential inhibitors to such use.

The central thread within government reports to date appears to be focused on asset recovery rather than a systematised approach to the implementation of financial investigation as an investigation tool to assist law enforcement at all levels. What has become known as the Payback Report (HMIC et al., 2004) makes the point that asset recovery must not simply be regarded as an income generation tool, rather it is a crime fighting tactic. It did not explain any implementation process to achieve that aim. A potential problem in embedding POCA across general law enforcement is commented on: "Most police forces currently lack an effective approach to cascade POCA activity into everyday policing. Typically, police forces have created small specialist teams to deal with confiscation and forfeiture" (HMIC et al., 2004: 87).

The NAO (2007) focused particularly on the number of cases under investigation (or resulted) at that time, as well as time frames to conclude orders and their enforcement. It is noticeable that the only section commenting on AFIs deals with the number trained for confiscation. No mention is made in the report regarding proceeds of crime training for general investigators. There is no mention or description of what a financial investigation skill set could involve, or any strategy of how to integrate financial investigation among general investigators to achieve increased asset recovery opportunities.

The theme of lack of general effectiveness by law enforcement in applying POCA continued in Home Office commissioned research two years later (Bullock et al., 2009). Areas for improvement were clearly identified. There should be greater clarity about the scope of POCA use, a more strategic and systematic approach to the use of confiscation, an improvement in co-ordination throughout the asset recovery system, effective tactical use of restraint orders and attention paid to the enforcement area of the regime (Bullock et al., 2009). The available evidence demonstrates continued focus upon asset recovery but without any apparent clear philosophy of how to better implement skills across law enforcement. It is noticeable that no detail was provided as to how the recommendations were to be achieved.

The ineffective use of financial investigation tools in general criminal investigations was a consideration of a joint thematic review of asset recovery one year later (HMCPSI et al., 2010). Government intentions that AFIs should work contemporaneously with investigation officers and prosecutors is recognised but, "links between FIs and the criminal investigation are less than clear in some areas, and there is an apparent lack of synchronization between them, in most cases within the police and HMRC" (HMCPSI et al., 2010: 8).

It is not just the confiscation element of financial investigation which is considered. CPS involvement with the POCA process was criticised: "Confiscation proceedings are subject to the Criminal Procedure Rules, but there is a lack of experience and know-how among generalist caseworkers in the CPS and the courts, and the parties are not held accountable for delays, which are considerable" (HMCPSI et al., 2010: 9).

Its conclusion for the future activity of asset recovery (and financial investigation) is fundamental to a more generic approach:

> The findings of this review suggest that agencies need to give further consideration to policy and the strategic issues which affect the recovery of criminally gained assets, in particular: how to ensure asset recovery represents value for money i.e. the cost of the process against what is gained and how that equation should affect the cases in which assets are pursued; whether adjustments to the incentivisation scheme are necessary; whether mainstreaming, while apparently desirable, is in fact truly achievable or cost effective; and whether targets are realistic.
>
> (HMCPSI et al., 2010: 10)

Focus seems to have remained upon the mainstreaming of asset recovery (not financial investigation) and why that endeavour had so far proven difficult.

Confiscation and financial investigation appear to be considered as one and the same, a clear and consistent pitfall of any attempt to export a clear message to general law enforcement practitioners. The findings may continue to be correct in the assertion that asset recovery in terms of the confiscation process is (and may have to remain) a specialist area but it fails to identify financial investigation as a separate skill base which can be generally applied. That same confusion appears to be endemic across law enforcement and clarifying the concepts involved in both areas (confiscation and financial investigation) would seem to be a distinct challenge to be overcome for policy makers and strategic decision makers who advocate wider use of the financial investigation skill set at a basic level.

The apparently unwavering political focus upon asset recovery and the seeming inability to differentiate between specialist and non-specialist AFI skill bases remains the dominant approach of policy makers and governmental review bodies (House of Commons, 2016; Transparency International, 2017b). The two skill bases are different in that AFIs receive training to enhance their previously general investigation ability and hone it to focus upon the complex area of law affecting assets post conviction of offenders. Non-specialist investigators do not receive such training but there seems no reason as to why they should not avail themselves of some of the more basic aspects of financial investigation in their routine investigations.

The Home Affairs Committee tasked with the review invited 22 written submissions and additional oral evidence from a range of agencies and commentators inside and outside the law enforcement arena (House of Commons, 2016). Most participants appear to be based in London potentially provoking a question as to whether the views expressed reflect a balanced presentation of confiscation and financial investigation issues nationally. As an example, the Serious Fraud Office representative discussed the issue of staff turnover, an issue in London but not necessarily a problem in the counties. A full list of commentators can be found in the House of Commons (2016: 7).

Primarily focused upon the several aspects of asset recovery, the House of Commons (2016) response is a good example of the seemingly confused political approach to the subject area. Advice from independent parties involved in the process is also open to criticism, particularly in not recognising that financial investigation should be integral to all criminal investigations and not solely concerned with asset identification and organised crime units (NPCC, 2016; Transparency International, 2016). Whether to establish a lead agency responsible for recovery of criminal proceeds is discussed within the report (notwithstanding the acknowledgement within the document that the Assets Recovery Agency (ARA) had been previously been tried) but once again confusion seems apparent. The Committee agrees that: "We therefore recommend that the National Crime Agency be made the lead agency for the recovery of criminal proceeds (House of Commons, 2016: 13). In the same section the report states: "The Government therefore does not agree that the NCA should be the lead agency for the recovery of criminal proceeds" (House of Commons, 2016: 13). Such contradictions do not seem helpful and are suggestive that political direction concerning confiscation and financial investigation remains unclear.

The myth that a financial investigation is somehow distinct from the evidential gathering process is perpetuated, particularly in the advice of one commentator to the Committee (a qualified barrister and an academic) who stated,

> The financial investigators should be working alongside the criminal investigators and they should be using the power that they have to discover the whereabouts of assets and then sweeping in at an early stage simultaneously with the execution of search warrants. There has to be a culture shift. They have to understand that just as it is important to get the evidence to prove the criminal case, they also need at the very same time the evidence to prove the existence of the assets and their whereabouts.
>
> (House of Commons, 2016: 8)

The perceived division between the criminal investigators and the AFIs is clear in the statement made. What is being commented on is asset recovery and not financial investigation. There does not seem to be any logical basis to separate criminal investigation process, financial investigation (pre conviction with the meaning that confiscation is a specialist and distinct aspect) and money laundering investigations. It is not clear in logic or practice whether they should be regarded as separate entities, but this seems to be a recurring and persistent theme at the strategic, tactical and practical levels. Detectives (and most constables) should be capable of using basic financial investigation skills to identify evidence and assets in the early stages of an investigation in order to present facts to an expert AFI if a restraint order is required (a specialist skill for which NCA accreditation is required). POCA and its stated intention of attempting to reduce crime seems to have been legislation intended for use by non-specialists in certain investigations. POCA (2002) money laundering provisions, cash detention provisions and an array of production orders were made available to all police constables and HMRC officers. The intention of legislators seems clear that those POCA powers should be used appropriately by all investigators at practitioner level. Use of POCA powers by general practitioners still appears to be ad hoc and the dependency on AFIs to conduct enquiries which appear to be financial in nature has persisted (HMCPSI et al., 2010; House of Commons, 2016; Howell, Horton and Gill, 2013).

Headline recommendations within the House of Commons (2016) demonstrate the preoccupation with asset recovery. Where the Committee advocated better financial investigation training for constables at entry level into policing, it was, "so that all officers are equipped to secure recovery at a much earlier stage and have a good understanding of the impact of charges, offences and pleas on asset recovery" (House of Commons, 2016: 10). For serving detectives, the recommendation was to undergo annual advanced training to be able to identify financial gain, "as well as criminal conduct in every investigation into a serious crime offering financial gain" (House of Commons, 2016: 10). This second recommendation illustrates the confusion (even after a wide range of opinions and advice had been considered) that politicians appear to consistently demonstrate when attempting to address the confiscation regime (and in particular, the *raison d'etre* for the wider and general application of financial investigation). The two recommendations (and the wider discussion of these in the report) confirm that asset recovery remains the primary focus, closely followed by a similar intensity upon serious crime. The broader aspects and benefits of financial investigation are mentioned in passing (as in the other reports discussed) but no clear way of implementing them is examined.

A feasible and effective government implementation strategy remains a clear problem, possibly due in part to the continuing focus upon the asset recovery and serious crime areas. It seems to be an impediment to the intention that financial investigation techniques should be consistently utilised at grass roots level across all UK law enforcement (House of Commons, 2016). Focus upon revenue streams (asset recovery) and serious criminality (organised crime) appears only part of the issue and the apparent lack of clear understanding at policy level is a severe impediment to successful implementation. There seems a lack of data within the available literature (and outside the scope of this project) to suggest the number of instances where financial investigation techniques are used generally compared with how they are utilised in cases which continue towards confiscation. There does not appear to be any available data as to the level or complexity of cases in which the powers are used for either reason. It is a concern that confiscation applies more often outside the organised crime remit but receives far less attention from researchers, strategists and policy makers (NAO, 2013).

A clear gap seems to have been identified by this work concerning structured attempts to ascertain the value of financial investigation outside of the confiscation and civil asset recovery processes. More research is required in addition to the specific areas previously targeted involving organised crime groups where financial investigation is more frequently used (Howell, Horton and Gill, 2013; Wood, 2017). Although the concept of financial investigation is generally mentioned in association with confiscation, there seems to be confusion at the policy level between confiscation (the asset recovery process) and the much wider field of financial investigation as a general skill set (House of Commons, 2016). Home Office focus on asset recovery and the returns from that process (the so-called "tin box") has arguably been debilitating to its own declared intention of embedding the process into general law enforcement investigations. The apparent confusion between the disciplines of confiscation and financial investigation, coupled with attaining (confiscation) financial targets set by the government may have contributed to a perception among general investigators that financial investigation is best left to AFIs (Davidson, Walker and Dayman, 2014).

Conclusion

It seems clear that the application of the confiscation process is fragmented and disparate, the settlement of confiscation orders appearing particularly weak and problematic (Wood, 2016). The situation is exacerbated by the apparently endemic lack of understanding at governmental level as to how the confiscation process functions and of peripheral inhibitors which constrict its effectiveness (particularly concerning enforcement of orders). The lack of a common set of criteria to ensure confiscation consistency is acknowledged at strategic level but problems are perpetuated by the inability at all levels to create an integrated approach in addressing the issues. The extent of the perception that financial investigation equates largely with confiscation within the general law enforcement community is unmeasured as is the impact upon its effective use by those practitioners.

5 International standards and independent commentators

International standards

It is important to realise that prior to 1986 there were limited provisions in modern UK legislation to deal with either asset recovery or money laundering. Historical reasons for the absence of the confiscation principle in UK law are not clear and are, at best, educated guesses (Alldridge, 2003). Until the late 19th century, the (common) law of forfeiture governed the power of the state to seize property (Kesselring, 2010; Taylor, 1998). There was no requirement to distinguish between property from proceeds of crime or from other property because all property was automatically forfeited to the Crown upon an individual's conviction (HMCPSI et al., 2010).

Until the Misuse of Drugs Act (1971) (MDA), it could be argued that the simple and long-standing objective of UK law (common law and statute) has singularly been the conviction and punishment of offenders, not asset recovery (confiscation), "the principal task of the system is to investigate, prosecute and punish perpetrators" (Naylor, 2003: 82). What does seem clear is that proceeds of crime legislation (and financial investigation) have developed sporadically in the UK since the passing of the MDA (1971). That Act seems to have been a government response to the, putatively, growing problem of domestic drug use and the publicity surrounding it. Its importance for financial investigation was that Section 27 of the Act provided the first legislated forfeiture power (available for all police officers) to deprive offenders of at least an element of their criminality (illicit drugs, paraphernalia and related cash). The limiting factor of the MDA whereby property subject of a forfeiture request at court had to be directly linked with the offending, reflected an earlier and similar premise in the Forfeiture Act of 1870. Since that time, forfeiture had been able to deal only with items immediately connected with a crime. That premise was simply transferred into the MDA seemingly without any consideration of the (then) emerging threat of drug trafficking on an international level (HMCPSI et al., 2010).

It is generally accepted that the drug trafficking case of *R v Cuthbertson* (1981) was the major prompt for legislators across the political spectrum to apply their minds to the (in)justice of allowing criminals to retain assets which

DOI: 10.4324/9781003438649-5

were clearly obtained from criminality (Hodgson, 1984). The Appeal Court decision resulted from a drugs investigation (Operation Julie) whereby investigators had identified approximately £750,000 of assets representing the proceeds of the criminal enterprise. As there was no confiscation regime at that time, the court proceeded to utilise section 27 of the MDA, strictly a forfeiture power (drug paraphernalia or cash from the arrest could be disposed of by the court), to deprive the offenders of their criminal gains nationally and internationally. The House of Lords eventually ruled, and apparently with some reticence, that s27 MDA was neither designed nor intended to deal with such matters and upheld the appeal (HMCPSI et al., 2010; R v Cuthbertson, 1981).

The case of R v Cuthbertson (1981) made the central issue clear. There was no provision in UK law to allow the removal of assets and criminal gain from convicted criminals, nor were offences available to indict offenders who organised the laundering of criminal funds. The focus at this stage remained upon drug trafficking.

The ensuing Hodgson Report (1984) led to the first UK drug trafficking legislation with confiscation powers included within it in the form of the Drug Trafficking Offences Act (DTOA, 1986). It introduced the new field of asset recovery by way of a confiscation regime to a law enforcement and judicial structure wholly inexperienced with the concept.

The aim of the legislators at this point was to combat drug trafficking and its profits rather than any wider objective of engaging against benefit from general acquisitive criminality (Cabinet Office, 2000). Garland (1996, 2001) might regard the DTOA as a display of punitive force against one criminal sector, a sovereign state response to public furore at the time. Nevertheless, it does appear to be a significant watershed. It was this very specific, target drug-related start to asset recovery (and the delimited application of financial investigation) that the authors have argued (within this book) became an important contributory factor in its marginalisation by way of its specialism within law enforcement. The point is one that is only briefly mentioned within the available subject literature. HMIC et al. (2004) describes financial investigation units (FIUs) as having originated from drugs teams and Gold and Levi (1994: 33) discussed relationships between financial institutions and police. They refer to the fact that FIUs were attached to drug squads, considering it an inhibiting factor in utilising financial investigation for other criminality types. The extent to which the origin of financial investigation in drug trafficking legislation has curtailed its trajectory as a general investigation skillset is an important consideration but one which remains unquantifiable.

The point has been made within that successive governments have continued to underline a desire to embed financial investigation into general law enforcement practices (Cabinet Office, 2000; HM Government, 2011). Why that continuing intention has apparently not yet been realised is important to understand.

The DTOA (1986) is also significant as it introduced the origin of contemporary money laundering offences by way of an offence of assisting another to retain benefits of drug dealing (DTOA, 1986: s42). Although this provided the foundation for future money laundering legislation consideration, it can also be regarded as one of the principal factors which constricted the trajectory of financial investigation from its outset. Not only was asset recovery primarily associated (in the longer term) with drug trafficking, but so too now was money laundering. Such singular concentration on the drug problem was contemporaneously reinforced in global terms (FATF, 1990; UN, 1988). The implementation of the DTOA coincided with an international recognition that drug trafficking had surpassed any individual law enforcement ability to control the problem in independent national jurisdictions. A more concerted effort was required, and it is against a backdrop of increasing international co-operation regarding the drug trafficking problem that UK legislation began to move forward (in terms of confiscation, asset recovery and financial investigation).

The Criminal Justice Act (CJA, 1988: Schedule 4) passed into legislation so that some non-drugs offences could also proceed to confiscation after conviction. Under the Act, confiscation was not mandatory, rather it was a duty of the court to consider confiscation when a defendant was convicted of a non-drug indictable offence (Leong, 2016). There were two types of confiscation determinations available to a court, a conviction determination where the benefit determined by the court could only be equal to the value of the offences committed (CJA, 1988: s72A) and a course of criminal conduct determination. For the latter process, it was incumbent upon the prosecutor to provide written notice to the court that the confiscation process was being triggered (CJA, 1988: s72AA). If the notice was not served, there could be no confiscation proceedings. Notwithstanding the UK had just passed the CJA attempting to broaden confiscation procedures to criminality other than drugs, international focus remained unshakeably concerned with drugs (UN, 1988).

The Vienna Convention 1988

By the mid-1970s and throughout the 1980s, drug trafficking had escalated into a problem of international proportions and governments worldwide recognised the need to collaborate to minimise and combat a growing threat to general social and economic stability. As previously mentioned in the money laundering section (2.3.5) of the literature review above, increasing international concern about drug trafficking resulted in the United Nations Convention Against Illicit Traffic in Narcotic Drugs and Psychotropic Substances of 1988 (the Vienna Convention). The Convention was attended by 106 countries and expressed its concerns about "the magnitude of and rising trend in the illicit production of, demand for and traffic in narcotic drugs and psychotropic substances" (UN, 1988: 1). Agreement was reached whereby participating countries would not only establish criminal offences of drug trafficking but also offences which form the basis of money laundering definitions used in the UK today.

Not only did Article 5 section 1 of the Convention advocate that the attending nations should adopt measures to confiscate proceeds derived from drug trafficking (UN, 1988), sections 6 (a), (b) and (c) recommended the same provisions in respect of proceeds which had been transformed into or disguised as, something else. In other words, for property that had been money laundered (although the term was not overtly used within the document).

Although the Vienna Convention was far reaching in so many positive respects it perhaps did not achieve a broader audience in the practical aspect of its intention. By limiting its accepted proposals to drug trafficking offences (and activities parallel to it), doing so immediately (but unintentionally) constricted the trajectory of financial investigation within general policing on an international level. Article 9 (e) of the Convention had been far sighted enough to advocate that "Methods used for the transfer, concealment or disguise of such proceeds, property and instrumentalities" should be initiated and developed (but only in relation to drug trafficking). The continuing dysfunction identified within this review between policy and strategic implementation of government intentions can be argued as having originated at the conclusion of the Vienna Convention. Two aspects remained unconsidered. First, how the intentions of the Convention were to be embedded at tactical and practical levels of law enforcement and, second, how isolated the practitioners of the new powers solely within the drugs environment would be. Failing to apply its mind to a broader approach and limiting the Convention proposals to one area of crime arguably ensured that from that point forward, financial investigation would be a specialist area (confiscation and money laundering) and of interest only to drug units (notwithstanding that the Criminal Justice Act had been enacted in the UK the same year).

The Financial Action Task Force (FATF)

It is important to recognise that the trajectory of UK financial investigation is not only affected by internally implemented policy and legislation, whether as a result of an independent recognition of a problem (such as the DTOA) or in response to an international accord to take action against a particular problem (such as the Vienna Convention or similar UN conventions). Other organisations have had their own effect upon the route which various aspects of financial investigation have taken, nationally within the UK and internationally upon the world stage.

The Vienna Convention was the catalyst for an international drive to begin to attempt to co-ordinate sovereign jurisdictions and focus on the two global problems it had identified, drug trafficking and the profits laundered as a result of it. The Convention reflected the international will to attack a problem but the potential abuse of world financial markets to launder those profits required a long-standing oversight which would outlast the transitional nature of governments, elected or otherwise. At the G7 Summit held in Paris in 1989, member nations in conjunction with the President of the European Commission convened the FATF (Li, 2009).

According to its own website, it was "given the responsibility of examining money laundering techniques and trends, reviewing the action which had already been taken at national or international level and setting out the measures that still needed to be taken to combat money laundering" (FATF, 2016: 1). Only one year after its formation, the FATF issued what was to become the keystone in the fight against global money laundering, 40 recommendations constituting an initiative to combat the misuse of financial systems by persons laundering drug money (FATF, 1990). Within 6 years, the 40 recommendations were revised (and endorsed by 130 countries) as it was realised that money laundering typologies continually evolved and international focus was beginning to move away from the narrow focus on drug trafficking (FATF, 1996, 2003). Eight special recommendations on terrorist financing followed in October 2001 and continued evolution of money laundering techniques have led to further revisions (FATF, 2003, 2016, 2018).

The focus of the FATF appears to be at the policy level where there is a necessity for very contrasting governmental regimes to work within similar parameters to combat the global problems of terrorism, organised criminality and money laundering (and other acquisitive criminality). This is reflected in its guidelines for assessing technical compliance with its recommendations and the level of effectiveness of national anti-money laundering systems (FATF, 2013, 2016).

It is of interest in terms of this book (and a clear gap identified in the literature) that the FATF methodology deals with two main components which it identifies as inter-linked. A technical compliance assessment (FATF, 2013) addresses each of the recommendations as they relate to national legal and institutional frameworks as well as the powers and procedures of competent authorities (FATF, 2012, 2013, 2016). An effectiveness assessment analyses whether a national legal and institutional framework is producing expected results (compared to a defined set of outcomes central to robust anti-money laundering measures) (FATF, 2013, 2016). There are four rating groups for each of the two categories. Compliant, largely compliant, partially compliant and non-compliant in respect of the technical assessment; this alongside high level, substantial level, moderate level and low level for the effectiveness assessment (FATF, 2013, 2016). The rating groups are indicators that a country is complying with agreed recommendations or that measures need to be put in place or revised in order to be more robust.

The gap in the available literature appears to be that FATF methodology does not focus upon how the recommendations (in any country) are translated into policing the perceived money laundering problem or at what levels. Simply adhering to the recommendations and legislating against money laundering does not mean that there is any kind of robust policing against it. The same can be said of the anti-money laundering regulations required to be in place by the FATF (such as exist in the UK). Having a SARs system in place (and comprehensive anti-money laundering regulations) seems desirable so long as the information reported because of it is used effectively (or at all) (Maxwell and Artingstall, 2017). In the UK, partly due to lack of real integration among general practitioners, that may not be the case and there appears to be a gap within the NIM, and therefore, it is potentially detrimental to better integrated financial investigation.

A question arises from the available literature as to whether successive UK and other governments have legislated more to achieve goals set by the FATF (or the UN) at the international policy level, rather than focusing on the nature of criminality within the UK and legislating specifically, rather than generally, to combat it. As a result, countries differ markedly in their implementation of FATF recommendations. Further reading on this point can be found in Hicks and Graycar (2019) who present an interesting comparison between the approaches of the UK and USA to demonstrate the point. Such a strategic concentration on policy and legislation (within government and law enforcement) rather than focusing on effective methods of implementation may partly explain the continued problem of integrating financial investigation and proceeds of crime practices within law enforcement. There does not appear to be any available empirical data to substantiate such a postulation, but the point may be demonstrated by considering a practical example. Money laundering has been the focus of policy advisors and policy makers for some years (Gov.UK, 2018; Home Office, 2016c; Transparency International, 2017c, 2017d) and yet there seems to be an absence in the available literature which demonstrates any type of implementation strategy to ensure the uptake of money laundering offences by non-specialist investigators, by the CPS, or by the judiciary. At the FATF (2022) conference in Berlin,, representatives continued to express concern that efforts to confiscate criminal proceeds remains insufficient to the task. This was seen as largely due to the availability of systems whereby criminals can move assets internationally with rapidity and a degree of anonymity (FATF, 2024).

Yet another example of policy not being transformed into practice is in the area of money laundering, a recognised problem within the UK (HM Government, 2013; House of Commons, 2016; NCA, 2017c). Despite money laundering being a constant source of debate by international agencies, governments, law enforcement at all levels and academics (HM Treasury and Home Office, 2015; Levi, 1991; Transparency International, 2015; UK Parliament, 2009; UNODOC, 2004) the UK does not have a national money laundering unit. In 2018, a National Economic Crime Centre (NECC) was "created to deliver a step change in the UK response to, and impact on, economic crime" (NCA, 2019f). The NECC is situated within the NCA (Home Office, 2017a; NCA, 2018). Whether it will investigate money laundering and to what degree remains unknown. Its remit will eventually be determined by an economic crime strategic board upon which the Home Secretary will be a participant (Home Office, 2017a). As yet, there does not appear to have been any direction from the FATF or the UN for countries to form money laundering investigation units and the UK government has shown no real interest in doing so. Regarding money laundering, there appears to be nothing evident within the available literature to explain the difference between government policy and law enforcement practice. Where this chapter is concerned, it is a puzzle that will require consideration if broader uptake of the potential offered by proceeds of crime legislation is to be achieved.

The United Nations Convention against Transnational Organised Crime 2000

(The Palermo Convention)

Contemporaneous with any sovereign state independent measures taken to combat money laundering or to assist asset recovery and the robust drivers of the FATF, the UN continued to be the aspect of international will to attempt to curtail the laundering of proceeds of crime. A decade after the Vienna Convention and the subsequent formation of the FATF, the Palermo Convention in 2000 became the key dictum in the realisation that organised crime was internationally endemic and a significant cause and effect of money laundering across the globe (UNODOC, 2004). The UN Office on Drugs and Crime (UNODC) synopsis of the Convention is succinct:

> States that ratify this instrument commit themselves to taking a series of measures against transnational organized crime, including the creation of domestic criminal offences (participation in an organized criminal group, money laundering, corruption and obstruction of justice); the adoption of new and sweeping frameworks for extradition, mutual legal assistance and law enforcement cooperation; and the promotion of training and technical assistance for building or upgrading the necessary capacity of national authorities.
>
> (UNODC, 2004: 1)

The UN had already convened regarding international terrorism – the International Convention for the Suppression of Terrorist Financing (1999) came into force in 2002 with the aim of protecting financial systems from those planning or engaged in terrorist activity (UNODC, 1999, 2018). The UN Convention against Corruption followed in 2004. The common thread in both conventions was their attempt to widen the scope of money laundering definitions and move away from drug trafficking to encompass proceeds from all serious crimes (UNODC, 1999, 2004, UN2016). The Palermo Convention helped to expand international agreement for money laundering controls to be applicable to the widest possible range of underlying offending as well as virtually any interaction with the proceeds of crime.

Independent influences on UK acquisitive crime policy and strategy

A third factor in the shaping of government policy is the effect of independent agencies such as Transparency International UK (TI-UK) originally formed in 2000 as a worldwide anti-corruption agency. There are in excess of 500 such internationally functioning groups (Free Government Information, 2012). TI-UK is perhaps one of the largest such organisations with over 100 chapters established around the world (TI-UK, 2017). Regarding the UK and proceeds of crime legislation, TI-UK has been involved in various government reviews and consultation papers (House of Commons, 2016: TI-UK, 2016) and regularly produces research papers concerning corruption, financial crime and confiscation (TI-UK, 2015, 2015a, 2017a).

The Basel Institute on Governance is another example of an influential non-governmental, non-law enforcement institution and (like TI-UK) it also produces research and advice regarding many of the issues so far discussed, particularly asset recovery for which it has its own International Centre (ICAR) established in 2006. Part of the ICAR's funding (although it is based in Switzerland as an associated Institute of Basel University) is actually from the UK's Department for International Development presumably supporting ICAR's work on strengthening technical capacity to trace assets (Basel Institute, 2009) and the intricacies of international co-operation (Basel Institute, 2017).

The available literature demonstrates that the concepts of money laundering, drug trafficking, terrorism and fraud have received continuing focus by the international community particularly in attempting to identify, understand and combat organised criminality. Institutions such as the FATF, UN and independent commentators such as TI-UK appear to have had a long-standing influence upon on UK government legislation and policies which deal with acquisitive crime (FATF, 1990, 2012; House of Commons, 2016). This brief precis of FATF, UN and independent agency activity demonstrates the plethora of recommended strategies, research and convention recommendations which have been the backdrop to UK proceeds of crime legislation since 1990. Concepts involved in tackling acquisitive crime, organised crime and financial crime may well appear to be understood and accepted by the international organisations and countries involved but only at policy level. The singular and continuing problem appears to be translating the concepts into general application.

There has been a constant flow of proceeds of crime legislation since POCA (2002), examples of which (though not an exhaustive list) are the Crime and Courts Act (2013), Criminal Finances Act (2017), Modern Slavery Act (2015), money laundering regulations (2007, 2017) and the Serious Crime Act (2015). Throughout that period there have been constant calls at the strategic and political level to keep adding to the legislative arsenal (Anderson, 2015; Home Secretary, 2016; Home Office, 2016b, 2016c; HM Government,

2016a). Such calls do not appear to alter an almost resigned acknowledgement (and a resigned acceptance) that successive government intentions to embed financial investigation, money laundering and financial crime objectives (including asset recovery) into general law enforcement still requires much work (House of Commons, 2016; NAO, 2013, 2016; Sproat, 2009). There seems to be no appreciation as to why by government policy makers, at the strategic level within law enforcement or by independent commentators. There appears to be one critical inhibitor to the general and effective use of financial investigation and proceeds of crime legislation, the lack of a generic philosophy by way of which it can be properly implemented into investigations at all levels of law enforcement. This is one of the important areas where this book may make a significant and original contribution to the field of financial investigation and general criminal investigation.

Continuing with the general historical perspective, other Acts of Parliament followed the DTOA (1986), beginning with the Criminal Justice Act (1988) (CJA) and the extension of confiscation legislation to combat acquisitive, indictable, non-drug offences. It did not, however, advance the concept of money laundering and it was not until the Criminal Justice Act (1993) created money laundering offences in respect of non-drug trafficking proceeds that they could potentially be more widely applied (Bell, 2002).

Shortcomings of the CJA were quickly apparent as it gave the court discretion as to whether to confiscate in non-drug trafficking cases and required service of notices dependent upon the type and scale of offences prosecuted (CJA, 1988: s72). What it did not attempt to address were the resourcing issues of law enforcement in implementing the legislation. Law enforcement appears to have been left to its own devices concerning how the new legislation could be implemented.

The discretion of the judiciary was removed by the Drug Trafficking Act (DTA, 1994) whereas the narrowness of the legislation was retained, and it continued to apply only to drug trafficking offences. Legislators refrained from connecting it to the existing CJA in any way. It was important in contributing to the development of money laundering in that it introduced offences of concealing, acquiring or assisting another to retain drug trafficking proceeds (DTA, 1994: Part III).

Neither the DTA or (and perhaps more importantly) the CJA were integrated into general law enforcement investigations, largely due to being ensconced within the drug squad environments. The original investigators given the task of dealing with the new drugs legislation under the DTOA within the police, were originally referred to as Drug Profit Confiscation Officers (Dorn, Murji and South, 1992; Metropolitan Police, 1988), a title which immediately segregated them from general investigators within Criminal Investigation Departments (CID) as well as from uniform officers. As other legislation was enacted and investigators were able to broaden the scope of their investigations to attack other criminal proceeds, the term financial investigator began to be more widely used to describe them. An opportunity to introduce financial investigation to a wider investigation field appears to have been missed, the repercussions of which arguably exist to the present day.

It was also unfortunate that the enforcement phase of the CJA and DTA provisions was particularly weak and problematic (Cabinet Office, 2000: 30). Between the DTA 1994 and the passing of the Anti-Terrorism, Crime and Security Act 2001, other legislative confiscation amendment provisions perhaps complicated the law enforcement approach to acquisitive crime and in particular asset recovery. Few people had expertise in deciding benefit and realisable assets and practitioners, the legal profession and courts regarded the process as confusing and difficult (Cabinet Office, 2000; Levi and Osofsky, 1995). In the wake of the Cabinet Office (2000) the government (and the courts) had recognised that separate treatment of drug trafficking from all other criminal activity made the legislation (prior to POCA) less applicable against what it termed criminal entrepreneurs (Hansard, 2001).

At no point did the legislation attempt to deal with the concept of financial investigation itself. Financial investigation remained undefined, and each new Act proceeded to set out new powers or definitions of offences. Detectives who utilised the financial aspects of the DTA and CJA received, in general law enforcement vocabulary, the esoteric label of financial investigator and financial investigation retained a strictly specialist nature within the police and HMCE.

The Cabinet Office (2000) had already recognised that financial investigation "is an important tool in the fight against crime...in addition to being the gateway to effective asset identification and recovery, it can provide new avenues for traditional law enforcement" (Cabinet Office, 2000: 51). Almost a decade later, the UK government was still insisting that it would "mainstream the use of financial investigation" (Cabinet Office, 2009: 55). Notwithstanding the continued key recognition of the potential of financial investigation, that strategy appears to remain problematic. Moreover, the inability of financial investigation to become embedded in mainstream investigations represents an unresolved puzzle, the hurdles of which represent a key focus in attempting to answer the issue of its more routine application.

The Proceeds of Crime Act (2002) was the definitive watershed for asset recovery legislation in the UK whereby the legislators were partly influenced by American legislation in properly attempting to draw together the civil and criminal legal frameworks in the UK to attack criminal assets (Cabinet Office, 2000). The USA had originally begun to attack organised criminality by introducing the Racketeer Influenced and Corrupt Organisations Act (1970) (RICO) and the Bank Secrecy Act (1970) (BSA). Money laundering controls were initially intended to combat the use of international banks for tax evasion but rapidly developed into a key mechanism against drug trafficking (Levi and Reuter, 2006).

The Americans had ceased to keep a sterile corridor between criminal and civil law and, using the RICO, US law enforcement agencies had a baseline from which to attack the proceeds of crime using criminal and/or civil frameworks, part of President Nixon's war on American organised crime (Woodiwiss, 2001). The BSA made it mandatory for banks to report currency transactions over $10,000 to the Department of the Treasury (in the UK providing the inspiration for the various money laundering regulations now in place and the issuing of SARs from financial institutions and the business sector). Notwithstanding its wider powers, the RICO is acknowledged as being rarely used throughout the 1970s and early 1980s (Levi and Reuter, 2006). Various reasons have been considered for that lack of use, particularly the work and length of time required to build a case, the length of trials and juries' ability to focus, a risk of abuse of powers and regional variations in application (Levi and Smiith, 2002). Implementation of the Money Laundering Control Act (1986) extended and clarified the powers of the Department of Treasury as well as criminalising money laundering offences (but only for funds generated from a prescribed list of offences) (Reuter and Truman, 2004; Madinger, 2012).

At the time of the Performance and Innovation Unit (PIU) Report (Cabinet Office, 2000) the UK government had an important luxury, the opportunity to observe what proceeds of crime legislation was in place in the USA and the time to conclude which parts of that legislation were deemed effective or otherwise. The PIU also examined how tax prosecutions worked in Australia, Ireland and France. Such an opportunity to review not only what had previously occurred within the UK but also how similar American legislation had worked, allowed legislators to construct strong, consolidating and quite flexible piece of legislation in the form of POCA.

Unlike the RICO, POCA resulted in considerable flexibility for investigators and prosecutors. Legislators had refrained from limiting either the new consolidated confiscation regime (civil and criminal) or the new money laundering offences to any kind of prescribed list of predicate (underlying) offending. They had also seen fit to include new money laundering offences in the same Act of Parliament as criminal, civil and tax investigatory powers which consolidated the previously disparate proceeds of crime arena. POCA powers and procedures could be brought to bear against the majority of offences across the whole spectrum of criminality (including money laundering committed abroad). American legislation was never really about the issue of reducing crime levels, rather it focused upon breaking the political and economic power of organised crime (Levi and Smith, 2002). The opposite was true of the UK and the fundamental objective of POCA was clearly intended to be the reduction of crime (POCA, 2002: 2).

The piecemeal growth of financial investigation resulting from each legislative change is likely to have contributed to differing application of it by law enforcement bodies. POCA enabled agencies such as the Department for Work and Pensions, Trading Standards and others with relevant statutory enforcement authorisation to utilise its powers. A singular problem, relevant to determining essential financial investigation characteristics has been that each agency has applied them in different ways and without any co-ordination

(Howell, Horton and Gill, 2013). This situation continues to the present day (HM Treasury, 2014; HMCPSI et al., 2010; National Audit Office, 2013). Other legislation has followed POCA, and the Serious Crime Act (2007) and the Serious Crime Act (2015) both added to the arsenal and tinkered with the confiscation regime. The already specialist area of confiscation (asset recovery) has become a complex and unwieldy area of law (Law Commission, 2017). Neither of these two enactments (like previous Acts) provided any definition of what a financial investigation might be or do. Financial investigation remains problematic and there seems "no understanding of what makes good performance" (House of Commons, 2014: 3). The Criminal Finances Act (2017) has also created new powers such as unexplained wealth orders (UWOs) but offers nothing to resolve the problem of financial investigation practice at all levels of law enforcement.

Since POCA (2002), there have been several other Acts of Parliament which continue to affect the trajectory of financial investigation. POCA has subsequently been amended to such an extent that it is arguable the asset recovery landscape in legislative terms, is perhaps as fragmented as it was prior to 2002. The consolidating effect (Cabinet Office, 2000) which POCA was intended to have (as the lead statutory authority for asset recovery and money laundering) seems short-lived.

Asset recovery seems perceived by all parties as a specialist area and altering that perception in the minds of general investigators and their supervisors has proven difficult (House of Commons, 2016). Why financial investigation is not embedded into wider law enforcement consciousness across all levels does not appear to have been fully addressed by any research (particularly involving general practitioners) and remains an unsolved conundrum (HMIC et al., 2004; Howell, Horton and Gill, 2013; House of Commons 2014). There appears to be limited empirical data apparent within the literature concerning the perspective of general practitioners and financial investigation, what their understanding of it and its parts may be and the extent to which it currently fits into their investigations.

This is conjoined with the lack of law enforcement vision to utilise its potential (House of Commons, 2016) and has prevented comprehensive strategic or tactical understanding or consideration of what makes essential financial investigation. Continuing legislative reluctance to define the term financial investigation (and the perception that it is a confiscation tool and thereby relevant only to asset recovery) appears to have contributed to a sporadic and fragmented implementation process across general law enforcement. It is arguable that it has also adversely affected how the confiscation regime is regarded by prosecutors and general practitioners (and its ensuing isolation from general law enforcement practice). This literature review has revealed a clear lack of empirical data as to the application of financial investigation techniques within the general investigation arena, from novice to highly experienced investigators. Money laundering offences still appear caught by their initial association with drugs legislation and the problems of predicate offences, a theme which directly correlates with apparent resistance to embrace it more broadly across law enforcement. POCA appears to have unintentionally reinforced the perception that money laundering is the domain of financial crime specialists, making the synthesis of a transferable financial investigation philosophy that much more difficult. The authors suggest, based upon available literature and strategic policy, that there is a lack of financial investigation strategy at all levels outside the area of confiscation and asset recovery, underuse of financial investigation techniques and minimal use of financial intelligence within the NIM by practitioners.

6 Financial intelligence and the National Intelligence Model

What is Intelligence?

Before considering what is meant by financial intelligence, the first question has to be, "What is intelligence?" Only then can the term financial intelligence be considered in relation to its routine use (and its understanding) by general investigators outside of the asset recovery arena. Laqueur (1985: 8) set out an initial problem regarding the field of intelligence in 1985 and is directly quoted by Warner (2002: 1): "all attempts to develop ambitious theories of intelligence have failed". Warner (2002) used Laqueur's (1985) summation to underline what he considered to be the recurring problem with attempts to define intelligence: "The term is defined anew by each author who addresses it and these definitions rarely refer to one another to build off. Without a clear idea of what intelligence is, how can we develop a theory to explain how it works?" (Warner, 2002: 15). Following a brief examination of some of the definitions of financial intelligence within the available literature it is the intention of these authors to postulate a definition of financial intelligence acknowledging the advice of building off existing definitions.

As might be expected, opinions differ widely, and definitions appear to depend upon which aspect of law enforcement, military or political direction the subject is approached from. It may be that arriving at a general definition of intelligence is an impossible challenge, and outside the scope of this project, although there is some consensus that intelligence can be split into two main types, strategic and tactical (operational) (Richards, 2010).

The American military advances the following description:

> Information is of greatest value when it contributes to the commander's decision-making process by providing reasoned insight into future conditions or situations. Intelligence provides the commander a variety of assessments and estimates that facilitate understanding the operational environment. Intelligence includes the organisations, capabilities, and processes involved in the collection, processing, exploitation, analysis and dissemination of information or finished intelligence.
>
> (Joint Force Intelligence Directorate, 2013: ix)

DOI: 10.4324/9781003438649-6

The principle described is a sound one; without the ability for the intelligence process to influence the thinking of decision makers who implement strategies impacting upon the criminal environment, there can be no intelligence led policing (Ratcliffe, 2010). The Association of Chief Police Officers (ACPO, 2005: 13) has a simpler definition: "information that has been subject to a defined evaluation and risk assessment process in order to assist with police decision making". Whereby the investigation process is well established across law enforcement, the same cannot be said of the relatively recent discipline of intelligence (Ratcliffe, 2009). This argument is based upon an assumption that senior police officers (in particular) have historically been former detectives and detectives see intelligence as an investigation aid. Such a view necessarily limits any strategic crime analysis and proactive intelligence output. Intelligence is not simply information collection and "It is what people do with data and information that gives them the special quality that we casually call intelligence" (Warner, 2002: 15).

There are many areas of law enforcement, and each one possesses its own types and sources of intelligence. Financial investigation is no different and information which is of a financial nature has ensconced itself in the general vernacular as financial intelligence. Whether that term is generally understood is open to question. Just as the general term intelligence continues to be debated, a collaborative consensus as to what constitutes financial intelligence continues to be just as elusive. Data is required to begin to understand how the term is interpreted across law enforcement at the strategic, tactical and practical levels where the authors believe the term financial intelligence is not generally understood. Consideration must also be given to its engagement with the NIM seemingly on a limited basis combined with limited use of SAR intelligence.

The National Financial Investigation Working Group (2011: 1), comprised of senior AFIs from different agencies (but primarily police and Home Office led), has its own definition of what can be considered as financial intelligence: "Any intelligence that is of a financial nature that can add value to an investigation". The definition prompts the question, what does "of a financial nature" mean?' Is the phrase referring to cash or credit card purchases, bank accounts, points cards, property investment or electronic data within the emerging digital environment (the internet)? How do operational officers recognise items of a financial nature during their normal duties (if they do so at all) and do they productively integrate with the NIM? The same questions could be asked of the AFIs.

The range of possibilities for items of a financial nature is as broad as the term seems vague and unhelpful. As a simple analogy, a bank statement found during the search of a premises may seem to be a straightforward example of financial intelligence. When the scenario is altered to consider an everyday patrol situation, financial intelligence may not be so apparent. The matter becomes more difficult to explain if an officer sees a new vehicle driven down a street by a known drug dealer. The officer may submit an intelligence item which detailed the description of the vehicle (registration plate, colour, make and so forth) and the report may even contain a description of the driver and what he was wearing. Whether the officer regards the sighting of the car as financial intelligence is a point for further study. If the officer does not make that connection and the report is submitted as a general sighting, the next question is whether any internal intelligence assessors make such a connection and inform their Financial Investigation Unit. There does not appear to be any research available within the literature to suggest how the NIM is used in connecting financial pieces of information and routing them to where they are best used to advantage.

The National Intelligence Model

Notwithstanding the importance of intelligence in military traditions, law enforcement in the UK has had to adapt to the requirements of obtaining intelligence and using it efficiently within a sound process. Richards (2010) recognises that intelligence is both a product and a business process and that: "Most observers define intelligence as the output of the process of analysis applied to information...Distinctions can be drawn between tactical (operational) and strategic intelligence" (Richards, 2010: 25). Tactical (operational) intelligence can perhaps be best described as "on the ground" intelligence where assessment and judgement are required to be contemporaneous with the situation (Coyne and Bell, 2011; Richards, 2010), for example, search warrant or kidnap and surveillance operations. Immediate response time margins dictated by live situations leave little time for all but rudimentary analytical processes. Strategic intelligence is the ability to use information to anticipate risk in general terms and to develop and inform strategies which are proactive in the longer term (for instance terrorism or public order) (Coyne and Bell, 2011a; Sheptycki, 2009). This is reflected by the NIM, designed as a business model to facilitate the organisation of knowledge, inform resource allocation and co-ordinate activity (Association of Chief Police Officers, 2005; Flood and Gaspar, 2009).

Since the Police Reform Act (2002), responsible for providing the statutory basis for the NIM, the model was made compulsory in police forces (England and Wales) in 2004 (Richards, 2010). The NIM has now been in general use for thirteen years but as observed by Flood and Gaspar (2009) why, if the NIM is central to today's police business to prioritise strategies, is it called an intelligence model. As two of the architects of the NIM, Flood and Gaspar (2009: 54) stated their model was an ideal one that, "would enable police commanders to understand and anticipate risks and threats across the public safety domain". They also maintain that at the time of writing the NIM, it would not have been acceptable for the government to support a business model for UK policing. The fact it was called NIM disguised the fact it was a business model for policing, the ruse being that it was sold as being an intelligence one: "The product was the same whatever the title, but consideration had to be given to the acceptability of its presentation" (Flood and Gaspar, 2009: 53).

If the NIM is concerned about the management and prioritisation of resources as much as it is concerned with the intelligence process (John and Maguire, 2012) a question must be raised as to the NIM's capability in processing intelligence and as to its operational effectiveness. The NIM in its initial and present form was certainly not seen as an end product by some of its creators: "The design of the National Intelligence Model was not the conclusion of this work, merely the beginning" (Flood and Gasper, 2009: 64). The point they make is relevant in as much as whether the NIM effectively processes (or otherwise) financial intelligence (a problematic term in itself) and whether law enforcement practitioners engage with the NIM to input, as well as access financial information (including the level of intelligence input from AFIs). Consideration will also be given to suspicious activity reports (SARs), the use that is made of them, and whether they are effective within their own (confiscation) or the NIM environment.

Intelligence and information handling is only taught during the initial 15 weeks of police basic training as one of a wide variety of law enforcement subjects. It appears to be addressed in a basic manner as part of the National Policing Curriculum (College of Policing, 2018a). Thereafter, (aside from a one-hour input on detective training courses) there appears to be no other training available from the College of Policing except for a three-day course for Chief Inspectors or above (strategic handling of intelligence). Chief Inspectors usually have a minimum of at least ten years' service, so it seems a little disconcerting that there is no additional training for general police officers apparently for the rest of their service. The lack of available and continuously updated training raises questions regarding the competency of general law enforcement practitioners in recognising, handling and using (financial) intelligence across the operational spectrum. Looking past the general observation to the more specific, for this book the question is whether constables (and similar ranks in other law enforcement agencies where there is even less training) understand what financial intelligence might mean and whether they recognise it when it presents itself.

Suspicious activity reports (SARs)

SARs are a particularly difficult area. The number that is followed up and lead to prosecution in high reporting jurisdictions (including the UK) is low, as was originally commented upon by Gold and Levi (1994). Accurate figures demonstrating how many SARs have led to criminal investigations and convictions in any particular year are unavailable. It is not clear from the available NCA literature that such specific records are kept or even feasible and it does not seem to be a point considered in the SARs Annual Reports (NCA, 2015, 2017e, 2018f). The observation of Gold and Levi (1994) was made prior to the increasingly high volume of SARs now being received annually from the regulated sector. The same problem of low yield still remains over two decades later and is not helped in any way by the Electronic Line Management Enterprise Recording (ELMER) system which was initially designed to handle 20,000 SARs in total (House of Commons, 2016). ELMER has been updated to reflect increased reporting, but SARs information technology resilience is recognised as an ongoing problem and replacement of the SARs IT systems remains a longer-term strategy for the NCA (Home Office and HM Treasury 2016; NCA, 2017e).

Although great emphasis is placed upon SARs, government (Home Office) expectations as to what they can be used for seems misplaced. SARs are the product of a mandatory process under the money laundering regulations (2007) whereby the financial sector submits otherwise confidential information to law enforcement agencies. SARs are not meant to underpin money laundering prosecutions, nor are they a stand-alone baseline for evidential conclusions. The empirical data for this research project intends to explore whether SARs are perceived within law enforcement as a specialist tool for AFIs and the extent to which they are used by general investigators. It is also of interest to ascertain whether general investigators understand the information SARs contain and how useful it may be to the general criminal investigative arena (engaging with NIM on a limited basis and limited use of SAR intelligence).

Paragraph 9.1 in Cabinet Office (2000: 74) reported in respect of SARs at that time, "an annual average of 15,000 such disclosures has led to only a handful of money laundering convictions. There are also significant delays in processing suspicious transaction reports".

This quote appears to contain several misunderstandings regarding money laundering and SARs.

Referring to money laundering convictions in the context of SARs seems misguided. A SAR is simply information from a financial institution which alerts law enforcement that a transaction has been suspicious in some way (NCA, 2015). Money laundering offences at the time of the Cabinet Office report (2000) were either indictable as part of drug trafficking investigations or dependent upon predicate offences as described in the Criminal Justice Act (1988) (offences such as theft, robbery or blackmail). Such offences would be the dominant prosecution charges and any money laundering charge treated as an add-on. If prosecution of the dominant (predicate) offence failed, then the money laundering offence perished by default. Government thinking about the concept of money laundering and how to combat it appears restricted from its outset. Even though POCA dispensed with predicate offences in 2002, the terminology and thought process of money laundering as a secondary offence seem to persist. This raises an important point which seems un-addressed in the available literature; the extent to which non-specialist investigators, CPS prosecutors and (some) AFIs still perceive that unless the criminality is drug trafficking or organised crime, money laundering is not considered. It is a continuing problem not only at the strategic, tactical and practical levels of law enforcement but politically, academically and judicially (House of Commons, 2016; NCA, 2017, 2017e).

There is a supposition in the quote that SARs are supposed to lead to money laundering offences which (as already described) was an impossibility without other offending. As discussed in more detail immediately below, SARs are not evidence. Financial institutions are required by the money laundering regulations (2007) to report suspicious activity (not money laundering offences per se) and the information they supply can be construed in many ways. As discussed by Levi and Reuter (2006), SARs are difficult to resolve without alerting the subjects of them and government expectations of high prosecution rates and asset stripping based upon them is unrealistic. SARs require careful handling and the information contained within them is retained in what the NCA describes as the strictest confidence (NCA, 2015c). SARs are considered to be sensitive intelligence and are not to be used in the prosecution of a case (Home Office, 2015). They are retained by the NCA for six years or until a SAR is proven not to be related to criminality (NCA, 2018). Their link with evidence is usually a tentative one. These issues may well contribute to the government thinking behind the new unexplained wealth orders (UWOs) whereby SARs could be used to attack unexplained assets reported by the regulated sector (Criminal Finances Act, 2017).

Recent newspaper articles describing foreign property investments in London which appear criminal and which the authorities have done nothing about, may be one of the reasons that the government and at least one independent commentator favoured new legislation to attack the funds being used (Collison, 2015; Evans, 2016; Mason and Travis, 2016; Transparency International, 2018). POCA enables civil recovery of property where a criminal prosecution has not succeeded. Civil recovery proceedings using POCA are considered to be in rem which is against the property itself and not the person who owns it. In other words, it is whether the property is guilty. The defining point is that a real attempt has been made to bring the individual to justice by the means of a criminal investigation and/or prosecution before civil recovery can be considered.

The Criminal Finances Act (2017) is different because that investigation aspect is no longer required to begin attacking the assets of an individual. A new investigative power in the law enforcement arsenal is the UWO. It is a power which seems primarily designed for where there is suspicion that an asset may have been purchased utilising criminal funds from abroad but where there is no realistic prospect of conviction or prosecution in the country of origin (Transparency International, 2018). In that regard, the legislation particularly focuses upon individuals defined as politically exposed persons (PEPs) (for example foreign politicians suspected of corruption) although a UWO can be used to investigate UK criminals in cases where “a person who is reasonably suspected of involvement in, or of being connected to a person involved in, serious crime to explain the nature and extent of their interest in particular property” (Home Office, 2018b: 1; 2023b).

A UWO is an investigation tool and is a civil power. It can only be obtained by application to the High Court and is available to the NCA, HMRC, SFO and the CPS (Home Office, 2018b). The term serious crime with regard to UWOs is defined within the Serious Crime Act (2007) and only applies to offences within Schedule 1 of that Act. Schedule 1 is a series of offences under the headings drug trafficking, slavery, people trafficking, firearms offences, prostitution and child sex, money laundering, fraud, bribery, offences in relation to public revenue, intellectual property, computer misuse, organised crime, environment and financial sanctions legislation. There seems to be an implicit expectation that SARs will be the primary source of intelligence which will lead to use of UWOs, particularly in money laundering investigations (Criminal Finances Act, 2017: s10). The POCA (2002) moratorium period of 31 days (the time allowed for law enforcement to investigate a SAR with regard to restraining assets) can be extended in the case of UWOs to a maximum of 186 days (six months) and during that time an interim freezing order can now be applied for to ensure the assets under investigation are not disposed of.

UWOs seem to be meant for use in complex investigations into serious crime (Keen, 2017) and although the Home Office (2018b) maintains they are not in their own right a power to recover assets, the intention seems to be exactly that (NCA, 2018e; Transparency International, 2018). The first two UWOs were obtained in February 2018 by the NCA to investigate assets totalling £22 million and thought to be owned by a politically exposed person (NCA, 2018e). In the reporting period 2022–2023, numbers of UWOs obtained continues to be low, with only one being obtained between 15 May 2022 and 14 May 2023 (Home Office, 2023). The limited number of agencies able to apply for UWOs and interim freeing orders suggests they are a specialist function rather than a general investigation tool. The title of the Act and the link between UWOs, asset recovery and restraint orders (interim freezing orders) suggest they fall into the remit of AFIs, already perceived as specialists (Howell, Horton and Gill, 2013; NPIA, 2008). It is arguable that the publicity about UWOs and property investigation and their value to serious and organised crime untouchables will not diminish the perception of general investigators that financial investigation is quite the opposite of a useable and generally available tool for non-specialists.

Since 2000, the number of SARs submitted by the financial sector of business seems voluminous. Between October 2013 to October 2014, 354,186 SARs were submitted, an increase on the previous period by 37,659 (National Crime Agency, 2014). The number of SARs submitted in 2014 was 23 times greater than in the millennium year and that number continues to increase. The increase may be due to the changing nature of banking (increased electronic and internet banking), wider coverage by the regulatory requirement (such as solicitors and estate agents), as well as reporting entities engaging in defensive reporting to minimise potential risks. To put SAR totals in perspective in terms of the UK financing system, in 2014 the average *daily* value of payments settled by supervised payment systems, Clearing House Automated Payment System (CHAPS), Bankers Automated Clearing System (BACS) and Faster Payment System (FPS) was £290 billion, from 28 million payment messages. CREST, the United Kingdom's securities settlement system, which is also supervised by the Bank of England, settled a *daily* average of £396 billion (Bank of England, 2015).

SARS therefore only represent a fraction of UK transactions each year but remain the focus of government attention and a sensitive problem for law enforcement (particularly police forces, where most SARS are dispatched for attention). SARs generally relate to domestic transactions but can be submitted from financial institutions regarding funds transferred to the UK from other countries (NCA, 2017a). Between October 2014 and September 2015, the number of SARs submitted increased again by 7.8% from 354,186 to 381,882 (NCA, 2015). Figures for the period October 2015 to September 2016 demonstrate the rise in SAR numbers continued, totalling 419,451, an increase of 9.14% for the same period (NCA, 2017e). From September 2016 to March 2017 a further 214,662 SARs were submitted (NCA, 2017a).

Under the current money laundering regulation regime, it is acknowledged by the NCA that SARs will continue to increase as more money laundering regulations are legislated and tightened (NCA, 2017e, 2018d). In 2022, the number of SARs reached a record high of 901,255. The volume problem of SARs does not appear a reducing one (NCA, 2023).

The continued rise in the volume of SARs might be attributable to financial institutions being statutorily obliged to accede to the money laundering regulations (2007, 2017) whereby any suspicious transactions must be submitted by way of a SAR to the UK Financial Intelligence Unit (UKFIU) a department within the NCA. The UKFIU is the single point of contact for the submission of SARs, conducts analysis of the information contained within them and is responsible for distribution of SAR intelligence to law enforcement agencies (NCA, 2019a). The definition of suspicious is subjective and is a matter for the institution concerned and the staff making the report. As the industry is heavily regulated, a very real concern is that institutions only submit SARs in order to avoid any risk or penalties as a result of not doing so (Levi and Reuter, 2006). Such reports are called defence against money laundering submissions (DAML) now recorded by the UKFIU (NCA, 2018d). A DAML involves a financial institution suspecting that something is wrong with a proposed transaction and requesting the NCA for permission to transact. If consent is given to transact by the NCA, then the financial institution will have a defence available to any subsequent allegation of money laundering which might be made against it. During the period 2015–2017, 27,471 DAML SARs were made (NCA, 2017a, 2018d). Although consent DAML SARs are recorded, it is not known how many other SARs are submitted by financial institutions (where consent is not overtly requested) as a general defensive reporting cover all, a just in case measure.

SARs have not been standardised in terms of what information should be reported or in the form it should be reported in. The quality of SARs varies so much that advice on how best to submit them has had to be explained within a specially prepared NCA document to attempt to address the problem (NCA, 2016, 2017a). SARs may also contain unclear reasons for suspicion or may relate to non-criminal activity such as tax avoidance or inheritance windfall (Fleming, 2005, 2007). Financial sector reporting may also inadvertently identify vulnerable individuals either actively being defrauded or who are potential victims (NCA, 2015). Suspicion is subjective and is based upon what the reporting individual within an institution considers normal or abnormal at the time a transaction is made. A simple example would be an individual walking into a bank with a carrier bag containing ten thousand pounds in cash. The bank teller should ask questions regarding the origin of the money and if a reasonable explanation is not forthcoming, or the individual becomes indignant or offensive, it is highly likely that a SAR would be submitted.

Poor quality of some SARs has long been an issue, possibly due within the corporate sector to very different and disparate training on what details to submit and why. To some extent the problem has been recognised by the NCA (2016) which, in an attempt to re-educate the corporate sector, has issued guidance to achieve a more standardised method of reporting. Empirical data does not appear available within the literature as to the proportion of SARs which can be termed low quality. Prior to the guidance being issued there was no established good practice for the regulated sector (financial institutions and companies subject to the UK money laundering regulations) to follow. Information within SARs could be as little as one line of information or several pages. The NCA guidance provides tips for best practice and (together with other advice) how to clearly identify the reason for the disclosure. Whether the guidance will lead to a more standardised disclosure of information remains to be seen. Historically, the NCA (and its predecessors) has lacked legal powers to obtain additional information from the institution submitting a SAR. The new Criminal Finances Act (2017) is intended (where SARs are concerned) to strengthen the hand of law enforcement and provide powers for the UKFIU to obtain additional information from the reporting institutions (NCA, 2017e). How such powers will affect use of SARs or increase investigation or intervention opportunities for law enforcement has not been posited.

SAR numbers increase annually (FTI consulting, 2018; NCA, 2017a). It is not known whether this results from tighter regulation controls, better recognition of suspicious transactions or an increase in numbers of transactions. A recent survey of AFIs established that the national SAR database is an important intelligence tool (Howell, Horton and Gill, 2013). Participants ranked credit reference reports as the primary intelligence tool of AFIs, followed by pre-production order checks with financial institutions and then Land Registry checks. SARs were considered the fourth most important tool for an investigating AFI. What is not made clear is how SARS are used in practice by AFIs and whether the information within them can be utilised other than in

Financial Units. Although outside the scope of this book, further research data in that area appears to be required. The FATF agrees that disclosures constitute a particularly valuable source of information for financial investigations (confiscation), furthermore, that national and international frameworks for providing access to such information are important in determining how intelligence can be made available to operational authorities and developed into investigative leads or evidence (FATF, 2012).

The SARs system has previously been observed to show, a "lack of strategic end to end processing in a loose-coupled law enforcement and regulatory system" (Levi and Reuter, 2006: 55). The HMIC (2015a) agreed that the SARs intelligence is still not a cohesive process. In a current national review being undertaken of the SARs regime, the question is whether that statement still holds true. The problem at least seems to have been recognised on both sides of the SARS system (the financial sector and law enforcement) that intelligence flow between them requires improving. The Joint Money Laundering Intelligence Taskforce (JMLIT) was set up as a one-year pilot in 2015 and continues to be extended (NCA, 2018b). Its constituent members attempt to engender a more cohesive approach to intelligence and co-operation between law enforcement and the regulatory sector by encouraging real-time iterative information sharing on serious crime and security threats (Ellis and de Oliveira, 2015).

There appears to be no available research data concerning certain points which need to be considered if inhibitors to routine practice are to be identified and a broader application of techniques is to be attempted. Whether general law enforcement investigators understand what SARs are and how they can be accessed and used is not clear in from the available literature. Nor is it clear how financial intelligence is integrated with the NIM at the practice level, or how it is considered by the strategic and tactical levels.

Theoretical considerations: the "culture of control"

Garland's (2001) "Culture of Control" is interesting if it is applied to financial investigation and confiscation as they are currently understood by government commentators (House of Commons, 2016). In a previous study, Garland (2000) summarised his argument regarding changing crime control strategies away from "vigorous policing and correctional penal measures" (Garland, 1996: 447). As a result of penal-welfare solutions falling into disrepute (Allen, 1991; Croft, 1978; Sparks, 1996). Garland (2000) theorised that two new lines of governmental action were evolving: "adaptive strategy stressing prevention and partnership and a sovereign strategy stressing enhanced control and expressive punishment". Politicians and law enforcement hierarchy were becoming more modest in claims to control crime and order, as Garland (1996: 447) previously summarised: "There is a new sense of the failure of criminal justice agencies, and a more limited sense of the state's powers to regulate conduct and prohibit deviance". Emphasis began to shift in the late

1990s towards proactively preventing crime (intelligence led policing) rather than punitive reaction through punishment (Garland, 2000). Whereby sovereign state strategy enhances control and directs policing and other criminal justice theatres (probation and prisons) towards punitive punishment (expressive justice), adaptive strategies require the organisational thrust of those agencies to be redefined, something governments are ambivalent about in certain political circumstances (Garland, 2001).

The limitations of the state's capacity to govern all details of modern social life is visible in its inability to deliver publicly expected levels of crime control (Garland, 2001). This has resulted in an attempt to face the problem by institutional reforms to overcome the problems or by creating new adaptive strategies which recognise the limitations and work within them (Garland, 2001). He maintains there are two politicised reactions to adaptive strategies. Politicians wilfully deny the issue and revert to sovereign state powers to punish perpetrators or they act out, "a mode that is concerned not so much with controlling crime as with expressing the anger and outrage that crime provokes" (Garland, 2001: 110).

Tony Blair in his campaign to become Prime Minister in 1997 stated, "Tough on crime, tough on the causes of crime" (Blair, 1995). It was a message that carried through to the review of proceeds of crime legislation instigated by him and published three years later (Cabinet Office, 2000). The sentiment seems to fit with theorising about sovereign state strategy and leads to a question of to what extent POCA (2002) was more a commanding gesture of public reassurance (Garland, 2001) than part of an adaptive strategy for its explicitly stated purpose, the reduction of crime. POCA is symbolically powerful, the message being clear that if you commit acquisitive crime then your benefit (asset base) could be forfeit. An additional sentence to the primary custodial term of up to 12 years can also be handed down by a court to be served in the case of non-payment of a confiscation order. The reality is that the symbolically powerful POCA message (taking the money out of crime) could be more robustly enforced at the post-confiscation order stage (NAO, 2013, 2016; Wood, 2017). Adaptive strategies for increased effective application of POCA requires agencies and governments to work together to achieve maximum effect. That co-operation has been shown by the literature to be lacking. Financial investigation continues to be perceived and treated as a specialist area associated with confiscation (asset recovery) rather than a focus for general investigation and crime reduction. Financial intelligence continues to also be perceived and treated as a specialist area rather than a focus for day-to-day law enforcement activities.

Garland (2000, 2001) makes three points concerning expressive justice, the "tough on crime" measures. First, any such measures are "populist and politicised" (Garland, 2000: 350), courting public opinion above views of criminal justice experts and professional groups. This seems to apply to the taking money out of crime intention where the government can be seen to be doing something about the problem of criminal benefit. Second, punishment for its own sake uses an expressive punitive scale (as does POCA in its default sentence prison scale) and, "an instrumental register attuned to public protection and risk management" (Garland, 2000: 350). Third is linking the strategy to victims who appear to be given greater (politicised) consideration in the prosecution system. These points provide any government with the escape route from adaptive strategies by allowing them to redefine success or failure in their own terms such as claiming falling crime rates at a time when digital offences were unrecorded (ONS, 2016).

Governments can just as effectively define deviance down in terms of tolerating behaviours which previously had been vigorously policed (Moynihan, 1993). An example would be the offence of simple possession of the drug cannabis now attracting a caution rather than prosecution. As Garland (2001) points out, it is easy enough for a government given the right circumstances to either filter offences out of the system or, as in this case, by lowering the criminal threshold for that particular and previously prosecuted behaviour. To assist the reader in understanding financial investigation powers against a theoretical context of sovereign and adaptive strategies of the "culture of control", Appendix Two sets them in the culture of control framework. The full extent of the theory which can be pursued by the reader in Garland (2001).

Conclusion

There has been a continuing stream of legislation which is claimed by successive governments to underpin POCA (2002) (see Appendix 1) but which may be a significant factor in the perceptions of general investigators that financial investigation is an end of process, asset-focused specialism (post conviction) of no use in general investigations. The continued calls for extra legislation from the strategic layer of policing does little to mitigate that perception while the lobbying of outside commentators for tighter confiscation and anti-money laundering mechanisms under the umbrella of financial investigation does little to integrate it as a general investigatory technique. This issue integrates with the theoretical framework of the "culture of control" (Garland, 2001) and is perhaps exacerbated by the seeming lack of a coherent and effective implementation strategy to separate financial investigation from asset recovery and facilitate its wider application.

Piecemeal growth of financial investigation resulting from each legislative change is likely to have contributed to differing application of it by law enforcement bodies. A singular problem has been that each agency has applied them in different ways and without any co-ordination (Howell, Horton and Gill, 2013). This situation continues to the present day (HMCPSI et al., 2010; National Audit Office, 2013) and training remains an issue for specialist and generalists alike. Other legislation has followed POCA, and the Serious Crime Act (2007) and the Serious Crime Act (2015) both added to the arsenal and tinkered with the confiscation regime. It has become a complex and unwieldy area of law (Law Commission, 2017). Neither of these two enactments (like previous Acts) provided any definition of what a financial investigation might be or do, something which this study attempts to address. Financial investigation remains problematic and there seems "no understanding of what makes good performance" (House of Commons, 2014: 3). The Criminal Finances Act (2017) has also created new powers (UWOs) but offers little to resolve the problem of financial investigation practice at all levels of law enforcement.

This section identifies parallel themes involving SARs and the NIM (as well as general financial intelligence flow) that relate particularly to generic use but with some relevance to broader financial investigation and intelligence characteristics. The literature indicates that SARS are not well utilised or investigated by law enforcement and this section has identified a clear disconnect between the compatibility and the integration of SARS within the NIM. Little information appears available to attempt to quantify to what extent financial information (SARS or otherwise) is disseminated into the operational echelons of everyday law enforcement and used by operational decision makers. The reverse is also true and there appears to be a gap in the literature concerning how frequently AFIs or non-specialist law enforcement practitioners submit financial intelligence or recognise what financial intelligence actually is. There remains a national and key evidence gap as to what extent the NIM is being used for financial intelligence at any level, as empirical data appears unavailable. There is also a clear requirement for empirical data regarding utilisation of SARS information across law enforcement (outside of the asset recovery process), the general awareness of financial intelligence at all levels (strategic, tactical and practice), and whether financial intelligence is actively utilised in the strategic planning of investigations.

There appears to be little or no empirical research available in the existing literature which might offer insight into the use of financial investigation strategy. Reliable data in this regard (which this book aims to offer) may provide opportunities to understand the current use of financial investigation techniques at all levels and to what extent those techniques are presently integrated into general investigations. This review has identified there seems a paucity of reliable information concerning general use of investigation strategy in criminal investigations, and specifically regarding financial investigation strategy. It is an aspect seemingly not included in research to date (Brown et al., 2012; Gale and Kelly, 2018; Howell, Horton, and Gill, 2013; Wood, 2017). It is one which may prove crucial to identifying and understanding inhibitors to strategic, tactical and practice level decision making concerning financial investigation, how financial intelligence is perceived and applied and why essential characteristics of financial investigation are traditionally tied to asset recovery.

Legislators have consistently resisted producing definitions of financial investigation and financial intelligence. It is a factor that may prove to be integral to the seeming inability of policy makers and practitioners to remove inhibitors preventing effective implementation of the acknowledged political and strategic desire to embed financial investigation within the standard investigation environment. The lack of a definition, when combined with the piecemeal introduction and amendments to proceeds of crime legislation described immediately above invites the question as to whether the legislation is in any way designed to promulgate essential financial investigationcharacteristics or integrated implementation at any level (strategic, tactical, practice). To move towards an answer to both issues, the postulation of relevant definitions for financial investigation and financial intelligence (offered by this book) may be a necessary process. Perhaps by clearly identifying the two areas in the minds of non-specialists can an understanding of the essential characteristics be properly achieved before moving on to the theorising of a generic philosophy. Without such definition, it seems likely that the pitfalls which currently exist will not be able to be properly negotiated.

It is with these points in mind, and as a result of clear gaps in the available literature, that at the conclusion of the literature review concerning financial investigation and financial intelligence this book advocates two definitions:

Proposed definition of (practical) financial investigation

In view of the continuing government intention to more effectively integrate financial investigation into non-specialist areas (House of Commons, 2016) it may be useful as an initial step, to alter the slant of the subject title. It may be more appropriate to refer to the subject area as *practical* financial investigation. If financial investigation can be de-mythologised from being perceived as a specialist area only useful in asset recovery cases, general investigators might begin to be persuaded that financial investigation is something they can utilise. A definition of *practical* financial investigation as a broad identification of the work area in question might be better explained as in Hughes (2021: 128):

> *Financial investigation is a technique to trace the complete or partial financial footprint of an individual or entity. It is a generic tool to inform strategic and tactical decision-making in the use of information, intelligence and evidence to support enquiries and investigations at all levels.*

Such a definition is designed to make financial investigation relevant for all investigations and enquiries, moving diametrically away from the generally held perception (validated by the majority of available literature) that it is something relevant only to the confiscation process and asset recovery.

Proposed definition of (usable) financial intelligence

Just as the technique of (practical) financial investigation needs to be clearly separated from the specialist area of confiscation (for which NCA accreditation is required in order to practice) a clear distinction may be similarly helpful regarding financial intelligence. As in the case of financial investigation, it may be useful as an initial step, to again alter the slant of the subject area's title. It may be more appropriate to refer to the subject area as *usable* financial intelligence. A definition of financial intelligence which associates closely with the proposed definition of financial investigation seems a sensible step forward in attempting to translate government intentions into practical investigation skill sets. After assessing the available literature about financial intelligence within this literature review, this research intends to attempt to fill the clear gap identified therein. A definition of (usable) financial intelligence as a generic identification of the work area in question might be better explained in Hughes (2021: 129) as:

> *Financial intelligence is any information which: assists in establishing the complete or partial financial footprint of individuals or entities and which can be utilised to inform strategic and tactical decision making for all investigation, prosecution and asset recovery purposes.*

This definition is designed to integrate with the NIM, but also to address day-to-day aspects of investigation rather than ad hoc or end of process confiscation focus. This book advocates the view that (usable) financial intelligence should be applied to identify intervention opportunities at any stage in any investigation in order to utilise suitable law enforcement powers (including the available POCA orders) and better target the use of cash detention provisions under POCA.

Such a definition is designed to make financial intelligence relevant for all investigations and enquiries, moving diametrically away from the generally held perception that it is something relevant only to the confiscation process and asset recovery. The suggested definition seems compatible with the NIM, offering a potential degree of integration demonstrated within this literature review to be lacking. It also purposefully steers away from the seemingly general perception across law enforcement and among policy makers that financial intelligence is somehow different to other intelligence and stems largely from bank accounts and the financial sector. The proposed definition intentionally aligns with and is complementary to that proposed for financial investigation.

The two areas seem parallel, financial investigation to support enquiries and investigations at all levels and financial intelligence to support all investigations, prosecutions and asset recovery purposes. Rudner (2004) suggests that in dealing with the international and complex terrorist threat which has developed since the New York World Trade Centre was destroyed on 11 September 2001, intelligence has bifurcated into a hunter as well as a gatherer. The more passive role for intelligence as a product gathered bilaterally from other activities, intelligence is now employed to proactively seek out and acquire information regarding hostile intentions and capabilities which can also be deployed as disruption tactics. For the purposes of this project a distinction can be made between the hunters (financial investigators in the general sense and not limited to AFIs) and gatherers (all law enforcement investigators rather than limited to intelligence specialists). Gatherers tend to be more desk-based and work behind the scenes. Hunters (Rudner, 2004) should be "hands-on" investigators who follow the cycle of investigation, identification and restraint of proceeds of crime beyond prosecution and conviction to confiscation, enforcement and in some cases civil recovery procedures. The two do not seem mutually exclusive and the scale of the problems and challenges of implementing proceeds of crime legislation appear to make clear the need for overlap and understanding of hunter/gatherer activities. This approach seems to link well with Garland (2000) on the scope of the challenges for implementing adaptive strategies in the areas of financial investigation and financial intelligence.

Both proposed definitions attempt to deal with the practicalities of applying financial investigation techniques to all investigations and the potential for them to be used strategically and tactically at all levels of law enforcement. As set out above, this review has established that asset recovery (confiscation) is regarded as a specialist environment which eclipses general usage of (applied) financial investigation. The two proposed definitions steer away from the notion of asset recovery and attempt to engender the two aspects (intelligence and investigation) with a practical appeal for all investigators. They are designed to de-mythologise the notion of complexity and reduce general perceptions of specialism. This book advocates that both proposed definitions should be an intrinsic component of developing a new and more routine approach to both areas and de-mystify their potential application for routine investigators.

All the above points inevitably question how the decision-making process for financial investigation is administered within government and law enforcement, and how strategic considerations (and expectations) translate through mid-tier chains of command (tactical) to wider policing methods (practical). There appears to be a pressing need for a comprehensive and integrated approach to financial investigation on a national scale and across the breadth of the law enforcement spectrum if it is to be utilised towards exploiting its potential.

The authors offer the identified gaps in the literature (and the disconnects in financial investigation) and the seemingly chronic need for empirical data as findings of this review. An eventual re-alignment of the strategic focus towards financial investigation techniques across the strategic (including policy makers), tactical and practice levels seems required.

7 Financial intelligence footprint and digital investigation and intelligence

The internet is a global phenomenon

Currently, there are estimated to be 5.8 billion internet users worldwide. It is arguable that the rise and expansion of the digital environment since the 1990s can be termed a contemporary Industrial Revolution in electronic form. The internet and digital devices offer a seemingly inexhaustible rate of expansion. Most aspects of modern life depend to some degree on their use, their security and an ability by users to apply themselves to the new digital reality which they bring. For law enforcement, already struggling to cope with traditional real-world crime, the digital environment poses a plethora of new issues to be reckoned with. In this regard, Her Majesty's Inspectorate of Constabulary (2015) concluded that a general perception was forming that the police were unprepared for cybercrime.

This book has previously dealt with the use of terminology and has set out why cybercrime as a descriptive title for offences using digital pathways is a misnomer. Having already drawn that particular line, this chapter will examine financial investigation through the lens of the current positioning of criminality using digital means, the perception of the internet by users and investigators and the impact that so-called cybercrime has had on law enforcement. It will do so against the backdrop of increasing numbers of cybercrimes reported and a comparatively small number of prosecutions of offenders (Wall, 2008). Governments would have us believe that crime is either under control or actually falling. It is an interesting exercise in any gathering of academics, students or the general public to ask a simple question in order to put the cybercrime "problem" in realistic context, "Who has not had a phishing email or text?". The reality is that everyone has, and every such message is an attempted crime. In attempting to gauge the number of such attempts and the real breadth of digital crimes such as fraud, the problem appears two-fold. First, digital criminal attempts are too many and too frequent to report. Second, such attempts are not recorded by either police of Action Fraud even if they were reported. The result is a gap in the evidence base concerning digital criminality and the non-acquisition of potentially very useful intelligence. It is arguable that governments and associated authorities are content not to record them as crime

DOI: 10.4324/9781003438649-7

would seem out of control, a point underpinned by Lewis (2018) maintaining as many as 80 billion automated scams are issued every day worldwide.

Current thinking ascribes two sub-species of internet criminality:

- Cyber-enabled crime, whereby real-world crimes such as fraud or blackmail are enhanced by digital technology (CPS, 2024; McGuire and Dowling, 2013).
- Cyber-dependent crime, meaning the crime can only be committed using technology. Without the digital pathway the crime could not be conducted, for example hacking or a virus attack (McGuire and Dowling, 2013).

The two degrees of separation seem clear at first glance but there are anomalies. In its "cyber choices" explanation, the NCA (2024: 1) states that cyber dependant criminality is where technological devices are used to commit the crime and are the target of the crime. Where does this leave offences such as bullying online? The action could not take place without the digital pathway, but the target is not a piece of technology at the other end. It is, instead, the end user, a human being. Bullying exists as a real-world circumstance but arguably can be categorised in either of the two cyber categories. The potential exists for investigators in all agencies to perceive cybercrime generally as the purview of specialists engaged in complex and time consuming enquiries (similar to the perception demonstrated earlier in this book about financial investigation).

There are also the needs of the victims of digital crime to be considered and whether there is a parity with the support provided to victims of real-world crime. In addressing the point raised by this statement, the authors of this work are in effect, admitting a distinction does exist, a hypothesis underpinned by the research of Leukfeldt, Notte and Malsch (2020), their conclusion being that the needs of digital crime victims are often not met and many crimes may not even be properly recorded. If this is the case, then the reliability of the current cybercrime threat data is immediately called into question. The evidence base for the term cybercrime, what exactly it may be referring to, the public perceptions of it and law enforcement reactions to it seem scant and fragmented (Curtis and Oxburgh, 2022). Politicians and other commentators appear to use the term with confidence but the paucity of reliable evidence-based research of the internet phenomenon seems lacking in the growing mythology of what it actually is.

All of this presents a problem for financial investigation and its application to the digital environment, locally, nationally and internationally. It also presents a problem by association, for what may be construed as financial intelligence concerning digital pathways. Just as every police force, HMRC and other law enforcement agencies have created financial investigation units (and by doing so underpinned the general perception of routine investigators that it is a specialist area of work), a similar situation has organically grown with cybercrime units. Each UK police force has a cybercrime unit, as do the Regional Organised Crime Units (ROCUs) and the NCA but cybercrime units are usually based away from divisional section officers who are at the front-line of policing. There is a growing body of research which suggests that the policing response to cybercrime (in its broadest sense and involving all law enforcement agencies) may be based in part on media representation of the problem (Cross et al., 2021; Curtis and Oxburgh, 2022). This relates to the earlier point above regarding the apparent lack of a reliable evidence-based approach to the cybercrime phenomenon.

The fact remains that police forces in particular have followed the route which financial investigation has travelled since some 30 years earlier; into the cul-de-sac of perceived complexity and specialist investigation. Similar to financial investigation, whether it reflects resource implications or other strategic reasoning, the general effect has been to effectively remove the topic from mainstream policing. This is further exacerbated because of the potential for confusion between cybercrime units and high-tech crime units (the latter responsible for interrogating technology itself and not directly related to investigations concerning the internet).

The digital (cyber) environment

Any research first needs to understand the way in which the internet functions although it is well beyond the scope of this book to delve into the technological machinations upon which it is created and operated. For the purpose of this chapter, it will be approached in terms of three distinct and widely accepted divisions within it; the surface web, the deep web and the dark web (Akbarialiabad, Dalfardi and Bastani, 2020). Drawing upon Essien (2019) as to the size of the world wide web, the estimate that the deep web is larger than the surface web by up to 500 times. The size of the dark web is unknown, just as the estimates of surface and deep sections seem best guess estimates with no real way to determine limits.

The surface web is generally accepted to be the internet environment which is primarily used by the general public in all countries (Essien, 2019). There is no exact percentage available as to how much of the internet lends itself to the surface web, but the consensus of web analytics seems to be between 4% and 6% (Khera, 2020; Traversals, 2024), a small amount considering that most of the world has integrated it into their social conscience on a daily basis. It is where search engines can be easily used, and many organisations have come to rely upon it for day-to-day business. For investigators, it does however, present an element of risk as much of the information (the digital footprint) inputted by general users is tracked and sold as commercial data. Many of the leading browsers are constructed to recover a breadth of information which may present a risk to the unwary investigator (Authentic8, 2024). The same tracking elements to recover commercially saleable or useful information could be used to identify the digital footprint of an investigator, particularly if criminals are cognisant that this can be done.

Of course, it involves a degree of expertise by the criminal, or a purchasing ability to buy in expertise from professional enablers (someone skilled in a particular remit who is willing to assist the perpetrator for a price). The scope of such activity by criminals is not known, nor do there appear to be any reliable estimates of the scale of such activity. It is an area where, once again, there appears to be a paucity of information or where reliable evidence-based research exists. It also poses a question as to how many times a day investigators at all levels access the internet without realising they have left their footprint to be found.

The deep web is the accepted transactional space which constitutes the major part of the digital environment but largely not indexed by the search engines, in contrast to the top 4%–6% surface web. Access to the general public is limited because the standard search engines do not routinely offer access as it is not an indexed space (unlike the surface web).

The dark web is accessible through specialised tools and associated software. These are often referred to as the Onion sites or to give the main dark web browser its common name – Tor (The Onion Router). In essence, Tor uses encrypted software with a seeming randomisation which camouflages user activity from internet service providers, other internet administrators and sovereign governments of all nation states (Collier and Stewart, 2021). A quick search of the surface web using Tor as the search term will immediately generate a number of responses which offer websites and search engines for use in the dark web space (Tor2Web, 2024). For example, Ahmia (2024) offers a directory of sites (none of which are verified by this work).

Aside from the need for some computing experience to enter the dark web, the risk within it is exacerbated by its widespread anonymity. Tor, run by anonymous volunteers, and similar to other aspects of the digital environment, has provided opportunities not just for users of it but researchers into it, and tutorials about how to proceed when using it is freely available (Tor Project Research, 2024). The perception of the dark web, perhaps because of its name in the first instance, is that it is a place solely of illegal and nefarious activity. In point of fact, it is estimated that almost three million users enter the dark web space every day (TorMetrics, 2024). Many of those users seek anonymity due to political activism (such as international dissidents to get their voice heard), for freedom of speech, knowledge exchange (such as the medical profession, scientists, political activists, etc) and for various other reasons which are not criminal (Moore and Rid, 2016). There is of course, a dearth of evidence that the dark web is also used for criminal activity inclusive of trade in drugs, weaponry, extremism, hacking and a plethora of other offences (Moore and Rid, 2016; UNODOC, 2023). It seems fair to suggest that the ramifications of all three sections of the digital environment present significant challenges for law enforcement and will continue to do so for the foreseeable future.

Policing the internet

Specific to investigations within the digital world, there appears to be a paucity of research about the daily routine of cybercrime investigators and the enquiries which take up their time (UK and internationally). At a pre COVID conference, the authors' own experience (based on talking informally to over 100 cyber investigators) indicated it is a myth that cybercrime investigators spend most of their time in the darkest corners of the dark web. In fact, a large number of the conference attendees had never actually entered the dark web. This was primarily due to their enquiries in the surface web, mainly on fraudulent activity or money laundering featuring money mules (a person who transfers criminal money via a bank account, usually their own). Although each UK police force (National Police Chief's Council, 2019) and some other prominent law enforcement agencies have cybercrime units, it remains largely unevidenced as to their effectiveness, workload, typology of crimes and levels of experience. It is also unknown as to their level of integration with routine policing on a daily basis. Do they all work to the same parameters or, because, for example, there are 43 police forces in the UK, do they all go about digital business in different ways?

A growing area of research appears to concentrate upon how the internet is policed, dispelling the accepted "truth" that the dark web in particular is invincible in its anonymity. Davies (2020: 1) concludes that although the dark web was once regarded as beyond the reach of law enforcement (in a global sense), that is no longer true. Law enforcement around the world now has the ability to deploy a "wide array of different techniques to identify, arrest and convict criminals of all types" who are using the dark space for their activity. (Davies, 2020: 1). Whether the available law enforcement methods routinely utilise financial investigation and to what extent, is not mentioned. It certainly seems evident that some commentators have established a link between corporate investigations and financial investigation to ascertain evidence relating to a wide array of offending not necessarily on the routine law enforcement radar and usually asset related (for example, chemical spills, illegal tipping of waste, and so forth) (Goetz, 2016).

There remains the question of intelligence concerning crimes using the internet and, notwithstanding any expertise which cybercrime investigators may have acquired, what is the level of training for police officers on the ground working with the public and is it sufficient to the task? The same question can be applied to all law enforcement agencies and there seems little evidence-based research on the matter to answer the question. Although there is some evidence that cybercrime is part of an initial training package to new recruits (ACPO, 2012; College of Policing, 2021), just as an hour of financial investigation is included in some police training schools, it remains unknown as to how officers are trained (or not) to interface with the public they serve. To a large degree, interaction with the public about cybercrime seems currently removed from much of routine policing due to the role of

Action Fraud, as fraud offences in particular can be directed by all forces to that agency. Whether reporting to Action Fraud is intended to keep fraud separate (and why) or whether it is a machination to keep crime figures contained may be fiercely contested if it were the subject of political debate. This work simply raises the point and suggests far more evidence-based research is required where real-world criminality escalates to the digital environment (cyber-enabled offending).

Where intelligence is concerned, a central question is whether the NIM is the correct vehicle for using cyber intelligence and whether that intelligence is routinely collected by general law enforcement investigators (as opposed to information collected as part of daily cyber intelligence gathering in specialist units). The same question has been posed earlier in this book regarding financial intelligence (see Chapter 6). There seems a lack of evidence as to how routine investigators interact with the NIM to either input information or download it. There is also little to find out how front line routine investigators interact with the public when taking reports of internet crimes. What questions does an officer ask at the scene, what evidence is an officer trained to look for, what exhibits should be taken, is a routine patrol officer sufficiently knowledgeable to know what evidence might be available at a scene? This is not an exhaustive list of questions but does demonstrate some of the issues facing 21st century law enforcement at all levels (strategic, tactical and practice).

As an example, consider the issue of volatile data, information which is temporarily stored in the random-access memory (RAM) of a computer while it is running. Although it may have a critical role to play in investigations, it only remains retrievable while a machine is switched on (Nyholm et al., 2022). When the machine is switched off, all volatile data is lost. Whether routine officers are generally aware of volatile data and, if so, whether they have the means to retrieve it and how to deal with it as evidence, or even as an exhibit, remains unknown. What is known is that until as recently as 2012 when volatile data is mentioned and practice changed (ACPO, 2012), the best practice for officers dealing with seizing computers was to switch the machine off at the plug to prevent data being interfered with or corrupted.

An expanding area of policing appears to be open source intelligence (OSINT). Equally, OSINT is a fast-expanding area of lucrative corporate business, the skills for which can be applied to assist law enforcement or corporate investigations. The essence of OSINT is that the information compiled from it is freely and publicly available, primarily via the surface web and to varying degrees the deep web. It does not rule out more traditional records such as land registry records pre computerisation around the turn of the millennium. These can still be paper records and investigators should be aware that not quite everything can be found online. Conduct a simple search using the search term OSINT and on one mainstream search engine alone, there are 13,900,000 results to sort through. From a corporate aspect, OSINT can be searched to find data that a rival company may not even realise has been made public or which has leaked via social media comments or via similar platforms

(Fruhlinger, Sharma and Breeden, 2023). For law enforcement, OSINT is searched for evidence, intelligence and intervention opportunities as well as being used to trace victims, witnesses and offenders (Rowley, 2021).

Internet jurisdiction

The internet is without borders making its use attractive to the modern criminal and with far less risk of being caught by law enforcement in any country. A criminal such as a fraudster can plan and orchestrate quite sophisticated criminality from anywhere in the world (Staniforth, 2017). Routing a fraud through several countries contemporaneously and using a simple programme such as a proxy server or virtual private network (VPN), a means of disguising location, exacerbates jurisdictional issues for those officers willing or able to investigate. The issue is a wider one than the single premise of jurisdiction (where and who can follow a crime committed using the internet without causing any type of diplomatic ripples). There is also the question of which agency and in which country will deal with a crime if several countries are involved. Law enforcement worldwide is usually funded from the public purse and managers who have access to very limited resources may question why it is their responsibility to pursue crimes which immediately seem to be routed offshore. This thought process may be exacerbated if a crime is low in value per victim but wider in the number of victims in the UK and abroad. For example, imagine if there is evidence a fraud is committed in the UK (apparently run by an offshore criminal) involving 27 identifiable victims nationwide, none of whom have lost more than £500. It then transpires that the same fraud has been perpetrated in 5 other countries across 4 continents but never affecting more than 50 victims in each, who will want to deal with pursuing the criminal? The problem is more complicated in the UK before it even becomes international as the same question exists if the UK victims live in 15 different counties.

This poses interesting questions which seem to have been subject to little research. For example, how many crimes are effectively written off by the Action Fraud avenue because of an international aspect perceived to be costly? How many times have investigations in cybercrime units been halted and closed based upon perceived cost effectiveness where international borders are involved using digital pathways? How many cybercrime investigations have utilised financial investigators and is there an argument based on the type of enquiries being run by cybercrime units to have a hybrid cyber/financial investigator? UK digital investigators claim that they are aware of and would use financial investigation (applying money laundering powers) but related convictions are rare and cross-fertilisation is impaired by rigid organisational structures (Donegan, 2019). Many also noted lack of prosecutor interest in charging money laundering offences as part of the rationale for limited application of proceeds of crime powers to digital investigations.

From an academic aspect, the jurisdictional issue allows academic theory to be applied in the form of the routine activity theory (RAT) originally articulated by Cohen and Felsen (1979) in a pre-internet environment. Simply put, for a crime to be realised (committed in full), there needs to be a motivated offender, a suitable victim and the absence of a capable guardian. There appears to be an assumption from Cohen and Felsen (1979) that criminals operate a rational decision-making model for their criminal choices (Kitteringham and Fennelly, 2012) presumably always choosing victims where capable guardianship is weakest. It is of course debatable whether criminals are capable of rationality if they are under the influence of mind affecting substances for example (such as alcohol or drugs), a point which tends to weaken the overall theory. That said, RAT may be useful to understanding gaps which may be present in the way criminals utilise the internet pathway to offending and the extent to which capable guardianship (law enforcement, for example) is or is not present.

The problem seems to be that once criminals pursue their criminality into the digital environment, offences seem largely to become the responsibility of cybercrime investigators who in the main are reacting to offending which is brought to their attention. The internet environment of course, does not have its own police force, something deemed impossible in the current operation of it. It also has no borders, and the RAT triangle adequately demonstrates that within the virtual internet environment, the absence of a capable guardian (policing) is likely quite common. Capable guardianship may exist in other forms of course, such as attempts at crime prevention both from law enforcement, corporate and business areas or from charities or vigilantes who work independently. Either way, there seems little cohesion to attempts at user protection within what is essentially a borderless, multilingual, jurisdictional grey area for international law enforcement at all levels. This is in the face of a constantly expanding criminality using digital pathways and with a rapidity which law enforcement in general terms will be hard pressed to match or cope with.

Conclusion

The digital environment is the challenge of our time for law enforcement. All aspects of the virtual world appear challenging from resourcing in terms of staff, hardware and up-to-date software, training required for investigators, crime prevention and knowledge of support available outside policing, generally in the corporate sector. Policing in general terms seems to need to acknowledge that financial investigation, in particular the financial footprint, and would allay to some extent, the duplication of time and resources if applied effectively.

There is no doubt in the minds of the authors of this book that financial investigation and the breadth of intelligence it is capable of generating beyond the world of asset recovery holds important potential for routine policing. The concept of following the financial footprint appears to us to be crucial for routine investigators understanding what financial investigation means in investigative terms. There is also little doubt that much more research into the remit of financial investigation beyond asset recovery is required, where it is currently used, how effective it might be and what can enhance its absorption into routine practice. That issue is exacerbated when applied to the digital environment as there seems to be a paucity of research concerning the various attributes of investigations, the depth to which those investigations reach, the experience and training of those involved and why (if the hypothesis that financial investigation and digital investigation are to some extent similar) cybercrime officers are not already hybrid in their training and skill sets.

Perhaps this has more to do with the perceptions of financial investigation at all levels as discussed in Chapter 2 of this book. The authors advance their definitions of financial investigation and financial intelligence as an initial step in beginning to properly embed the investigative benefits of them into the routine policing psyche. This is particularly important for the virtual environment. With understanding will hopefully come the change in mindset and eventually to practice but this change cannot occur without a thorough research analysis of the existing system and perceptions at all levels and in regard to both environments, traditional and virtual.

8 Conclusion

Introduction

This book has focused upon areas within law enforcement where financial investigation is currently applied and whether perceptions of it at all levels (strategic, tactical and practice) affects its trajectory as a general technique to be utilised by all investigators and to support most investigations. In doing so, it has examined the apparent juxtaposition of governmental ambition for general and integrated financial investigation and an acknowledged problem in its (and law enforcement's) ability to deliver on its objective (House of Commons, 2016; Levi and Maguire; 2011).

Financial investigation within the literature, does not appear to have been often considered as a central theme. Where it has been considered in more detail, it appears to be dependent on the depth of study into specific criminal typologies such as money laundering or organised crime (Brown et al., 2012; Howell, Horton and Gill, 2013) predominantly using AFIs as the source of information. This status offers an interesting parallel to the understanding and application of the concept by strategic and tactical decision makers and practitioners. More recent attempts to consider financial investigation focus upon training implications (Chave, 2017) or begin by expressing the wider potential of financial investigation, then proceeding to discuss serious organised crime, asset recovery or what AFIs can do to inform non-specialists of its potential (ECORYS, 2015; Gale and Kelly, 2018; Woods, 2017).

Government and strategic thinking concerning financial investigation does recognise the mainstream potential of financial investigation (Gale and Kelly, 2018; HM Inspectorate of Constabulary, HM Crown Prosecution Service Inspectorate, HM Magistrates Court Inspectorate, 2004; House of Commons, 2016), but asset recovery still appears to take precedence in the legislation being passed (Criminal Finances Act, 2017). It is against this national strategic outlook that the aim of this work was to systematically examine the influence of proceeds of crime policy, terminology and legislation upon mainstream law enforcement's relationship with financial investigation and to attempt to identify effective financial investigation practice and the possibility of it being better integrated into investigations.

DOI: 10.4324/9781003438649-8

This work has resulted in the provision of a baseline of evidence which draws together information from a wide spectrum of generalists and specialists at all levels. It offers an indication of the divergencies of practice, perception, training and understanding concerning financial investigation.

Contribution to the literature and the field of practice

This book has aimed to offer an original contribution to the literature and the field. Adding knowledge to this field would only offer a modest contribution given the limited directly relevant research, hence the need for a broad base synthesis across a diverse terrain of parallel literature. This work has sought to develop and refine the concepts of financial investigation and financial intelligence. It has situated it in a theoretical context and considered models for the integration of enhanced conceptual understanding, policy development and practice. It has consistently been the authors' intention to synthesise secondary data and provide critical and original analysis of all data to provide the first real analysis of the history of financial investigation and to understand why it remains confined largely to asset recovery (confiscation).

Conceptual clarity has been offered to the reader by developing and refining the subject area of financial investigation using a clear epistemological approach and ontological understanding. The historical trajectory of financial investigation has been explored to understand current perceptions towards it at all levels of law enforcement and among external commentators (government ministers, policy makers and academics). Consideration has been given to the theoretical context of available research, particularly in regard to the "culture of control" theory (Garland, 2001) and the extent to which the financial investigation skill set has been accepted into general investigation strategy. In that context, there appears to be a powerful mandate for proceeds of crime powers at a legislative and theoretical level. On a practical level this review has indicated that (regardless of symbolic sovereign state headlines) the use and impact of financial investigation remains primarily a function of knowledge and applied interaction between specialists and general investigators and their supervisors (adaptive strategies). Such adaptive strategies appear non-generic (differing regionally across law enforcement), nor do they seem founded upon national policing directives supported by managers who are well informed about (or generally supportive of) the potential financial investigation may offer.

The authors consistently provide a much-needed distinction between financial investigation in its generalist sense (potential application to all investigations) and the specialist area of confiscation (asset recovery). This book consistently reiterates the principle that the two are separate concepts and has considered in detail whether the idea of general financial investigation has been swallowed and obscured by the leviathan of asset recovery. As advocated by Burrell and Morgan (1979) the methodology of this work provides an epistemological framework through which the reality of financial investigation can be understood, and the meaning of this undertaking conveyed.

The review of literature throughout this work explicitly focuses on legislation, policy, regulation, literature and other secondary data relevant to the UK to orient the research to a fixed reference point in which the author had the capacity to guide the reader. That is, the secondary data available in academic journals and books, professional and government publications, grey literature, domestic and international legislation, and case law. It also included component elements involving international issues and entities.

This work includes a focus on the terminology used within the subject area of financial investigation. Beginning with an assessment of several commonly used phrases by law enforcement investigators, the public, government policy makers and research academics, it examines the extent to which they are perceived as, or associated with, financial investigation. It then questions the effect of accepted terminology within law enforcement relevant to this research and upon the wider use of financial investigation skills separate to asset recovery. Several key themes of significance to what essential characteristics of financial investigation might be and how it might be more broadly applied, have emerged. There appears to be continuing dysfunction within and between the strategic, tactical and practice levels, which is underpinned by the lack of a comprehensive national UK financial investigation strategy or any concerted effort to go beyond the traditional focus on confiscation and asset recovery. This is not mitigated by the partial coverage of financial investigation in the national UK Organised Crime Strategy. Terminological confusion in the literature (alongside policy and practice) has conspired to maintain a myth of financial investigation as a specialist silo.

The book also explores typologies commonly associated with asset recovery and thereby financial investigation. It begins by considering the phrase financial investigation and the difficulties in defining what it means. It continues the literature review from the perspective of five areas of law enforcement where references to it are more usually to be discovered: confiscation, asset recovery, drug trafficking, money laundering and cash detention. Consideration is given to potential issues within and between the strategic, tactical and practice levels of law enforcement and comments upon the national UK financial investigation strategy. Discussion identified other key issues. First is the lack of a legislative definition of financial investigation. A clear distinction from confiscation appears requisite and the authors offer a possible definition of what can be termed *practical* financial investigation in Chapter 6, linked to a potential definition of financial intelligence. The authors' intention is to modify the gap in the literature and suggest a definition which can be used to de-mythologise financial investigation at all levels (strategic, tactical and practice) and the perception that it is a specialist area only useful in asset recovery cases. The existing gap in the general utilisation of financial investigation techniques is underpinned by the lack of comprehensive identification and disparate discussion within the available literature concerning characteristics that constitute effective aspects of it.

There is no general or bespoke training strategy which will underpin the implementation of financial investigation techniques into mainstream law enforcement investigation and management practice. There is also little or no data in the available literature upon which to base a general training requirement. Adding to the theme of training is the inadequacy of proceeds of crime and financial investigation training across law enforcement at all levels, the judiciary, the court service, the CPS and other prosecuting authorities. There appears to be a clear problem from a political perspective and at all levels (strategic, tactical and practice) in recognising and understanding factors negatively influencing the trajectory of financial investigation. This contributes to the absence of a clear and effective implementation process by way of which its techniques can be accessed and routinely applied by investigators at all levels and regardless of specialisation or generalised application.

Linking directly to a broader generic financial investigation philosophy is the clear gap identified concerning structured attempts to ascertain the value of financial investigation outside of the confiscation and civil asset recovery processes. The apparent confusion between the disciplines of confiscation and financial investigation coupled with attaining (confiscation) financial targets set by the government may have contributed to the perception that it is something best left to experts in the minds of general investigators.

The work further considers the literature from the perspectives of international standards and financial intelligence, adding to the previously discussed themes. Insights are also offered regarding the influence of bodies outside of the UK upon domestic proceeds of crime legislation and their possible effect upon the trajectory of financial investigation outside the confiscation regime.

The book examines what the term financial intelligence might mean (it remains undefined), and the authors offer an alternative definitional possibility for this concept as well as financial investigation. Both proposed definitions attempt to deal with the practicalities of applying financial investigation techniques to all investigations and the potential for them to be used strategically and tactically at all levels of law enforcement. Both proposed definitions steer away from the notion of asset recovery and attempt to engender the two aspects (intelligence and investigation) with a practical appeal for all investigators. They are designed to de-mythologise the notion of complexity and reduce general perceptions of specialism. Before advancing these two definitions, the work offers a discussion on the relationship between financial intelligence and the National Intelligence Model (NIM) and the understanding of the concept from the perspectives of specialists and general investigators at all levels (strategic, tactical, practice). In doing so, some insight is provided as to how suspicious activity reports mandatorily supplied by the financial sector are used in policing (lending support to the theory that financial investigation is only engaging with the NIM on a limited basis and with limited use of SAR intelligence) and whether the UK anti-money laundering structure integrates at any level with financial intelligence or financial investigation. This adds to the theme previously identified in involving NIM application and financial intelligence, in that the NIM (or its operators in intelligence units) seems inefficient in processing information to present intervention opportunities in general investigations. At the strategic and tactical levels there appears to be little use of investigative strategy to better facilitate the use of financial investigation techniques across all criminal investigations as a generic skill set (House of Commons, 2016).

Parallel themes involving SARs and the NIM are identified (as well as general financial intelligence flow) that relate particularly to applying techniques more broadly but with some relevance to essential characteristics of financial investigation. The literature indicates that SARS are not well utilised or investigated by law enforcement and this section has identified a clear disconnect between the compatibility and the integration of SARS within the NIM. Little information appears available to attempt to quantify to what extent financial information (SARS or otherwise) is disseminated into the operational echelons of everyday law enforcement and used by operational decision makers. The reverse is also true and there appears to be a paucity of information concerning how frequently AFIs or non-specialist law enforcement practitioners submit financial intelligence or recognise what financial intelligence actually is. There remains a national (and key) evidence gap as to what extent the NIM is being used for financial intelligence at any level, as empirical data appears unavailable. In view of the indications from the literature which lend credence to the hypothesis that financial investigation engages with the NIM only on a limited basis, as indicated by this book, there is a clear requirement for empirical data regarding utilisation of SARS information across law enforcement (outside of the asset recovery process). This in conjunction with concern about the general awareness of financial intelligence at all levels (strategic, tactical and practice) and whether financial intelligence is actively utilised in the strategic planning of investigations.

A continuing stream of legislation claimed by successive governments to underpin POCA (2002) may be a significant factor in the continuing perception of general investigators that financial investigation is an end of process, asset-focused specialism (post conviction) of little use in general investigations. Continued calls for extra legislation from the strategic layer of policing does not encourage the mitigation of that perception while the lobbying of outside commentators for tighter confiscation and anti-money laundering mechanisms under the umbrella of financial investigation does little to integrate it as a general investigatory technique.

This work demonstrates that the topic area appears to resonate with the theoretical framework of the "culture of control" (Garland, 2001) perhaps exacerbated by the seeming lack of a coherent and effective implementation strategy to separate financial investigation from asset recovery and facilitate its wider and routine application. Applying this theory questions whether proceeds of crime legislation and financial investigation (confiscation) are to some extent symbolic (therefore under-utilised) and employed intentionally or unwittingly by policy makers and politicians as a sovereign state strategy, the big stick with which to convince the public that criminality is subject to draconian punitive sanctions in the form of asset recovery (confiscation).

Confiscation as a specialism can be argued to be a sovereign state strategy but financial investigation is likely inhibited by its close affiliation with the specialist domain of the AFIs. Affiliating proceeds of crime legislation in such a way (as a sovereign state denial strategy) underpins the point that successive governments may be under a continuing dénouement of their own making, that because POCA and associated legislation is so stringent in their own philosophy of crime and order, then it must (ergo) be working. Further value added from this book is that by modelling the concept of financial investigation using the theoretical framework of "culture of control" (Garland, 2001) the authors' continued assertion that it is distinct from confiscation can be made clear. The dichotomy seems to be that governmental and strategic drive for draconian measures (arguably a sovereign state strategy) centred around asset recovery (such as unexplained wealth orders (UWOs) under the Criminal Finances Act (2017) conflicts with a continuous desire to embed financial investigation techniques into all investigations as practical adaptive strategies (House of Commons, 2016). The specialist versus generalist training requirements are therefore not assisted, perhaps a reason that current training opportunities do not reflect the frequency with which strategic policy makers laud the potential plaudits of financial investigation with only mitigated practical uptake.

All the above points inevitably question how the decision-making process for financial investigation is administered within government and law enforcement, and how strategic considerations (and expectations) translate through mid-tier chains of command (tactical) to wider policing methods (practical). There appears to be a pressing need for a comprehensive and integrated approach to financial investigation on a national scale and across the breadth of the UK law enforcement spectrum if it is to be utilised towards exploiting its potential. The identified gaps in the literature (and the disconnects in financial investigation) and the seemingly chronic need for empirical data are key findings of this review. Critical analysis of the key themes within this review responds directly to what constitutes essential financial investigation characteristics. The points arising from that examination are intrinsic to theorising and synthesising a generic and comprehensive (transferable) philosophy of financial investigation, which would allow the skill base to be utilised more broadly across law enforcement.

The authors remind the reader that, due to the lack of empirical data concerning financial investigation and its interface with general investigation techniques (and perceptions) identified within the literature review, this work does not propose to provide solutions on a micro-scale. The intention of the review has always been to collect enough information across all levels (strategic, tactical, practice) to provide a baseline to begin to understand what essential financial investigation might be and any factors which limit its trajectory. The collected information would then be useful in deciding whether a generic philosophy of financial investigation is potentially attainable. The broader scale of this work compared to the arguable narrowness of Gale and Kelly (2018), for example, has allowed it to provide more robust indications of good or bad practice, misunderstanding, gaps or consensus or variable practice within specialisms.

This book questions the implied presumptions of policy makers that financial investigation is a concept understood by investigators and managers, and that financial investigation strategy is widely used (College of Policing, 2019; NCA, 2019). It also suggests that the concept of financial intelligence is not widely understood within law enforcement and that it and SARs are only partially integrated with the NIM for general use. Other research has focused upon finding the value of financial investigation rather than asking what it is (Howell, Horton and Gill, 2013) or what the outcome is if applied to organised crime (Brown et al., 2012). This may be part of the reason that financial investigation (as a skill set) seems confused with asset recovery and the confiscation process. It may also be why continuing attempts by policy makers and successive governments have difficulty in widening the use of financial investigation techniques and (instead) continue to pass ever more draconian legislation (CFA, 2017; SCA, 2015) which is little used by the AFIs it is meant for (Gale and Kelly, 2018).

This book has illuminated the lack of focused and creative debate concerning the nature of financial investigation in all its aspects and how it (as a subject) is perceived within law enforcement at all levels. Examining financial investigation in its current state of unclear definition, understanding, and application within that environment has been no simple task. Its origins were the product of a politically motivated reaction to a 1970s drug trafficking epidemic (Hodgson, 1984) and its characteristics have gradually been extracted from the plethora of disparate literature; a difficulty exacerbated by a lack of empirical data outside of confiscation focused information. An additional factor is the constant habit of commentators, practitioners and policy makers to amalgamate financial investigation with confiscation, an emasculation of their own intentions to integrate it beyond the traditional focus of asset recovery. Identifying essential characteristics of effective financial investigation in this study has never been about the minutiae of investigation, the practical aspects of which are endless. It has remained focused upon identifying the central tenets of effectiveness, somewhat elusive in the literature and where an original contribution of this book lies.

Training remains a central theme within the literature but the debated approach to it remains disparate and unresolved (Chave, 2017; House of Commons, 2016). There is little doubt that the current intention is to (at some point) provide detectives with proceeds of crime training (House of Commons, 2016) but without any rational approach to the problem and the benefit of the broader implications identified within this project. Without imparting understanding to general investigators and engaging them as to the benefits of financial investigation (and how to apply basic skills), training in bespoke areas of policing seems consigned to making the same mistakes which limit it in the first place. The authors of this work suggest that training cannot simply be about the investigators themselves and without strategic and tactical recognition of the potential financial investigation offers for all investigations the problem is that much more exacerbated. The real question may be a conceptual one regarding the division of labour as to expectations of specialists, generalists and their managers. The big stick of confiscation has not proven an effective deterrent to criminals (House of Commons, 2014; NAO, 2013).

Applying the framework of Garland (2001), the sovereign state strategy of asset recovery has arguably not worked as well as anticipated and is acknowledged to have been applied in an other-than-wholly effective manner by investigators, specialist or otherwise (House of Commons, 2016). This appears to have been compounded by successive government denial strategies (Garland, 2001) whereby rigorous legislation continues to be passed but without a general investigation uptake to make it practically applicable (examples being usage of the section 357 Disclosure Order under POCA, 2002 and the unexplained wealth order (UWO) of the Criminal Finances Act, 2017).

This book attempts to bring together the different aspects and perceptions and identify strong and weak areas of knowledge and practice. In the future it may contribute to finding ways to integrate financial investigation into the existing law enforcement pathways, currently outside its scope. There is value in providing a baseline towards how to figure out how to work together rather than disparately. This does connect with the "culture of control" theory of Garland (2001) in as much as each group should still be able to execute its distinct mandate notwithstanding any uptake of financial investigation techniques. The debate should perhaps not be about legislation, strategy and policing and place emphasis upon the adaptive and practical implementation challenges of "getting on with the job". Perhaps it should concern the overarching synergy between strategic, tactical and practical policing, and, once those are made clear, embedding best practice across broader law enforcement.

Financial investigation (and strategy) and financial intelligence

Put simply, the emergent essential characteristics of effective financial investigation in this book can be identified in six categories. The first is definitional and the authors offer a definition of (practical) financial investigation for the purpose of clarifying the concept for investigators and enabling them to learn and understand it and integrate the concept within their investigation skillset and baseline training. The second is terminological and the separation of financial investigation from confiscation at all levels seems crucial if the wider application of the skillset is to be progressed. This seems simple in principle but has proven more difficult in practice due to current embedded use of terminology in the legislation and policing culture. Change in this regard may be assisted by the definitional clarity advocated by the authors and generic baseline training in identifying financial footprints for evidential purposes.

The third category is intelligence, a key facet of financial investigation and one which, if properly integrated with established NIM practice, holds significant potential for law enforcement investigations. This book has postulated a definition of financial intelligence as it is considered by the authors to apply to all investigators and one which interlinks with that postulated for financial investigation. It is advocated that defining the two concepts will enable a more comprehensive integration with the NIM at all levels and allow intelligence specialists to identify more intervention opportunities for police action in the general criminal environment (recognition, gathering, input analysis and dissemination). It will also encourage general investigators to recognise information which may constitute financial intelligence at a basic level.

In this regard, SARs perhaps have a role to play in enhancing the more general use of financial intelligence and should be recognised as an essential characteristic of financial investigation. SARs should also be a mandatory requirement of any money laundering operation, therefore requiring all investigators to be trained in their availability, content and methods of use. This does not appear to currently be the case, even among specialists and that limited understanding of what might constitute financial intelligence is inhibitive to the NIM process, evidential gathering and identifying intervention points, for example, cash detention and general arrest opportunities. The authors openly question the implicit presumption of policy makers and commentators within the available literature that SARs are widely understood and used broadly across law enforcement (Hughes, 2021). A preliminary indication from the data in Hughes (2021) (though a larger sample in any further research would be required to confirm that indication), is that covert human source handlers may not be interrogating their assets regarding financial intelligence opportunities.

Category four is educational and (from a management perspective) not necessarily one specifically about training courses. Policy makers' perceptions that concepts such as financial intelligence and financial investigation strategy are known and understood by all investigators are contested by the authors. Education also concerns the wider understanding and appreciation of financial investigation skills (including within the judiciary and among prosecuting authority lawyers) and how managers offer opportunities to enhance investigations from strategic and tactical aspects (utilising financial investigation strategy). This means a step away from asset recovery and the perception of financial investigation as a specialist skill set. The authors believe this will require a step-change in the way current managers approach not only proceeds of crime legislation and financial investigation techniques but investigations in general. Traditional silo methods of investigation (one specialist unit, one type of crime) no longer seem pertinent to the digital globalisation which has transformed the nature of crime in recent decades. This book advocates what seems obvious (but which remains problematic), a more integrated approach at all levels for financial investigation and perhaps for policing methods in general.

The fifth category concerns the managerial aspect of financial investigation and this book suggests there is a clear training (educational) requirement for all management levels. Consistent strategic and tactical consideration at both levels across all investigations is required, moving away from the traditional focus upon asset recovery and leading to effective application as a generic and routinely applied skillset to uncover financial footprints (not asset recovery) for evidential purposes. Again, this does not appear to simply be a traditionally recognised training requirement. To be truly effective, it appears to require a step-change in the philosophy of law enforcement leadership.

It currently appears that senior and mid-tier leadership across law enforcement only seem to have knowledge of certain aspects of financial investigation, mostly related to asset recovery audit trail (Hughes, 2021). There are some limited exceptions such as missing persons enquiries, but most supervisors appear to miss the relevance financial investigation has for investigations outside the confiscation and the serious and organised crime criminal genres. The authors believe that for real change to occur, management must first embrace the concept to provide the opportunity for financial investigation to embed more broadly across law enforcement as an everyday tool. This is possibly the most essential characteristic. Without supervisory support at all levels (very much lacking generally to date) and despite what government and College of Policing ambitions might be, financial investigation has not been able and will continue to be unable to embed in the minds of all investigators that it is something they themselves can use effectively.

Category six concerns policy and the clear need to re-align focus on financial investigation and move away from asset recovery to clearly delineate both areas. For this to be achieved the authors believe that it would be helpful to provide clear legislative definitions for the terminological use of financial investigation and financial intelligence and to move away from a continuing governmental focus upon asset recovery. In principle this seems linked to the development of an implementation plan which goes beyond the traditional focus of AFIs and is inclusive of all law enforcement, judiciary and prosecuting authorities.

If the essential characteristics as described above can be recognised and acted upon, financial investigation may begin to be afforded the cohesive and interactive approach it requires across all levels of law enforcement.

Any generic philosophy of financial investigation will of necessity include all the characteristics discussed in this work. They represent rudimentary group pillars originating around factors from which a transferable generic philosophy might be engendered. The authors have identified the clear distinction between financial investigation and the confiscation regime notwithstanding the investigatory skillset operates from the same baseline in both theatres. Hughes (2021) reveals the distinction is only realised by a small number of AFI respondents and non-specialist personnel a valuable point seemingly unrecognised by previous research (Brown et al., 2012; Gale and Kelly, 2018;

Howell, Horton and Gill, 2013). Although AFIs are the main protagonists, there is enough evidence which points to some use of their skill set by non-AFI trained investigators beyond the traditional theatre of asset recovery. This is encouraging but most of that activity does seem to involve acquisitive crime or serious and organised criminality (Brown et al., 2012), though some officers are aware that financial investigation can be used to identify evidence and locate suspects, witnesses, and victims for non-financial offences.

The authors pose the question as to whether the formulation of a generic philosophy is possible and although convinced that it is, this book indicates the current financial investigation mechanism within law enforcement is working in a limited and disparate fashion. Numerous and significant issues in financial investigation practice at all levels of law enforcement have been discussed. If financial investigation is to be de-mythologised from asset recovery and considered as an effective adaptive strategy across law enforcement, a generic philosophy will only be achieved by using informed empirical data about the issues identified in this work. Its value as advocated by the authors, is its probative value, its function as a lens through which to confirm the disparate nature of financial investigation and to demonstrate the concept of it at all levels appears widely misunderstood. This has enabled the authors to probe and question terminologies and methods of investigation traditionally accepted by policy makers and commentators as being well-established. It also serves as a significant indication as to why the declared intention of successive governments and their policy makers to embed financial investigation outside the theatre of asset recovery has remained problematic.

The beginnings of a transferable philosophy can be drawn from the essential characteristics explained above as a guiding principle for future behaviour. The baseline of examination provided in this book indicates much more is required. The definitions of financial investigation and financial intelligence must be an integral part of any generic philosophy and although presented in this research by authors confident of their legitimacy and applicability, research to test their compatibility with the subject area is perhaps a prerequisite of them being accepted. What is clear is that as a guiding principle, financial investigation can only realise its greater potential by fully integrating with general investigations (and the NIM) and be recognised at all levels of law enforcement as an evidence gathering standard investigation tool. How this is to be accomplished remains unanswered.

Training and education will be a critical factor if views within law enforcement are to change and access the potential that financial investigation techniques offer. This book identifies where there are some areas of good practice as well as areas identified where some inhibitors to better application of financial investigation and financial intelligence might lie. Unlike previous literature in this arena (Brown et al., 2012; Gale and Kelly, 2018; Howell, Horton and Gill, 2013) the authors move away from AFIs and serious and organised crime considerations as the primary source of information and application of financial investigation beyond asset recovery. Insight has now been offered into the application of financial investigation and financial intelligence beyond that conveyed by national statistics, political, social and academic commentators. It also appears to be the first time that any examination of the relationship between generalists and specialists in their perceptions and practice within the field of financial investigations has been made in this form. If this initial baseline of information can be built upon in the future, the authors are confident that financial investigation can realise the potential it offers to all investigators for evidential gathering.

Selected strategic and tactical level managers receive a one-day training course which only deals with how to authorise production and restraint orders. Training does not deal with investigation strategy and how to effectively apply financial investigation outside of asset recovery (including money laundering investigations and cash detention opportunities). The available training needs properly scoping not only to the needs of specialists and non-specialists which will involve a review of current content and availability and its suitability to generic use across law enforcement. It must also include strategic and tactical level managers who are intrinsic to investigative decision making and who need to be able to support and advise general investigators from a position of knowledge. The separation of financial investigation from the asset recovery perception of it which currently exists, seems essential to such a review. This would include how the FISS site is currently utilised. It would also, of course have to include the judiciary and prosecuting authorities whose support appears limited at present (House of Commons, 2016).

It is perhaps time for governments and associated hierarchies to stop implicitly assuming that because legislation or policies are created, they are therefore understood and effective. The legislative intent of the Proceeds of Crime Act (POCA, 2002) to foster crime reduction remains an unresolved challenge. A sustained focus on adaptive implementation and routine application to general investigation and intelligence offers a path to promote the public interest in reducing crime.

References

Action Fraud (2016) *Fraud and Cybercrime Cost UK Nearly £11 Billion in Past Year.* Available at: http://www.actionfraud.police.uk/news/fraud-and-cybercrime-cost-UK-nearly-11bn-in-past-year-oct16 [Accessed 03 March 2017].

Ahmia (2024) *Onion Domain List.* Available at: https://ahmia.fi/address/ [Accessed 29 April 2024].

Akbarialiabad, H., Dalfardi, B., and Bastani, B. (2020) The Double-edged Sword of the Dark Web: Its Implications for Medicine and Society. *Journal of General Internal Medicine,* 18 May 2022. Available at: https://www.ncbi.nlm.nih.gov/pmc/articles/PMC7661673/ [Accessed 29 April 2024].

Albanese, J. S. (2010) North American Organised Crime. *Global Crime Journal,* Vol. 6, No. 1, pp. 8–18.

Alldridge, P. (2003) *Forfeiture, Confiscation, Civil Recovery, Laundering and Taxation of the Proceeds of Crime.* Oxford: Hart Publishing.

Allen, R. (1991) Out of Jail: The Reduction in the Use of Penal Custody for Male Juveniles 1981–88. [pdf] *Howard Journal of Criminal Justice,* Vol. 30, No. 1, pp. 30–52. Available at: https://doi.org/10.1111/j.1468-2311.1991.tb00694.x [Accessed 20 June 2018].

Allum, F., and Gilmour, S. eds. (2012) *Routledge Handbook of Transnational Organised Crime,* pp. 52-64.

Alpna, S. M. (2016) Cyber Crime – Its Types, Analysis and Prevention Techniques. [pdf] *International Journal of Advanced Research in Computer Science and Software Engineering,* Vol. 6, No. 5, pp. 145–150. Available at: http://ijarcsse.com/Before_August_2017/docs/papers/Volume_6/5_May2016/V6I5-0315.pdf [Accessed 01 May 2018].

Anderson, D. (2015) *A Question of Trust. Report of the Investigatory Powers Review.* [pdf] Available at: https://assets.publishing.service.gov.uk/government/uploads/system/uploads/attachment_data/file/434399/IPR-Report-Web-Accessible1.pdf [Accessed 24 May 2018].

Assets Recovery Agency (2006) *Resource Accounts 2005-06.* Available at: https://assets.publishing.service.gov.uk/media/5a7caa46ed915d6969f467b7/1341.pdf [Accessed 3rd May 2017].

Association of Chief Police Officers (2005) *Guide to the National Intelligence Model.* [pdf] Bedford: National Centre for Policing Excellence. Available at: https://whereismydata.files.wordpress.com/2009/01/national-intelligence-model-20051.pdf [Accessed 12 April 2014].

Association of Chief Police Officers (2006) *Practice Advice on Financial Investigation.* Bedfordshire: Centrex.

Association of Chief Police Officers (2012) *ACPO Good Practice Guide for Digital Evidence.* Available at: https://www.digital-detective.net/digital-forensics-documents/ACPO_Good_Practice_Guide_for_Digital_Evidence_v5.pdf [Accessed 25 April 2024].

Association of Police and Crime Commissioners (2018) *About the APCC.* [pdf] Available at: http://www.apccs.police.uk/about-the-apcc/ [Accessed 14 May 2018].

Atkinson, J. (1978) Criminal Law. Racketeer Influenced and Corrupt Organisations, 18 U.S.C.1961–68: Broadest of the Federal Criminal Statutes. [pdf] *The Journal of Law and Criminology,* Vol. 69, No. 1, pp. 1–18. Available at: https://scholarlycommons.law.northwestern.edu/cgi/viewcontent.cgi?referer=https://www.google.com/&httpsredir=1&article=6055&context=jclc [Accessed 26 April 2018].

Attorney General (2016) *The Threat Faced Today from Economic Crime and How the UK Government Is Addressing It.* [pdf] Available at: https://www.gov.uk/government/speeches/attorney-general-jeremy-wright-speech-to-the-cambridge-symposium-on-economic-crime [Accessed 07 June 2018].

Authentic8 (2024) *What Is the Surface Web?* Available at: https://www.authentic8.com/glossary/what-is-surface-web [Accessed 29 April 2024].

Bank of England (2015) *The Bank of England's Supervision of Financial Market Infrastructures — Annual Report.* [pdf] London: Bank of England Publications. Available at: http://www.bankofengland.co.uk/publications/Documents/fmi/annualreport2015.pdf [Accessed 10 October 2015].

Basel Institute on Governance (2009) *Tracing Stolen Assets – A Practitioner's Guide.* [pdf] Available at: https://www.baselgovernance.org/sites/collective.localhost/files/publications/asset-tracing_web-version_eng.pdf [Accessed 09 September 2017].

Basel Institute on Governance (2017) *Asset Recovery.* Available at: https://www.baselgovernance.org/theme/icar [Accessed 10 September 2017].

Bean, P. (2008) *Drugs and Crime.* 3rd edition. Devon: Willan Publishing.

Bell, R. E. (2002) Abolishing the Concept of 'Predicate Offence'. *Journal of Money Laundering Control,* Vol. 6, No. 2, pp. 137–140.

Berdal, M., and Serrano, M. eds. (2002) *Transnational Organised Crime and International Security.* London: Lynne Rienner Publishers Inc.

Blair, A. (1995) *Leader's Speech.* Brighton, 01 October. Available at: http://www.britishpoliticalspeech.org/speech-archive.htm?speech=201 [Accessed 13 June 2019].

Brenner, S. (2001) Is There Such a Thing as "Virtual Crime"? [pdf] *California Criminal Law Review*, Vol. 4. No. 1, pp. 1–72. Available at: http://ssrn.com/abstract=1611839 [Accessed 17 June 2015].

British Bankers Association (2016) *Written Response CFB06.* Available at: https://publications.parliament.uk/pa/cm201617/cmpublic/CriminalFinances/memo/CFB05.pdf [Accessed 23 June 2018].

British Broadcasting Corporation (2013) *National Crime Agency to 'Relentlessly Pursue' Organised Crime.* Available at: http://www.bbc.co.uk/news/uk-24418847 [Accessed 03 May 2024].

Brown, R., Evans, E., Webb S., Holdaway, S., Berry, G., Chenery, S., Gresty, B., and Jones, M. (2012) *The Contribution of Financial Investigation to Tackling*

Organised Crime: A Qualitative Study. [pdf] Research Report 65. London: Home Office. Available at: https://www.gov.uk/government/uploads/system/uploads/attachment_data/file/116518/horr65.pdf [Accessed 20 November 2013].

Bullock, K. (2010) The Confiscation Investigation: Investigating the Financial Benefit Made from Crime. *Policing: A Journal of Policing and Practice*, Vol. 4, No. 1, pp. 7–14.

Bullock, K., Mann, D., Street, R. and Coxon, C. (2009) *Examining Attrition in Confiscating the Proceeds of Crime.* [pdf] Research Report 17. London: Home Office. Available at: https://assets.publishing.service.gov.uk/government/uploads/system/uploads/attachment_data/file/116617/horr17-report.pdfhttps://assets.publishing.service.gov.uk/government/uploads/system/uploads/attachment_data/file/116617/horr17-report.pdf [Accessed 14 June 2016].

Burrell, G., and Morgan, G. (1979) *Sociological Paradigms and Organisational Analysis.* London: Taylor and Francis.

Button, M., Johnston, l., Frimpong, K., and Smith, G. (2007) New Directions in Policing Fraud: The Emergence of the Counter Fraud Specialist in the United Kingdom. *International Journal of the Sociology of Law*, Vol. 35, No. 4, pp. 192–208.

Cabinet Office (2000) *Recovering the Proceeds of Crime.* [pdf] London: Cabinet Office. Available at: http://webarchive.nationalarchives.gov.uk/+/http:/www.cabinetoffice.gov.uk/media/cabinetoffice/strategy/assets/crime.pdf [Accessed 14 June 2013].

Cabinet Office Strategy Unit (2009) *Extending Our Reach: A Comprehensive Approach to Tackling Serious and Organised Crime.* [pdf] London: Home Office. Available at: https://www.gov.uk/government/uploads/system/uploads/attachment_data/file/228946/7665.pdf [Accessed 17 June 2015].

Cabinet Office (2011) *The Cost of Cyber Crime.* [pdf] London: Home Office. Available at: https://www.gov.uk/government/publications/the-cost-of-cyber-crime-joint-government-and-industry-report [Accessed 01 May 2018].

Chambliss, W. J., and Williams, E. (2012) Transnational Organised Crime and Social Science Myths. In: F. Allum and S. Gilmour, eds. *Routledge Handbook of Transnational Organised Crime*, pp. 52–64. Oxon, UK.

Chave, D. (2017) Proceeds of Crime Training: Bringing it up to Date. [pdf] *Journal of Financial Crime*, Vol. 24, No. 3, pp. 437–448. Available at: https://doi.org/10.1108/JFC-04-2017-0028 [Accessed 17 May 2018].

Christians, A. (2017) Distinguishing Tax Avoidance and Evasion: Why and How. [pdf] *Journal of Tax Administration*, Vol. 3, No. 2, pp. 5–21. Available at: http://jota.website/article/view/141/106 [Accessed 07 May 2018].

City of London Police (2018) *Economic Crime Academy Prospectus 2017/2018.* [pdf] Available at: https://academy.cityoflondon.police.uk/images/prospectus [Accessed 08 May 2018].

City of London Police (2018a) *Money Laundering Investigation Unit.* Available at: https://www.cityoflondon.police.uk/advice-and-support/fraud-and-economic-crime/fraudsquads/Pages/Money-Laundering-Investigation-Unit-(MLIU).aspx [Accessed 07 June 2018].

City of London Police (2018b) *Advice and Support: Fraud and Economic Crime.* Available at: https://www.cityoflondon.police.uk/advice-and-support/fraud-and-economic-crime/Pages/default.aspx [Accessed 20 June 2018].

Cohen, L. E., and Felson, M. (1979). Social Change and Crime Rate Trends: A Routine Activity Approach. *American Sociological Review*, Vol. 44, No. 4, pp. 588–608. https://doi.org/10.2307/2094589.

College of Policing (2015) *Leadership Review.* [pdf] Available at: http://www.college.police.uk/What-we-do/Development/Promotion/the-leadership-review/Documents/Leadership_Review_Final_June-2015.pdf [Accessed 16 June 2017].

College of Policing (2018) *Intelligence Management.* [pdf] Available at: https://www.app.college.police.uk/app-content/intelligence-management/ [Accessed 14 April 2018].

College of Policing (2018a) *Investigation. Training and Accreditation.* [pdf] Available at: https://www.app.college.police.uk/app-content/investigations/investigative-strategies/financial-investigation-2/training-and-accreditation/ [Accessed 15 April 2018].

College of Policing (2018b) *Investigation Process.* Available at: https://www.app.college.police.uk/app-content/investigations/investigation-process/ [Accessed 20 September 2018].

College of Policing (2019) *Financial and Telephone Enquiries.* Available at: https://www.app.college.police.uk/app-content/major-investigation-and-public-protection/missing-persons/missing-person-investigations/#financial-and-telephone-enquiries- [Accessed 8 May 2019].

College of Policing (2024) *Phases of an Investigation.* Available at: https://www.college.police.uk/app/investigation/investigation-process [Accessed 21 March 2024].

College of Policing (2024a) *Effective Financial Investigation.* Available at: https://www.college.police.uk/app/investigation/investigative-strategies/financial-investigation/effective-financial-investigation [Accessed 17 July 2017].

Collier, B., and Stewart, J (2021) Privacy Worlds: Exploring Values and Design in the Development of the Tor Anonymity Network. *Sage Journals*, Vol. 47, No. 5. Available at: https://journals.sagepub.com/doi/10.1177/01622439211039019?icid=int.sj-abstract.citing-articles.10 [Accessed 29 April 2024]

Collinson, P. (2015) Is it Time to Close the Door to Foreign Buyers of British Property? *The Guardian*, 21 November. Available at: https://www.theguardian.com/money/blog/2015/nov/21/foreign-buyers-british-property [Accessed 29 June 2018].

Council of Europe (2014) *White Paper on Transnational Organised Crime.* [pdf] Strasbourg: Council of Europe. Available at: https://edoc.coe.int/en/organised-crime/6837-white-paper-on-transnational-organised-crime.html [Accessed 20 April 2018].

Cowell, F. A. (1990) *Cheating the Government. The Economics of Evasion.* London; MIT Press.

Coyne, J. W., and Bell, P. (2011) The Role of Strategic Intelligence in Anticipating Transnational Organised Crime: A Literary Review. *International Journal of Law, Crime and Justice*, Vol. 39, No. 1, pp. 60–78.

Coyne, J. W., and Bell, P. (2011a) Strategic Intelligence in Law Enforcement: A Review. *Journal of Policing, Intelligence and Counter-Terrorism*, Vol. 6, No. 1, pp. 23–29.

Croall, H. (1989) Who Is the White-collar Criminal? *The British Journal of Criminology*, Vol. 29, No. 2, pp. 157–174.

Croall, H. (2001) *Understanding White Collar Crime.* Buckingham: Open University Press.

Croft, J. (1978) *Research in Criminal Justice.* Home Office Research Study No. 44. London: Home Office.

Cross, C., Holt, T., Powell, A., and Wilson, M. (2021). Responding to Cybercrime: Results of a Comparison between Community Members and Police Personnel. *Trends and Issues in Crime and Criminal Justice* [Electronic Resource], Vol. 635, pp. 1–20. Available at: https://search.informit.org/doi/10.3316/agispt.20211101056193 [Accessed 26 April 2024].

Crown Prosecution Service (2014) *CPS Asset Recovery Strategy.* [pdf] Available at: https://www.cps.gov.uk/sites/default/files/documents/publications/cps_asset_recovery_strategy_2014.pdf [Accessed 15 May 2018].

Crown Prosecution Service (2018) *Organised Crime Strategy.* Available at: https://www.cps.gov.uk/organised-crime-strategy [Accessed 15 April 2018].

Crown Prosecution Service (2018a) *Private Prosecutions – Legal Guidance.* Available at: https://www.cps.gov.uk/legal-guidance/private-prosecutions [Accessed 10 July 2018].

Crown Prosecution Service (2018b) *Proceeds of Crime Act 2002 Part 7 – Money Laundering Offences.* Available at: https://www.cps.gov.uk/legal-guidance/proceeds-crime-act-2002-part-7-money-laundering-offences [Accessed 02 October 2018].

CPS (2024) *Cybercrime – Prosecution Guidance.* Available at: https://www.cps.gov.uk/legal-guidance/cybercrime-prosecution-guidance [Accessed 26 April 2024].

Curtis, J., and Oxburgh, G. (2022) Understanding Cybercrime in Real-world Policing and Law Enforcement. *The Police Journal: Theory, Practice and Principles*, pp. 1–20. Available at: https://researchportal.northumbria.ac.uk/ws/portalfiles/portal/70677416/0032258x221107584.pdf [Accessed 24 April, 2024].

Davidson, I., Walker, R., and Dayman, I. (2014) *Money Laundering in England and Wales: A Response to Academic Research ~ "Generating Evidence to Inform Practice".* Unpublished.

Davies, G. (2020) Shining a Light on Policing of the Dark Web: An Analysis of UK Investigatory Powers. *Sage Journals,* Vol. 84, No. 5. Available at: https://journals.sagepub.com/doi/full/10.1177/0022018320952557#fn9-0022018320952557 [Accessed 30 April 2024].

Donegan, M. (2019) *Perceptions of Money Laundering in Digital Crime Investigations* (MSc Dissertation). Derby: University of Derby. Available at: https://library.college.police.uk/docs/theses/Donegan_2019_money_laundering.pdf [Accessed 31 May 2024].

Dorn, N., Murji, K., and South, N. (1992) *Traffickers, Drug Markets and Law Enforcement.* London: Routledge.

Durham Constabulary (2015) *Police Seize £100K under Proceeds of Crime Law.* [pdf] Available at: https://www.durham.police.uk/news-and-events/Pages/News%20Articles/Police-seize-%C2%A3100k-which-was-%27under-proceeds-of-crime-.aspx [Accessed 27 June 2018].

East Midlands Police Collaboration (2016) *Police and Crime Commissioner Candidate Briefing Document.* [pdf] Available at: https://www.derbyshire-pcc.gov.uk/Document-Library/Taking-Part/PCC-Elections-2016/PCC-Briefing-Pack-EMSOU-Final.pdf [Accessed 13 April 2018].

ECORYS (2015) *Needs Assessment on Tools and Methods of Financial Investigation in the European Union.* Available from: https://www.wodc.nl/binaries/2612-summary_tcm28-74130.pdf [Accessed 10 June 2019].

Edmonds, T., and Jugnarain, D. (2016) *Private Prosecutions: A potential Anticorruption Tool in English Law.* [pdf] Open Society Foundations: Legal remedies for Grand Corruption. Available at: https://www.justiceinitiative.org/uploads/cb5149bf-6ea8-449a-8260-cea5d8590dfb/legal-remedies-4-edmonds-jugnarain-20160505.pdf [Accessed 19 December 2019].

Edwards, A., and Gill, P., eds. (2004) *Transnational Organised Crime. Perspectives on Global Security.* London: Routledge.

Ellis, C., and de Oliveira, I. S. (2015) *Tackling Money Laundering: Towards a New Model for Information Sharing.* [pdf] London: Royal United Services Institute for Defence and Security Studies. Available at: https://rusi.org/sites/default/files/201509_op_tackling_money_laundering.pdf [Accessed 01 September 2015].

Essien, E. E. (2019) Relevance of the Deep Web. *International Journal of Natural and Applied Science*, Vol. 12, pp. 107–113. Available at: https://www.researchgate.net/publication/344333231_Relevance_of_the_Deep_Web_to_Academic_Research [Accessed 25 April 2024].

European Commission (2018) *Financial Investigation* Available at: https://ec.europa.eu/home-affairs/what-we-do/policies/organized-crime-and-human-trafficking/financial-investigation_en [Accessed 19 April 2018].

Europol (2014) *The Internet Organised Crime Threat Assessment (IOCTA).* [pdf] Available at: http://www.europol.europa.eu [Accessed 25 April 2018].

Evans, J. (2016) How Laundered Money Shapes London's Property Market. *Financial Times*, 6 April. Available at: https://www.ft.com/content/f454e3ec-fc02-11e5-b5f5-070dca6d0a0d [Accessed 29 June 2018].

Fafinski, S. (2011) Public Policy Responses to Cybercrime. [pdf] *Policy and Internet.* Vol. 3, No. 2, Article 1. Available at: http://www.psocommons.org/policyandinternet/vol3/iss2/art1 [Accessed 07 May 2018].

Fafinski, S., Dutton, W. H., and Margetts, H. (2010) Mapping and Measuring Cybercrime. [pdf] *Oxford Internet Institute*, OII Forum Discussion Paper No. 18. Available at: http://www.law.leeds.ac.uk/assets/files/staff/FD18.pdf [Accessed 30 April 2018].

FATF (2022) *FATF Conference on Digital Transformation.* Available at: https://www.fatf-gafi.org/en/publications/Digitaltransformation/Conference-digital-transformation.html [Accessed 29 October 2024].

Federal Bureau of Investigation (2015) *White Collar Crime.* [pdf] Available at: https://www.fbi.gov/about-us/investigate/white_collar [Accessed 20 September 2015].

Federal Bureau of Investigation (2017) *Internet Crime Report.* Available at: https://www.ic3.gov/Media/PDF/AnnualReport/2017_IC3Report.pdf [Accessed 1 June 2019].

Federal Bureau of Investigation (2024) *What Is White Collar Crime and How is the FBI Combatting it?* Available at: https://www.fbi.gov/about/faqs/what-is-white-collar-crime-and-how-is-the-fbi-combating-it [Accessed 03 April 2024].

Fernandez-Steinko, A. (2008) *The False Tracks of Organised Crime.* Cataract: Barcelona.

Financial Action Task Force (1990) *The Forty Recommendations of the Financial Action Task Force on Money Laundering 1990.* [pdf] Available at: http://www.fatf-gafi.org/media/fatf/documents/recommendations/pdfs/FATF%20Recommendations%201990.pdf [Accessed 25 April 2017].

Financial Action Task Force (1996) *Annual Report 1995–1996.* Available at: https://www.fatf-gafi.org/content/dam/fatf-gafi/annual-reports/1995%201996%20ENG.pdf [Accessed 26 April 2017].

Financial Action Task Force (2003) *FATF 40 Recommendations October 2003, Incorporating All Subsequent Amendments Until October 2004.* [pdf] Available at: .http://www.fatfgafi.org/media/fatf/documents/FATF%20Standards%20-%2040%20Recommendations%20rc.pdf [Accessed 25 April 2017].

Financial Action Task Force (2005) *International Best Practices: Detecting and Preventing the Illicit Cross-border Transportation of Cash and Bearer Negotiable Instruments* [pdf] Paris: FATF. Available at www.fatf-gafi.org/topics/fatfrecommendations/documents/bestpracticescashcourierssrix.html [Accessed 10 October 2015].

Financial Action Task Force (2010) *The Review of the Standards-Preparation for the* 4th *Round of Mutual Evaluations.* Available at: https://www.fatf-gafi.org/content/dam/fatf-gafi/public-consultation/First%20public%20consultation%20document.pdf [Accessed 13 May 2024].

Financial Action Task Force (2012) *Operational Issues – Financial Investigations Guidance.* [pdf] Paris: FATF. Available at http://www.fatf-gafi.org/media/fatf/documents/reports/Operational%20Issues_Financial%20investigations%20Guidance.pdf [Accessed 09 September 2015].

Financial Action Task Force (2012a) *International Standards on Combatting Money Laundering and the Financing of Terrorism and Proliferation.* The FATF Recommendations. [pdf] Available at: http://www.fatf-gafi.org/media/fatf/documents/recommendations/pdfs/FATF%20Recommendations%202012.pdf [Accessed 14 May 2018].

Financial Action Task Force (2013) *Annual Report 2012–2013.* Available at: https://www.fatf-gafi.org/content/dam/fatf-gafi/annual-reports/FATF%20Annual%20Report%202012%202013.pdf.coredownload.inline.pdf [Accessed 13 May 2024].

Financial Action Task Force (2016) *History of the FATF* [pdf] Available at: http://www.fatf-gafi.org/about/historyofthefatf/ [Accessed 05 May 2017].

Financial Action Task Force (2018) *International Standards on Combatting Money Laundering and the Financing of Terrorism and Proliferation.* The FATF Recommendations. [pdf] Available at: http://www.fatf-gafi.org/media/fatf/documents/recommendations.html [Accessed 22 May 2019].

Financial Action Task Force (2024) *Amendments to the FATF Standards to Strengthen Global Asset Recovery.* Available at: https://www.fatf-gafi.org/en/publications/Fatfrecommendations/amendment-FATF-standards-global-asset-recovery.html [Accessed 26 March 2024].

Financial Action Task Force and Middle East and North Africa Financial Action Task Force (2015) *Money Laundering through the Physical Transportation of Cash.* Available at:https://www.fatf-gafi.org/content/dam/fatf-gafi/reports/money-laundering-through-transportation-cash.pdf [Accessed 29 October 2024].

Financial Conduct Authority (2016) *Financial Crime: A Guide for Firms. Part1: A Firm's Guide to Preventing Financial Crime.* Available at: https://www.handbook.fca.org.uk/handbook/document/fc/FC1_FCA_20160703.pdf [Accessed 11 September 2019].

Fijnaut, C., and Paoli, L. eds. (2004) *Organised Crime in Europe. Concepts, Patterns and Control Policies in the European Union and Beyond.* Dondrecht: Springer.

FinCen (2016) *Gudiance.* Available at: https://www.fincen.gov/sites/default/files/shared/FIN-2016-G001.pdf [Accessed 20 January 2018].

Finckenauer, J. O. (2005) Problems of Definition: What Is Organised Crime? *Trends in Organised Crime*, Vol. 8, No. 3, pp. 63–83.

Fleming, M. H. (2005) *UK Law Enforcement Agency Use and Management of Suspicious Activity Reports: Towards Determining the Value of the Regime.* [pdf] London: University College London. Available at: http://www.jdi.ucl.ac.uk/downloads/pdf/Fleming_LEA_Use_and_Mgmt_of_SARs_June2005.pdf [Accessed 31 August 2015].

Fleming, M. H. (2007) Issues in Measuring the Efficacy of a Suspicious Activity Reports (SARs) Regime. *Amicus Curiae*, No. 70, pp. 9–12.

Flood, B., and Gaspar, R. (2009) strategic Aspects of the UK National Intelligence Model. In J. Ratcliffe, ed. *Strategic Thinking in Criminal Intelligence.* 2nd edition. New South Wales: Federation Press.

Free Government Information (2012) *Global Freedom of Information and the National Security Archive.* Available at: https://freegovinfo.info/?s=number+of+agencies+similar+Transparency+International&submit= [Accessed 29 June 2018].

Fruhlinger, J., Sharma, A., and Breeden, J. (2023) *15 Top Open-Source Intelligence Tools.* CSO. Available at: https://www.csoonline.com/article/567859/what-is-osint-top-open-source-intelligence-tools.html [Accessed 30 April 2024].

FTI Consulting (2018) *Preparing for the New SARs Regime.* Available at: http://www.fticonsulting-emea.com/~/media/Files/emea--files/insights/articles/the-new-sars-regime.pdf [Accessed 25 May 2018].

Gale, E., and Kelly, J. (2018) *Exploring the Role of the Financial Investigator.* London: Home Office.

Garland, D. (1996) The Limits of the Sovereign State. Strategies of Crime Control in Contemporary Society. *The British Journal of Criminology*, Vol. 36, pp. 445–471.

Garland, D. (2000) The Culture of High Crime Societies. *The British Journal of Criminology*, Vol. 40, pp. 347–375.

Garland, D. (2001) *The Culture of Control.* Oxford: Oxford University Press.

Garland, J., and Terry, C. (2012) *How Not to Run an Election. The Police and Crime Commissioner Elections 15 November 2012.* [pdf] London: Electoral Reform Society. Available at: https://www.electoral-reform.org.uk/wp-content/uploads/2017/06/2012-England-and-Wales-Police-Crime-Commissioner-Elections.pdf [Accessed 06 July 2018].

Gibson, W. (1984) *Neuromancer.* London: Gollancz.

Giles, A. (2013) The Assessment of Benefit Under Part 2 of the Proceeds of crime Act 2002: A Sledgehammer to Crack a Nut? [pdf] *Plymouth Law and Criminal Justice Review*, Vol. 1, pp. 85–109. Plymouth: Plymouth University Press. Available at: http://www.pbs.plymouth.ac.uk/plr/Vol5/Amy%20Giles%20Article%20EDITED.pdf [Accessed 03 November 2015].

Gilmour, P. (2020). Exploring the Barriers to Policing Financial Crime in England and Wales. *Policing: A Journal of Policy and Practice*, Vol. 15, No. 2, June 2021, pp. 1507–1521. https://doi.org/10.1093/police/paaa081

Goetz, K. (2016) *An Introduction to Internet-based Financial Investigations.* Boca Raton, FL: CRC Press.

Gold, M., and Levi, M. (1994) *Money-Laundering in the UK: An Appraisal of Suspicion-Based Reporting.* London: The Police Foundation.

Goldsmith, M., and Linderman, M. J. (1989) Asset Forfeiture and Third-Party Rights: The Need for Further Law Reform. [pdf] *Duke Law Journal.* Vol. 38, No. 5, pp. 1254–1301. Available at: https://scholarship.law.duke.edu/dlj/vol38/iss5/3/ [Accessed 26 April 2018].

Golobinek, R. (2006) *Financial Investigation and Confiscation of Proceeds of Crime: Training Manual for Law Enforcement and Judiciary.* [pdf] Strasbourg: Council of Europe. Available at: https://www.coe.int/t/dghl/cooperation/economiccrime/specialfiles/CARPO-ManualFinInv_eng.pdf [Accessed 14 December 2014].

Gordon, S., and Ford, R. (2006) On the Definition and Classification of Cybercrime. [pdf] *Journal in Computer Virology*, Vol. 2, No. 1, pp. 13–20. Available at: https://link.springer.com/article/10.1007/s11416-006-0015-z [Accessed 07 May 2018].

Gottschalk, P., and Rundmo, T. (2014) Crime: The Amount and Disparity of Sentencing – A Comparison of Corporate and Occupational White-collar Criminals. *International Journal of Law, Crime and Justice*, Vol. 42, No. 3, pp. 175–187. Available at: https://brage.bibsys.no/xmlui/bitstream/handle/11250/277628/Gottschalk_Rundmo_IJLCJ_2014.pdf?sequence=1 [Accessed 07 May 2018].

Gov.UK (2011) *The UK Cyber Security Strategy: Protecting and promoting the UK in a Digital World.* Available at: https://assets.publishing.service.gov.uk/media/5a78a991ed915d04220645e2/uk-cyber-security-strategy-final.pdf [Accessed 29 October 2024].

Gov.UK (2018) *UK Launches New Anti-money Laundering Watchdog.* Available at: https://www.gov.uk/government/news/uk-launches-new-anti-money-laundering-watchdog [Accessed 28 June 2018].

Gov.UK (2020) *Assets Recovery Agency.* Available at: https://www.gov.uk/government/organisations/assets-recovery-agency [Accessed 13 March 2020].

Greer, C. (2007) News Media, Victims and Crime. In P. Davies, P. Francis, and C. Greer, eds. *Victims, Crime and Society.* 2nd edition. London: Sage, pp. 20–49.

Gunn, A. (1978) Tax Avoidance. [pdf] *Scholarly Works.* Paper 134. Notre Dame Law School. Available at: http://scholarship.law.nd.edu/law_faculty_scholarship/134 [Accessed 07 May 2018].

Gurule, J. (1995) The Money Laundering Control Act of 1986: Creating a New Federal Offence or Merely Affording Federal Prosecutors an Alternative Means of Punishing Specified Unlawful Activity. [pdf] *American Criminal Law Review*, Vol. 32, pp. 823–854. Available at: https://scholarship.law.nd.edu/law_faculty_scholarship/21/ [Accessed 26 April 2018].

Hall, M. (2012) One Step Forward (Six Steps Back). In Proceeds of Crime Review. *The Journal of Assets Forfeiture and Money Laundering*, Vol. 7, pp. 16–25.

Hansard (2001) *Proceeds of Crime Bill: Order for Second Reading in Hansard 1803-2005 HC Deb 30 October 2001 vol 373 cc757–852.* [pdf] London: House of Commons. Available at: http://hansard.millbanksystems.com/commons/2001/oct/30/proceeds-of-crime-bill [Accessed 14 November 2016].

Her Majesty's Courts and Tribunals Service (2016) *Trust Statement 2015–2016.* [pdf] Available at: https://www.gov.uk/government/uploads/system/uploads/attachment_data/file/536077/hm-courts-and-tribunals-service-trust-statement-2015-16.pdf [Accessed 16 September 2017].

Her Majesty's Crown Prosecution Service Inspectorate, Her Majesty's Inspectorate of Court Administration and Her Majesty's Inspectorate of Constabulary (2010) *Joint Thematic Review of Asset Recovery: Restraint and Confiscation Casework.* [pdf] Available at: https://www.justiceinspectorates.gov.uk/hmic/media/joint-thematic-review-of-asset-recovery-restraint-and-confiscation-casework-full-report-20100324.pdf [Accessed 10 December 2014].

Her Majesty's Government (2010) *Cyber Crime Strategy*. [pdf] Available at: https://www.gov.uk/government/uploads/system/uploads/attachment_data/file/228826/7842.pdf [Accessed 12 June 2015].

H.M. Government (2011) *Human Trafficking: The Government Strategy*. [pdf] Available at: https://assets.publishing.service.gov.uk/government/uploads/system/uploads/attachment_data/file/97845/human-trafficking-strategy.pdf [Accessed 06 July 2018].

H.M. Government (2013) *Serious and Organised Crime Strategy*. [pdf] Available at: https://www.gov.uk/government/uploads/system/uploads/attachment_data/file/248645/Serious_and_Organised_Crime_Strategy.pdf [Accessed 7 December 2013].

H.M. Government (2016) *National Cyber Security Strategy 2016–2021*. [pdf] Available at: https://www.gov.uk/government/uploads/system/uploads/attachment_data/file/567242/national_cyber_security_strategy_2016.pdf [Accessed 10 June 2017].

H.M. Government (2016a) *Queen's Speech 2016*. Available at: https://www.gov.uk/government/speeches/queens-speech-2016 [Accessed 24 May 2018].

H.M. Government (2018) *Home Secretary Announces New National Economic Crime Centre to Tackle High Level Fraud and Money Laundering*. Available at: https://www.gov.uk/government/news/home-secretary-announces-new-national-economic-crime-centre-to-tackle-high-level-fraud-and-money-laundering [Accessed 30 April 2018].

Her Majesty's Government (2022) *Government Cyber Security Strategy*. Available at: https://assets.publishing.service.gov.uk/media/61f0169de90e070375c230a8/government-cyber-security-strategy.pdf [Accessed 2 April 2024].

H.M. Inspectorate of Constabulary (2014) *Crime Recording: Making the Victim Count. The Final Report of an Inspection of Crime Data Integrity in Police Forces in England and Wales*. [pdf] Available at: https://www.justiceinspectorates.gov.uk/hmic/wp-content/uploads/crime-recording-making-the-victim-count.pdf [Accessed 29 November 2016].

Her Majesty's Inspectorate of Constabulary (2015) *Regional Organised Crime Units. A Review of Capability and Effectiveness*. [pdf] Available at: https://www.justiceinspectorates.gov.uk/hmicfrs/wp-content/uploads/regional-organised-crime-units.pdf [Accessed June 2017].

Her Majesty's Inspectorate of Constabulary (2016) *State of Policing. The Annual Assessment of Policing in England and Wales*. [pdf] Available at: www.justiceinspectorates.gov.uk/hmic/ [Accessed 10 January 2017].

Her Majesty's Inspectorate of Constabulary (2016a) *PEEL: Police Effectiveness 2015. An Inspection of Derbyshire Constabulary*. [pdf] Available at: https://www.derbyshire-pcc.gov.uk/Document-Library/Transparency/Public-Information/HMIC-Publications/2016/police-effectiveness-2015-derbyshire.pdf [Accessed 03 May 2018].

Her Majesty's Inspectorate of Constabulary (2017b) *State of Policing: The Annual Assessment of Policing in England and Wales 2016*. [pdf] Available at: https://www.justiceinspectorates.gov.uk/hmicfrs/wp-content/uploads/state-of-policing-2016-double-page.pdf [Accessed 15 may 2018].

H.M. Inspectorate of Constabulary, H.M Crown Prosecution Service Inspectorate, H.M. Magistrates Court Inspectorate (2004) *Payback Time: Joint Review of Asset Recovery since the Proceeds of Crime Act 2002*. [pdf] Available at: https://www

.justiceinspectorates.gov.uk/cjji/inspections/payback-time-joint-review-of-asset-recovery-since-the-proceeds-of-crime-act-2002/ [Accessed 07 September 2016].

Her Majesty's Treasury (2007) *The Financial Challenge to Crime and Terrorism.* London: Her Majesty's Stationery Office.

Her Majesty's Treasury (2014) *Review of Enforcement Decision-making at the Financial Services Regulators.* Available at: https://assets.publishing.service.gov.uk/media/5a7ecd2c40f0b62305b8344a/enforcement_review_response_final.pdf [Accessed 20 January 2019].

HM Treasury and Home Office (2015) *UK National Risk Assessment of Money Laundering and Terrorist Financing.* [pdf] Available at: https://assets.publishing.service.gov.uk/government/uploads/system/uploads/attachment_data/file/468210/UK_NRA_October_2015_final_web.pdf [Accessed 24 May 2018].

HM Treasury and Home Office (2017) *National Risk Assessment of Money Laundering and Terrorist Financing 2017.* [pdf] Available at: https://assets.publishing.service.gov.uk/government/uploads/system/uploads/attachment_data/file/655198/National_risk_assessment_of_money_laundering_and_terrorist_financing_2017_pdf_web.pdf [Accessed 18 June 2018].

Hicks, D.C. (2010) Money Laundering. In: F. Brookman, M. Maguire, H. Pierpoint, and T. Bennett, eds. *Handbook on Crime.* Cullompton, Devon: Willan, pp. 712–725.

Hicks, D., and Graycar, A. (2019) Money Laundering. In: M. Natarajan, ed. *International and Transnational Crime and Justice.* Cambridge: Cambridge University Press, pp. 80–85.

Hicks, D., Tolkovsky, N., and Hughes, C. (2017) *Systematic Evidence Review of Cybercrime.* Paper Presented to the Society of Evidence-Based Policing, Organised by the East Midlands Police Academic Collaborative (EMPAC), Institute for Public Safety, Crime and Justice, and the University of Cambridge, Northampton, 2 March.

Hicks, T. (2016) *Written Evidence Submitted by Tristram Hicks.* House of Commons Home Affairs Committee Proceeds of Crime: Fifth Report of Session 2016–2017. [pdf] Available at: https://www.publications.parliament.uk/pa/cm201617/cmselect/cmhaff/25/25.pdf [Accessed 4 February 2017].

Hodgson, D. (1984) *Profits of Crime and their Recovery: Report of a Committee Chaired by Sir Derek Hodgson.* London: Heineman.

Home Office (2003) *The Role of Police Authorities in Public Engagement.* [pdf] Available at: http:/library.college.police.uk/docs/hordsolr/rdsolr3703.pdf [Accessed 18 June 2018].

Home Office (2004) *One Step Ahead.* [pdf] Available at: https://assets.publishing.service.gov.uk/government/uploads/system/uploads/attachment_data/file/251075/6167.pdf [Accessed 30 April 2018].

Home Office (2007) *Asset Recovery Action Plan. A Consultation Document.* London: Her Majesty's Stationery Office.

Home Office (2010) *Report of the Appointed Person for England and Wales and Northern Ireland: (Proceeds of Crime Act 2002, Part 5, Chapter 3) 2009–2010.* Available at: https://www.gov.uk/government/uploads/system/uploads/attachment_data/file/97822/poca-appointed-persons-0910.pdf [Accessed 17 November 2016].

Home Office (2011) *Report of the Appointed Person for England and Wales and Northern Ireland 2010–2011.* Available at: https://www.gov.uk/government/uploads/system/uploads/attachment_data/file/97821/appointed-persons-report-201011.pdf [Accessed 17 November 2016].

Home Office (2011a) *Future Directions for Organised Crime Research.* [pdf] Available at: https://assets.publishing.service.gov.uk/government/uploads/system/uploads/attachment_data/file/116653/future-organised-crime-res-2011.pdf [Accessed 27 April 2018].

Home Office (2011b) *Deprivation of Criminal Assets.* [pdf] Available at: https://www.gov.uk/government/publications/deprivation-of-criminal-assets [Accessed 14 May 2018].

Home Office (2012) *Asset Recovery Incentivisation Scheme 2012-2013: Arrangements for Implementation and Payment. Disclosure 22.* [pdf] Available at: https://www.cps.gov.uk/publications/docs/foi_disclosures/2013/disclosure_22_supporting_data_2.pdf [Accessed 09 March 2017].

Home Office (2013) *Report for 2012 - 2013 of the Appointed Person for England and Wales under Section 291 of the Proceeds of Crime Act 2002.* Available at: https://www.gov.uk/government/publications/report-for-2012-to-2013-of-the-appointed-person-under-the-proceeds-of-crime-act-2002 [Accessed 17 November 2016].

Home Office (2014a) *Home Secretary at APCC Partnership Summit.* Speech. London. Available at: https://www.gov.uk/government/speeches/home-secretary-at-apcc-partnership-summit [Accessed 01 November 2016].

Home Office (2014b). *Report for 2013 - 2014 of the Appointed Person for England and Wales under Section 291 of the Proceeds of Crime Act 2002.* Available from: https://www.gov.uk/government/uploads/system/uploads/attachment_data/file/332982/AppointedPerson2013-14_PRINT.pdf [Accessed 17 November 2016].

Home Office (2015) *Circular 022/2015: Money Laundering: The Confidentiality and Sensitivity of Suspicious Activity Reports (SARs) and the Identity of Those Who Make Them.* [pdf] Available at: https://www.gov.uk/government/publications/circular-0222015-money-laundering-the-confidentiality-and-sensitivity-of-suspicious-activity-reports-sars-and-the-identity-of-those-who-make-them/ [Accessed 24 May 2019].

Home Office (2016) *Code of Practice Issued under Section 377 of the Proceeds of Crime Act 2002 Investigations.* London: Her Majesty's Stationery Office.

Home Office (2016a) *Modern Crime Prevention Strategy.* London: Her Majesty's Stationery Office.

Home Office (2016b) *Home Secretary Theresa May Launches the Modern Crime Prevention Strategy.* [pdf] Speech at International Crime and Policing Conference 2016. Available at: https://www.gov.uk/government/speeches/home-secretary-theresa-may-launches-the-modern-crime-prevention-strategy [Accessed 24 May 2018].

Home Office (2016c) *Action Plan for Anti-money Laundering and Counter-terrorist Finance: Consultation on Legislative Proposals.* [pdf] Available at: https://assets.publishing.service.gov.uk/government/uploads/system/uploads/attachment_data/file/559957/Action_Plan_for_anti_money-laundering_and_counter-terrorist_finance_-_consultation_on_legislative_proposals.pdf [Accessed 24 May 2018].

Home Office (2017) *Asset Recovery Statistical Bulletin 2011/12 – 2016/17.* London: Her Majesty's Stationery Office.

Home Office (2017a) *Home Secretary Announces New National Economic Crime Centre to Tackle High Level Fraud and Money Laundering.* Available at: https://www.gov.uk/government/news/home-secretary-announces-new-national-economic-crime

-centre-to-tackle-high-level-fraud-and-money-laundering [Accessed 20 February 2018].

Home Office (2018) *Understanding the Costs of Cyber Crime*. A report of the key findings from the Costs of Cyber Crimes Working Group. Research Report 96. London: Her Majesty's Stationery Office.

Home Office (2018a) *Explanatory Memorandum to the Proceeds of Crime Act 2002 (References to Financial Investigators) (Amendment) (England and Wales) Order 2018* No. 318. [pdf] Available at: http://www.legislation.gov.uk/uksi/2018/318/pdfs/uksiem_20180318_en.pdf [Accessed 14 June 2018].

Home Office (2018b) *Unexplained Wealth Orders*. Circular 003/2018 [pdf] Available at: https://www.gov.uk/government/publications/circular-0032018-criminal-finances-act-unexplained-wealth-orders/circular-0032018-unexplained-wealth-orders [Accessed 02 July 2018].

Home Office (2018c) *Commonwealth Countries Unite to Stamp Out Human Trafficking and Child Exploitation*. Available at: https://www.gov.uk/government/news/commonwealth-countries-unite-to-stamp-out-human-trafficking-and-child-exploitation [Accessed 6 July 2018].

Home Office (2018d) *Circular 006/2018: Criminal Finances Act: Disclosure Orders*. Available at: https://www.gov.uk/government/publications/circular-0062018-criminal-finances-act-disclosure-orders/circular-0062018-criminal-finances-act-disclosure-orders [Accessed 06 July 2018].

Home Office (2023) *Asset Recovery Statistical Bulletin: Financial Years Ending March 2018 to 2023*. Available at: https://www.gov.uk/government/statistics/asset-recovery-statistical-bulletin-financial-years-ending-2018-to-2023/asset-recovery-statistical-bulletin-financial-years-ending-march-2018-to-march-2023 [Accessed 25 March 2024].

Home Office (2023a) *Government Response to the Law Commission's Review of Confiscation*. Available at: https://www.gov.uk/government/publications/government-response-to-the-law-commissions-review-of-confiscation/government-response-to-the-law-commissions-review-of-confiscation [Accessed 13 May 2024].

Home Office (2023b) *Unexplained Wealth Orders: 2022–2023 Annual Report*. Available at: https://www.gov.uk/government/publications/unexplained-wealth-orders-2022-to-2023-annual-report/unexplained-wealth-orders-2022-to-2023-annual-report [Accessed 14 May 2024].

Home Office and HM Treasury (2016) *Action Plan for Anti-money Laundering and Counter Terrorist Finance*. [pdf] Available at: https://www.ifa.org.uk/media/631299/Home-Office-and-HM-Treasury-6-2118-Action_Plan_for_Anti-Money_Laundering__print_.pdf [Accessed 29 June 2018].

Home Secretary (2016) *Home Secretary's Speech to the FCA's Financial Crime Conference*. [pdf] Available at: https://www.gov.uk/government/speeches/home-secretarys-speech-to-the-fcas-financial-crime-conference [Accessed 14 June 2017].

Hopkins, M., and Shelton, N. (2019) Identifying Money Laundering Risk in the United Kingdom. Observations from National Risk Assessments and a proposed Alternative Methodology. *European Journal of Criminal Policy*, Vol. 25, pp. 63–82.

House of Commons (2003) *Crown Prosecution Service Resource Accounts 2002–2003* [pdf] Available at: https://www.cps.gov.uk/publications/docs/resourceaccs02-03.pdf [Accessed 02 October 2016].

House of Commons (2004) *Crown Prosecution Service Resource Accounts 2003–2004* [pdf] Available at: https://www.cps.gov.uk/publications/docs/resourceaccs03-04.pdf [Accessed 02 October 2016].

House of Commons (2005) *Crown Prosecution Service Resource Accounts 2004–2005* [pdf] Available at: https://www.cps.gov.uk/publications/docs/resourceaccs04-05.pdf [Accessed 02 October 2016].

House of Commons (2006) *Organised Crime in Northern Ireland: Third Report of Session 2005–2006, Vol 2: Oral and Written Evidence.* [pdf]. (HC886-II) Available at: https://publications.parliament.uk/pa/cm200506/cmselect/cmniaf/886/886ii.pdf [Accessed 24 May 2018].

House of Commons (2007) *Assets Recovery Agency. Fiftieth Report of Session 2006–2007.* [pdf] (HC391). Available at: https://publications.parliament.uk/pa/cm200607/cmselect/cmpubacc/391/391.pdf [Accessed 14 May 2018].

House of Commons (2008) *Assets Recovery Agency Resource Accounts 2007–2008.* [pdf] (HC661). Available at: https://assets.publishing.service.gov.uk/government/uploads/system/uploads/attachment_data/file/250222/0661.pdf [Accessed 28 June 2018].

House of Commons Committee of Public Accounts (2014) *Confiscation Orders. Report Together with Formal Minutes, Oral and Written Evidence.* [pdf] London: The Stationery Office (HC942 2013-14). Available at: http://www.publications.parliament.uk/pa/cm201314/cmselect/cmpubacc/942/942.pdf [Accessed 30 March 2014].

House of Commons (2016) *Proceeds of Crime: Fifth Report of Session 2016–2017 to Home Affairs Committee* [pdf]. (HC25). Available at: https://www.publications.parliament.uk/pa/cm201617/cmselect/cmhaff/25/25.pdf [Accessed 17 October 2016].

House of Commons (2016a) *Proceeds of Crime: Government Response to the Committee's Fifth Report of Session 2016–2017.* [pdf] (HC805). Available at: https://publications.parliament.uk/pa/cm201617/cmselect/cmhaff/805/805.pdf [Accessed 15 April 2018].

House of Commons (2016b) *Criminal Finances Bill.* Explanatory Notes. [pdf] Available at: https://publications.parliament.uk/pa/bills/cbill/2016-2017/0075/en/17075en.pdf [Accessed 18 June 2019].

Howell, C., Horton, T., and Gill, M. (2013) *Financial Investigation: Identifying the Value.* Leicester: Perpetuity Research and Consultancy International (PRCI) Ltd.

Hughes, C. (2021) *Financial Investigation: Establishing the Principles of a Generic and Effective Philosophy.* Unpublished.

Hughes, C., and Brown, R. (2022) Financial Investigation for Routine Policing in Australia. *Trends and Issues in Crime and Criminal Justice*, Australian Institute for Criminology, No. 649, pp. 1–12. Canberra: Australian Institute of Criminology. https://doi.org/10.52922/ti78603

Insidetime (2014) *Confiscation Orders.* Available at: https://insidetime.org/confiscation-orders-7/ [Accessed 27 June 2018].

Institute of Chartered Secretaries and Administrators (2018) *UK Economic Crime Strategy Specifics Remain Unclear.* Available at: https://www.icsa.org.uk/knowledge/governance-and-compliance/analysis/economic-crime-strategy [Accessed 07 May 2018].

International Monetary Fund (2001) *Financial System Abuse, Financial Crime and Money Laundering – Background Paper.* [pdf] Available at: https://www.imf.org/external/np/ml/2001/eng/021201.htm [Accessed 10 May 2018].

Interpol Website (2015) *Cybercrime* [pdf] Available at: http://www.interpol.int/Crime-areas/Cybercrime/Cybercrime [Accessed 12 November 2015].

Interpol (2017) *Annual Report.* Available at: https://www.google.com/search?q=Interpol+2017&rlz=1C1GCEU_enGB893GB893&oq=Interpol+2017&gs_lcrp=EgZjaHJvbWUyBggAEEUYOTIICAEQABgWGB4yCAgCEAAYFhgeMg0IAxAAGIYDGIAEGIoFMg0IBBAAGIYDGIAEGIoFMg0IBRAAGIYDGIAEGIoFMgoIBhAAGIAEGKIEMgoIBxAAGIAEGKIEMgoICBAAGIAEGKIEMgoICRAAGIAEGKIE0gEKMzYzODBqMGoxNagCCLACAQ&sourceid=chrome&ie=UTF-8 [Accessed 9 October 2019].

Jarvis, P., and Earis, R. (2015) Participating in the Activities of an Organised Crime Group: The New Offence. *Criminal Law Review,* Vol. 10, pp. 766–788. London: Sweet and Maxwell.

Jeremie, J. (2015) The Financial Crisis, Economic Crime and Development. In: B. Rider, ed. *Research Handbook on International Financial Crime.* London: Edward Elgar Publishing.

Jewkes, Y. (2007) *Crime Online.* Devon: Willan Publishing.

John, T., and Maguire, M. (2003) Rolling Out the National Intelligence Model: Key Challenges. In: K. Bullock and N. Tilley, eds. *Crime Reduction and Problem-Oriented Policing.* Cullompton: Willan.

John, T., and Maguire, M. (2012) Criminal Intelligence and the National Intelligence Model. In: T. Newman, T. Williamson, and A. Wright, eds. *Handbook of Criminal Investigation.* London: Routledge, pp. 199–221.

Johnston, I. (2014) Police for Hire: Judge Hits Out at Met's Agreement to aid Virgin Media in a Private Prosecution. *The Independent,* 30 January. Available at: https://www.independent.co.uk/news/uk/crime/police-for-hire-judge-hits-out-at-mets-agreement-to-aid-virgin-media-in-a-private-prosecution-9094705.html [Accessed 06 July 2018].

Joint Force Intelligence Directorate (2013) *Joint Intelligence, JP 2.0: ix.* [pdf] Available at: http://www.dtic.mil/doctrine/new_pubs/jp2_0.pdf [Accessed 02 September 2015].

Keatinge, T. (2023) *Money Laundering: The Beating Heart.* Royal United Services Instifute, 27 November 2023. Available at: https://www.rusi.org/explore-our-research/publications/commentary/money-laundering-beating-heart-organised-crime [Accessed 25 March 2024].

Keen, F. (2017) *Unexplained Wealth Orders. Global Lessons for the UK Ahead of Implementation.* [pdf] Royal United Services Institute, Occasional Paper. Available at: https://rusi.org/sites/default/files/201709_rusi_unexplained_wealth_orders_keen_web.pdf [Accessed 10 May 2018].

Kesselring, K. J. (2010) Felony Forfeiture and the Profits of Crime in Early Modern England. *The Historical Journal,* Vol. 53, No. 2, pp. 271–288.

Khera, V. (2020) *The Web Layers: Introduction to Surface, Deep and Darknet.* Cyber Protection Magazine. Available at: https://cyberprotection-magazine.com/the-web-layers-introduction-to-surface-deep-and-darknet [Accessed 29 April 2024].

Kirby, S., and McPherson, I. (2004) Integrating the National Intelligence Model with a Problem-solving Approach. *Community Safety Journal,* Vol. 3, No. 2, pp. 36–46.

Kirby, S., Northey, H., and Snow, N. (2015) New Crimes – New Tactics: The Emergence and Effectiveness of Disruption in Tackling Serious Organised Crime. *The Journal of Political Criminology,* Vol. 1, No. 1, pp. 33–44.

Kirchler, E., Maciejovsky, B., and Schneider, F. (2003) Everyday Representations of Tax Avoidance, Tax Evasion and Tax Flight: Do Legal Differences Matter? [pdf] *Journal of Economic Psychology*, Vol. 24, No. 4, pp. 535–553. Available at: https://edoc.hu-berlin.de/bitstream/handle/18452/4223/43.pdf?sequence=1 [Accessed 08 May 2018].

Kitteringham, G., and Fennelly, L. J. (2012) Routine Activity Theory. In: L. J. Fennelly, ed. *Handbook of Loss Prevention and Crime Prevention,* 6th edition. Oxford: Butterworth-Heineman, pp. 577–607.

Kuhns, J. B., Blevins, K. R., and Lee, S. Z. (2012) *Understanding Decisions to Burglarise from the Offenders' Perspective.* [pdf] University of North Carolina: UNC Charlotte. Available at: https://www.researchgate.net/profile/Joseph_Kuhns/publication/268444817_Understanding_Decisions_to_Burglarize_from_the_Offender%27s_Perspective/links/546b48410cf2f5eb18091770/Understanding-Decisions-to-Burglarize-from-the-Offenders-Perspective.pdf [Accessed 17 May 2018].

Laqueur, W. (1985) *A World of Secrets. The Uses and Limits of Intelligence.* New York; Basic Books.

Law Commission (2017) *Confiscation.* Available at: http://www.lawcom.gov.uk/confiscation/ [Accessed 24 April 2017].

Law Commission (2019) *Anti-money Laundering: The SARs Regime.* London: Her Majesty's Stationery Office. (HC2098 2018).

Law Commission (2022) *Confiscation of the Proceeds of Crime after Conviction: A Final Report.* HC828 Law Com No 410. Available at: https://cloud-platform-e218f50a4812967ba1215eaecede923f.s3.amazonaws.com/uploads/sites/30/2022/11/Confiscation-of-the-proceeds-of-crime-after-conviction-a-final-report_web.pdf [Accessed 13 May 2024].

Leicestershire Police (2018) *Economic Crime Unit.* Available at: https://leics.police.uk/about-us/our-departments/crime-and-intelligence-directorate/economic-crime-unit [Accessed 21 June 2018].

Leong, A. V. M. (2016) *The Disruption of Organised Crime: An Analysis of Legal and Non-Legal Strategies.* London: Routledge.

Leukfeldt, E. R., Notté, R. J. (Raoul), and Malsch, M. (Marijke). (2020). Exploring the Needs of Victims of Cyber-dependent and Cyber-enabled Crimes. *Victims & Offenders*, Vol. 15, No. 1, pp. 60–77. https://doi.org/10.1080/15564886.2019.1672229 [Accessed 26 April 2024].

Levi, M. (1991) Regulating Money Laundering. The Death of Bank Secrecy in the UK. *The British Journal of Criminology,* Vol. 31, No. 2, pp. 109–125.

Levi, M. (2013) *Drug Law Enforcement and Financial Investigation Strategies.* Modernising Drug Law Enforcement Report 5 [pdf] London: International Drug Policy Consortium. Available at: http://static1.1.sqspcdn.com/static/f/650429/23655284/1381248515913/MDLE+Report+5+_+Drug+Law+Enforcement+and+Financial+Investigation+Strategies.pdf?token=5l8HdjmCP2N8K6okKhp65wROxQA%3D [Accessed 20 January 2017].

Levi, M., Innes, M., Reuter, P., and Gundur, R. V. (2013) *The Economic, Financial and Social Impacts of Organised Crime in the EU.* [pdf] Brussels: European Parliament. Available at: http://www.europarl.europa.eu/RegData/etudes/etudes/join/2013/493018/IPOL-JOIN_ET(2013)493018_EN.pdf [Accessed 24 April 2018].

Levi, M., and Maguire, M. (2004) Reducing and Preventing Organised Crime: An Evidence-based Critique. *Crime, Law and Social Change,* Vol. 41, No. 5, pp. 397–469.

Levi, M., and Maguire, M. (2011) Financial and Organised Crime in Europe: Converging Paradigms of Control? In: T. Spapens, M. Groehijsen, and T. Kooijmans, eds. *Universalis. Liberamicorum Cyrille Fijnaut.* Cambridge: Intersentia, pp. 723–733.

Levi, M., and Osofsky, L. (1995) *Investigating, Seizing and Confiscating the Proceeds of Crime.* Crime Detection and Prevention Series Paper 61. London: Home Office.

Levi, M., and Reuter, P. (2006) Money Laundering. *Crime and Justice: A Review of Research*, Vol. 34, pp. 1–90. Chicago: The University of Chicago Press. Available at: http://www.jstor.org/stable/10.1086/501508 [Accessed 02 February 2013].

Levi, M., and Smith, A. (2002) *A Comparative Analysis of Organized Crime Conspiracy Legislation and Practice and their Relevance to England and Wales.* London: Home Office Online Report, 17/02.

Levi, M., Doig, A., Gundur, R., Wall, D., and Williams, M. (2015) *The Implications of Economic Cybercrime for Policing.* [pdf] London: City of London Corporation. Available at: https://www.cityoflondon.gov.uk/business/economic-research-and-information/research-publications/Documents/Research-2015/Economic-Cybercrime-FullReport.pdf [Accessed 21 March 2017].

Lewis, J. A. (2018) *Economic Impact of Cybercrime—No Slowing Down.* Washington, DC: The Center for Strategic and International Studies (CSIS) Report.

Lilley, P. (2003) *Dirty Dealing. The Untold Truth about Global Money Laundering, International Crime and Terrorism.* London: Kogan Page.

Li, X. B. (2009) *Money Laundering and its Regulation in China* (PhD Thesis). Cardiff University, Cardiff. https://orca.cardiff.ac.uk/id/eprint/54966/1/U585355.pdf [Accessed 15 May 2024].

Long, A. V. M. (2016) *The Disruption of International Organised Crime: An Analysis of Legal and Non-Legal Strategies.* London: Routledge.

Madinger, J. (2012) *Money Laundering: A Guide for Criminal Investigators*, 3rd edition. Boca Raton: CRC Press.

Maguire, M., and John, T. (2006) Intelligence Led Policing, Managerialism and Community Engagement: Competing Priorities and the Role of the National Intelligence Model in the UK. *Policing and Society*, Vol. 16, No. 1, pp. 65–85.

Malani, A. (1999) The Scope of Criminal Forfeiture under RICO: The Appropriate Definition of Proceeds. [pdf] *University of Chicago Law Review*, Vol. 1289 pp. 1291–1316. Available at: https://chicagounbound.uchicago.edu/cgi/viewcontent.cgi?article=2639&context=journal_articles [Accessed 26 April 2018].

Mason, R., and Travis, A. (2016) Ultimate Owners of UK Property May Be Forced into Spotlight. *The Guardian*, 21 April. Available at: https://www.theguardian.com/uk-news/2016/apr/21/ministers-consider-forcing-disclosure-of-true-ownership-of-uk-property [Accessed 29 June 2018].

Maxwell, N. J., and Artingstall, D. (2017) *The Role of Financial Information-Sharing Partnerships in the Disruption of Crime.* London: Royal United Services Institute.

McBarnet, D. (1992) Legitimate Rackets: Tax Evasion, Tax Avoidance and the Boundaries of Legality. [pdf] *The Journal of Human Justice*, Vol. 3, No. 2, pp. 56–74. Available at: https://link.springer.com/article/10.1007/BF02619290 [Accessed 08 May 2018].

McGuire, M., and Dowling, S. (2013) *Cyber Crime: A Review of the Evidence.* [pdf] Research Report 75. London; Home Office. Available at: https://assets.publishing.service.gov.uk/media/5a74fc06e5274a59fa716800/horr75-summary.pdf [Accessed 15 May 2024].

Mecone, J. M., Shapiro, J. B., and Martin, T. (2006) Racketeer Influenced and Corrupt Organisations. [pdf] *American Criminal Law Review*, Vol. 43, pp. 869–919. Available at: https://scholarship.law.berkeley.edu/cgi/viewcontent.cgi?article=3155&context=facpubs [Accessed 26 April 2018].

Metropolitan Police (1988) *Drug Trafficking Offences Act 1986 Training Manual*. London: Metropolitan Police.

Mills, H., Skodbo, S., and Blyth, P. (2013) *Understanding Organised Crime: Estimating the Scale and the Social and Economic Costs*. [pdf] Research Report 73. London: Home Office. Available at: https://www.gov.uk/government/uploads/system/uploads/attachment_data/file/246390/horr73.pdf [Accessed 23 October 2014].

Milosevic, B. (2016) Money Laundering as a Form of Economic Crime in the Role of Financing Terrorism. [pdf] *Law and Politics*, Vol 14, No. 4, pp. 549–560. Available at: casopisi.junis.ni.ac.rs/index.php/FULawPol/article/download/2423/1581 [Accessed 30 January 2018].

Ministry of Housing, Communities and Local Government (2016) *Fighting Fraud and Corruption Locally: The Local Government Counter Fraud and Corruption Strategy 2016 to 2019*. [pdf] London: Chartered Institute of Public Finance and Accountancy. Available at: https://assets.publishing.service.gov.uk/government/uploads/system/uploads/attachment_data/file/503657/Fighting_fraud_and_corruption_locally_strategy.pdf [Accessed 07 May 2018].

Ministry of Justice (2016) *Departmental Overview 2015–2016*. [pdf]. Available at: https://www.nao.org.uk/wp-content/uploads/2016/10/Departmental-Overview-2015-6-Ministry-of-Justice.pdf [Accessed 28 April 2017].

Minkes, J. (2017) *Income Tax Evasion*. [pdf] Oxford Bibliographies. Available at: http://www.oxfordbibliographies.com/view/document/obo-9780195396607/obo-9780195396607-0188.xml [Accessed 08 May 2018].

Mokhiber, R. (1988) *Corporate Crime and Violence*. San Francisco: Sierra Club.

Moore, D., and Rid, T. (2016) Cryptopolitik and the Darknet. Survival. *Journal of Global Politics and Strategy*, Vol. 58, No. 1. Available at: https://www.tandfonline.com/doi/full/10.1080/00396338.2016.1142085 [Accessed 29 April 2024].

Morris, D., E. (1982) An Introductory Examination of the Racketeer Influenced and Corrupt Organisations Act. [pdf] *Akron Law Review*, Vol. 15, No. 4, pp. 771–790. Available at: http://ideaexchange.uakron.edu/cgi/viewcontent.cgi?article=1941&context=akronlawreview [Accessed 26 April 2018].

Moynihan, D. P. (1993) Defining Deviance Down. How We've Become Accustomed to Alarming Levels of Crime and Destructive Behaviour. [pdf] *The American Scholar*, Winter, pp. 17–30. Available at: https://timemilitary.files.wordpress.com/2012/03/defining-deviancy-down-amereducator.pdf [Accessed 16 June 2019].

Mujuzi, J., D. (2015) The Right to Institute a Private Prosecution. *International Human Rights Law Review*, Vol, 4. No. 2, pp. 222–255. Available at: https://brill.com/view/journals/hrlr/4/2/article-p222_3.xml [Accessed 26 November 2019].

National Archives (2011) *Taking the Cash Out of Crime*. [pdf] Available at: http://webarchive.nationalarchives.gov.uk/video/ukhomeoffice/Z22JAaftt5U [Accessed 27 June 2018].

National Audit Office (2007) *The Assets Recovery Agency*. [pdf] Available at: https://www.nao.org.uk/wp-content/uploads/2007/02/0607253.pdf [Accessed 23 September 2016].

National Audit Office (2013) *Confiscation Orders.* [pdf] London: Stationery Office Limited. Available at: https://www.nao.org.uk/wp-content/uploads/2013/12/10318-001-Confiscation-Book.pdf [Accessed 14 January 2014].

National Audit Office (2016) *Confiscation Orders: Progress Review.* [pdf] Available at: https://www.nao.org.uk/wp-content/uploads/2016/03/Confiscation-orders-progress-review-Summary.pdf [Accessed 28 March 2017].

National Audit Office (2017) *Online Fraud.* [pdf] HC45 Available at: https://www.nao.org.uk/wp-content/uploads/2017/06/Online-Fraud.pdf [Accessed 01 May 2018].

National Centre for Policing Excellence (2005) *Practice Advice on Core Investigative Doctrine.* Available at: http://library.college.police.uk/docs/acpo/Core-Investigative-Doctrine.pdf [Accessed 02 July 2018].

National Crime Agency (2014) *SARS Annual Report.* [pdf] Available at: http://www.nationalcrimeagency.gov.uk/publications/464-2014-sars-annual-report/file [Accessed 03 October 2015].

National Crime Agency (2014a) *National Strategic Assessment of Serious and Organised Crime 2014.* [pdf] Available at: http://nationalcrimeagency.gov.uk/publications/207-nca-strategic-assessment-of-serious-and-organised-crime/file [Accessed 24 April 2018].

National Crime Agency (2014b) *High End Money Laundering: Strategic and Action Plan.* [pdf] Available at: http://www.nationalcrimeagency.gov.uk/publications/625-high-end-money-laundering-strategy/file [Accessed 18 June 2018].

National Crime Agency (2015) *Suspicious Activity Reports (SARs) Annual Report 2015.* [pdf] Available at: http://www.nationalcrimeagency.gov.uk/publications/677-sars-annual-report-2015/file [Accessed 07 January 2016].

National Crime Agency (2015a) *Senior Appropriate Officer Financial Investigation Training Pre-read Material.* London: NCA.

National Crime Agency (2015b) *The NCA Commitment to Working in Partnership with UK Operational Partners.* [pdf] Available at: http://www.nationalcrimeagency.gov.uk/publications/178-the-nca-commitment-to-working-in-partnership-with-uk-operational-partners/file [Accessed 30 April 2018].

National Crime Agency (2015c*) Introduction to Suspicious Activity Reports.* [pdf] Available at: http://www.nationalcrimeagency.gov.uk/publications/suspicious-activity-reports-sars/550-introduction-to-suspicious-activity-reports-sars-1/file [Accessed 24 May 2018].

National Crime Agency (2016) *Guidance on Submitting Better Quality Suspicious Activity Reports (SARs).* [pdf] Available at: http://www.nationalcrimeagency.gov.uk/publications/732-guidance-on-submitting-better-quality-sars/file [Accessed 11 June 2017].

National Crime Agency (2016a) *National Strategic Assessment of Organised Crime 2016.* [pdf] Available at: http://www.nationalcrimeagency.gov.uk/publications/731-national-strategic-assessment-of-serious-and-organised-crime-2016/file [Accessed 27 June 2017].

National Crime Agency (2016b) *Cyber Crime Assessment 2016. The Need for a Stronger Law Enforcement and Business Partnership to Fight Cyber Crime.* [pdf] Available at: http://www.nationalcrimeagency.gov.uk/publications/709-cyber-crime-assessment-2016/file [Accessed 16 April 2018].

National Crime Agency (2017) *Economic Crime Command*. Available at: http://www.nationalcrimeagency.gov.uk/about-us/what-we-do/economic-crime [Accessed 11 March 2017].

National Crime Agency (2017a) *SARs Reporter Booklet* [pdf] London; NCA. Available at: http://www.nationalcrimeagency.gov.uk/publications/694-suspicious-activity-reports-reporter-booklet-may-2016/file [Accessed 14 November 2017].

National Crime Agency (2017b) *National Strategic Assessment of Serious and Organised Crime*. [pdf] London: NCA. Available at: http://www.nationalcrimeagency.gov.uk/publications/807-national-strategic-assessment-of-serious-and-organised-crime-2017/file [Accessed 27 April 2018].

National Crime Agency (2017c) *NCA Annual Plan 2017–2018*. Available at: http://www.nationalcrimeagency.gov.uk/publications/790-nca-annual-plan-2017-18/file [Accessed 30 April 2018].

National Crime Agency (2017e) *Suspicious Activity Reports (SARs) Annual Report 2017*. [pdf] London: NCA. Available at: http://www.nationalcrimeagency.gov.uk/publications/826-suspicious-activity-reports-annual-report-2017/file [Accessed 10 October 2017].

National Crime Agency (2018) *UK Financial Intelligence Unit*. Available at: http://www.nationalcrimeagency.gov.uk/about-us/what-we-do/economic-crime/ukfiu [Accessed 23 May 2018].

National Crime Agency (2018b) *Joint Money Laundering Intelligence Task Force*. Available at: http://www.nationalcrimeagency.gov.uk/about-us/what-we-do/economic-crime/joint-money-laundering-intelligence-taskforce-jmlit [Accessed 11 June 2018].

National Crime Agency (2018c) *National Strategic Assessment of Serious and Organised Crime 2018*. [pdf] Available at: https://nationalcrimeagency.gov.uk/who-we-are/publications/173-national-strategic-assessment-of-serious-and-organised-crime-2018/file [Accessed 27 June 2018].

National Crime Agency (2018d) *SARs Regime Good Practice. Frequently Asked Questions Defence Against Money Laundering*. [pdf] Available at: http://www.nationalcrimeagency.gov.uk/publications/902-defence-against-money-laundering-faq-may-2018/file [Accessed 29 June 2018].

National Crime Agency (2018e) *NCA Secures First Unexplained Wealth Orders*. Available at: http://www.nationalcrimeagency.gov.uk/news/1297-nca-secures-first-unexplained-wealth-orders [Accessed 04 June 2018].

National Crime Agency (2018f) *Suspicious Activity Reports (SARs) Annual Report 2018*. [pdf] Available at: https://nationalcrimeagency.gov.uk/who-we-are/publications/256-2018-sars-annual-report/file [Accessed 22 May 2019].

National Crime Agency (2019) *Financial Investigation*. [pdf] Available at: https://nationalcrimeagency.gov.uk/what-we-do/how-we-work/investigating-and-disrupting-the-highest-risk-serious-and-organised-criminals/criminal-asset-denial/financial-investigation-training-courses [Accessed 13 May 2019].

National Crime Agency (2019a) *Suspicious Activity Reports*. Available at: https://nationalcrimeagency.gov.uk/what-we-do/crime-threats/money-laundering-and-terrorist-financing/suspicious-activity-reports [Accessed 22 May 2019].

National Crime Agency (2019c) *National Economic Crime Centre Leads Push to Identify Money Laundering Activity*. Available at: https://nationalcrimeagency.gov.uk/news/national-economic-crime-centre-leads-push-to-identify-money-laundering-activity [Accessed 27 May 2019].

National Crime Agency (2019d) *National Strategic Assessment of Serious and Organised Crime.* [pdf] Available at: https://nationalcrimeagency.gov.uk/who-we-are/publications/296-national-strategic-assessment-of-serious-organised-crime-2019/file [Accessed 05 June 2019].

National Crime Agency (2019f) *National Economic Crime Centre.* Available at: https://nationalcrimeagency.gov.uk/what-we-do/national-economic-crime-centre?view=article&id=43:current-vacancies&catid=10 [Accessed 18 June 2019].

National Crime Agency (2020b) *Financial Investigation Training Courses.* Available at: https://www.nationalcrimeagency.gov.uk/what-we-do/how-we-work/investigating-and-disrupting-the-highest-risk-serious-and-organised-criminals/criminal-asset-denial/financial-investigation-training-courses [Accessed 29 July 2020].

National Crime Agency (2023) *Suspicious Activity Reports (SARs) Annual Report 2022.* Available at: https://www.nationalcrimeagency.gov.uk/news/suspicious-activity-report-sars-annual-report-2022 [Accessed 26 March 2024].

National Crime Agency (2024) *Cyber Choices.* Available at: https://nationalcrimeagency.gov.uk/cyber-choices [Accessed 26 April 2024].

National Financial Intelligence Working Group (2011) *Agreed Working Definition of 'Financial Investigation'.* Unpublished.

National Fraud Authority (2011) *Fighting Fraud Together* [pdf] Available at: https://assets.publishing.service.gov.uk/government/uploads/system/uploads/attachment_data/file/118501/fighting-fraud-together.pdf [Accessed 16 September 2016].

National Fraud Authority (2013) *Annual Fraud Indicator.* [pdf] Available at: https://assets.publishing.service.gov.uk/government/uploads/system/uploads/attachment_data/file/206552/nfa-annual-fraud-indicator-2013.pdf [Accessed 16 September 2016].

National Police Chiefs Council (2016) *Financial Investigation and Proceeds of Crime Portfolio- written evidence.* [pdf] Available at: https://www.parliament.uk/business/committees/committees-a-z/commons-select/home-affairs-committee/inquiries/parliament-2015/proceeds-of-crime/publications/ [Accessed 07 June 2018].

National Police Chief's Council (2019) *Dedicated Cybercrime Units Get Million Pound Cash Injection.* Available at: https://news.npcc.police.uk/releases/dedicated-cybercrime-units-get-million-pound-cash-injection#:~:text=as%20part%20of%20the%20Team,being%20drawn%20into%20committing%20cybercrime. [Accessed 28 April 2024].

National Policing Improvement Agency (2008) *Practice Advice on the Management and Use of Proceeds of Crime Legislation.* [pdf] Available at: http://library.college.police.uk/docs/npia/Proceeds-of-crime-2008.pdf [Accessed 01 May 2016].

Naylor, R. T. (2003) Towards a General Theory of Profit Driven Crimes. *British Journal of Criminology*, Vol. 43, pp. 81–101.

Naylor, R. T. (2004) *Wages of Crime. Black Markets, Illegal Finance and the Underworld Economy.* London: Cornell University Press.

Nevitt, P. (2013) We Must Bring an End to Information Silos. [pdf] *Police Oracle.* Available at: https://www.policeoracle.com/news/Investigation/2013/Nov/27/Viewpoint-We-must-bring-an-end-to-information-silos_74082.html/specialist [Accessed 10 May 2018].

Ngai, G. (2012) Money Laundering. *American Criminal Law Review*, Vol. 49, No. 2, pp 1011–1036. Available at: https://www.ncjrs.gov/App/Publications/abstract.aspx?ID=262059 [Accessed 20 April 2018].

Northumbria Police (2009) *Operation Payback 3.* Available at: http://www.northumbria.police.uk/z_unpublished_content_archive/payback3/ [Accessed 27 June 2018].

Nottinghamshire Police (2018) *Freedom of Information Request 005432/14.* [pdf] Available at: https://www.nottinghamshire.police.uk/sites/default/files/documents/files/FOI%20005432%2014.pdf [Accessed 20 June 2018].

Nyholm, H., Monteith, K., Lyles, S., Gallegos, M., De Santis, M., Donaldson, J., and Taylor, C. (2022) The Evolution of Volatile Memory Forensics. *Journal of Cybersecurity and Privacy,* Vol. 2, No. 3, pp. 556–572. Available at: https://www.mdpi.com/2624-800X/2/3/28 [Accessed 26 April 2024].

Office for National Statistics (2014) *Police Workforce, England and Wales, 31 March 2014.* [pdf] Available at: https://www.gov.uk/government/publications/police-workforce-england-and-wales-31-march-2014/police-workforce-england-and-wales-31-march-2014 [Accessed 01 October 2015].

Office for National Statistics (2015) *Crime in England and Wales – Year Ending March 2015.* [pdf] Available at: http://www.ons.gov.uk/ons/rel/crime-stats/crime-statistics/year-ending-june-2015/index.html [Accessed 10 October 2015].

Office for National Statistics (2016) *Crime in England and Wales: Year Ending June 2016.* [pdf] Available at: https://www.ons.gov.uk/peoplepopulationandcommunity/crimeandjustice/bulletins/crimeinenglandandwales/yearendingjune2016 [Accessed 05 December 2016].

Office for National Statistics (2016a) *Crime in England and Wales: Year Ending Sept 2016.* [pdf] London. Available at: https://www.ons.gov.uk/peoplepopulationandcommunity/crimeandjustice/bulletins/crimeinenglandandwales/yearendingsept2016 [Accessed 14 March 2017].

Office for National Statistics (2023) *Crime in England and Wales: Year Ending March 2023.* Avaialble at: https://www.ons.gov.uk/peoplepopulationandcommunity/crimeandjustice/bulletins/crimeinenglandandwales/yearendingmarch2023 [Accessed 21 March 2024].

Office for National Statistics (2023a) *Crime in England and Wales: Year Ending June 2023.* Available at: https://www.ons.gov.uk/peoplepopulationandcommunity/crimeandjustice/bulletins/crimeinenglandandwales/yearendingjune2023#:~:text=Computer%20misuse,-The%20Crime%20Survey&text=The%20latest%20CSEW%20estimates%20showed%20that%20fewer%20than%20one%20in,850%2C000%20offences%20of%20computer%20misuse [Accessed 24 April 2024].

O'Nwafor, A. (2013) Corporate Criminal Responsibility. [pdf] *Journal of African Law*. Vol. 57, No. 1, pp. 81–107. Available at: https://www.cambridge.org/core/journals/journal-of-african-law/article/corporate-criminal-responsibility-a-comparative-analysis/1520B222AD93A5B0436459D3E0870344 [Accessed 10 May 2018].

Parliament UK (2018) *Economic Crime Inquiry Launched.* Available at: https://www.parliament.uk/business/committees/committees-a-z/commons-select/treasury-committee/news-parliament-2017/economic-crime-launch-17-19/ [Accessed 30 January 2018].

Pascual, D. S. R. (2017) Measuring Organised Crime: Complexities of the Quantitative and Factorial Analysis. In: H. L. Larsen, J. M. Blanco, R. P. Pastor, and R. R. Yager, eds. *Using Open Data to Detect Organised Crime Threats*. New York: Springer International Publishing, pp. 25–44.

Platt, S. (2015) *Criminal Capital: How the Finance Industry Facilitates Crime*. Hampshire: Palgrave Macmillan.

Police and Crime Commissioners' Treasurers' Society (2012) *Police Authorities: How They Were Established and Their Role in Policing*. [pdf] Available at: https://paccts.org.uk/uploads/files/the.../police_authorities_-_paccts_briefing.doc [Accessed 18 June 2018].

Price Waterhouse Cooper (2016) Adjusting the Lens on Economic Crime. *Global Economic Crime Survey*. [pdf] Available at: https://www.pwc.com/gx/en/economic-crime-survey/pdf/GlobalEconomicCrimeSurvey2016.pdf [Accessed 16 February 2017].

Price Waterhouse Cooper (2018) Pulling Fraud out of the Shadows. *Global and Economic Crime Survey*. [pdf] Available at: https://www.pwc.com/gx/en/forensics/global-economic-crime-and-fraud-survey-2018.pdf [Accessed 03 May 2018].

Public Bill Committee (2001) *Clause 3 Accreditation and Training Proceeds of Crime Bill*. [pdf] Available at: https://www.theyworkforyou.com/pbc/2001-02/Proceeds_of_Crime_Bill/02-0_2001-11-13a.3.0 [Accessed 03 October 2016].

Quinney, E. R. (1964) The Study of White-Collar Crime: Toward a Reorientation in Theory and Research. [pdf] *Journal of Criminal Law, Criminology and Police Science*, Vol. 55, June, pp. 208–214. Available at: http://scholarlycommons.law.northwestern.edu/cgi/viewcontent.cgi?article=5230&context=jclc [Accessed 07 September 2015].

Quirk, P. J. (1997) *Money Laundering: Muddying the Macroeconomy*. [pdf] Finance and Development. Washington: International Monetary Fund. Available at: https://www.imf.org/external/pubs/ft/fandd/1997/03/pdf/quirk.pdf [Accessed 20 April 2018].

Ratcliffe, J. H. (2009) *Strategic Thinking in Criminal Intelligence*. 2nd edition. Sydney: The Federation Press.

Ratcliffe, J. (2010) Intelligence-led Policing and the Problems of Turning Rhetoric into Practice. *Policing and Society*, Vol 12, No. 1, pp. 53–66. Available at: https://www.tandfonline.com/doi/abs/10.1080/10439460290006673?src=recsys [Accessed 21 February 2020].

Rawlinson, P. (2016) Organised Crime Mythologies. [pdf] *Criminology and Criminal Justice*. Oxford Research Encyclopedias. Available at: http://criminology.oxfordre.com/view/10.1093/acrefore/9780190264079.001.0001/acrefore-9780190264079-e-157?result=73&rskey=5U9vhR [Accessed 27 April 2016].

Reuter, P. and Truman, M. (2004) *Chasing Dirty Money: The Fight against Money Laundering*. Washington, DC: Peterson Institute for International Economics.

Richards, J. (2010) *The Art and Science of Intelligence Analysis*. Oxford: Oxford University Press.

Rider, B. (2009) *Market Abuse and Insider Dealing*. Indiana: Tottel Publishing Limited.

Robinson, J. (1998) *The Laundrymen*. London: Pocket Books.

Rowley, M. (2021) *Open Source Intelligence: The Cinderella of the Investigative Family?* Available at: https://www.police-foundation.org.uk/2021/10/open-source-intelligence-the-cinderella-of-the-investigative-family/ [Accessed 14 May 2024].

Royal United Services Institute (2019) *Welcome to RUSI*. Available at: https://rusi.org/ [Accessed 23 December 2019].

Rudner, M. (2004) Hunters and Gatherers: The Intelligence Coalition Against Islamic Terrorism. *International Journal of Intelligence and Counter-Intelligence*, No. 17, pp. 193–230. Available at: https://www.tandfonline.com/doi/abs/10.1080/08850600490274890 [Accessed 20 July 2020].

R v Cuthbertson [1981] AC 470;2 All ER. 401

(R (Virgin Media Ltd) v Zinga [2014] EWCA Crim 52, [2014] All ER (D) 211 (Jan)

Ryder, N. (2013) To Confiscate or Not to Confiscate? A Comparative Analysis of the Confiscation of the Proceeds of Crime Legislation in the United States of America and the United Kingdom. *Journal of Business Law*, No. 8, pp. 767–798.

Ryder, N. (2014) The Good, the Bad and the Downright Ugly. *Criminal Lawyer*, Vol. 221. pp. 5–6.

Ryder, N. (2018) *Is There Something Missing? Terror Finances and the UK Review of Economic Crime*. [pdf] Centre for Research and Evidence on Security Threats. Lancaster. Lancaster University. Available at: https://crestresearch.ac.uk/comment/economic-crime-ryder/ [Accessed 30 April 2018].

Saviano, R. (2012) *Italy's other Mafia*. Gomorrah. London: Picador.

Schelling, T. (1984) *Choice and Consequence*. Cambridge, MA: Harvard University Press.

Schneider, F., and Enste, D. H. (2013) *The Shadow Economy: An International Survey*. Cambridge: Cambridge University Press.

Scottish Government (2009) *Independent Review of Policing*. Available at: https://www2.gov.scot/Publications/2009/01/23133505/0 [Accessed 6 May 2017].

Shapiro, S. P. (1990) Collaring the Crime, not the Criminal: Re-considering the Concept of White-collar Crime. [pdf] *American Sociological Review*, Vol. 55, pp. 346–365. Available at: http://psycnet.apa.org/doi/10.2307/2095761 [Accessed 27 September 2015].

Sheptycki, J. (2009) Policing, Intelligence Theory and the New Human Security Paradigm. In: P. Gill, S. Marrin, and M. Pythian, eds. *Intelligence Theory: Key Questions and Debates*. New York: Routledge, Taylor and Francis Group.

Shore, H. (2015) *London's Criminal Underworlds, c.1720 – 1930. A Social and Cultural History*. London: Palgrave Macmillan.

Smith, R. (2009) A Call for the Integration of 'Biographical Intelligence' into the National Intelligence Model. *Policing: A Journal of Policy and Practice*, Vol. 3, No. 2, pp. 191–199.

Sparks, R. (1996) Penal Austerity: The Doctrine of Less Eligibility Reborn. In: R. Matthews and P. Francis, eds. *Prisons 2000: An International Perspective on the Current State and Future of Imprisonment*, pp. 74–93. London: Palgrave MacMillan.

Sproat, P. A. (2009) To What Extent Is the UK's Anti-money Laundering and Asset Recovery Regime Used against Organised Crime? *Journal of Money Laundering Control,* Vol 12, No. 2, pp. 134–150.

Staniforth, A. (2017) *Blackstone's Handbook of Cyber Crime Investigation*. Oxford: Oxford University Press.

Suleh-Yusuf, M. (2017) Corporate Criminal Liability: Reviewing the Adequacy of Wilful Blindness of Mens Rea. [pdf] *International Journal of Law*, Vol. 3, No. 2, pp. 24–32. Available at: http://www.lawjournals.org/archives/2017/vol3/issue2/3-2-12 [Accessed 10 December 2017].

Sutherland, E. H. (1940) The White-Collar Criminal. *American Sociological Review*, Vol. 5, No. 1, pp. 1–12.

Taylor, D. (1998) *Crime, Policing and Punishment in England, 1750–1914*. London: MacMillan Press Ltd.

Tett, G. (2016) *The Silo Effect*. London: Abacus.

Thames Valley Police (2018) *Departments and Teams*. Available at: https://www.thamesvalley.police.uk/about-us/who-we-are/departments/ [Accessed 20 June 2018].

Tolkovsky, N. (2018) *The 'Duality of Fraud'*. Available at: http://hdl.handle.net/10545/623029 [Accessed 20 August 2020].

Tor2Web (2024) *Tor2Web Browser*. Available at: https://www.tor2web.org/ [Accessed 29 April 2024].

TorMetrics (2024) *Users*. Available at: https://metrics.torproject.org/userstats-relay-table.html?start=2023-1-01&end=2024-01-01 [Accessed 30 April 2024].

Tor Project research (2024) *Home Page*. Available at: https://research.torproject.org/ [Accessed 29 April 2024].

Transparency International (2015) *Curbing Illicit Financial Flows to Unlock a Sustainable Future*. [pdf] Available at: https://www.transparency.org/whatwedo/publication/curbing_illicit_financial_flows_to_unlock_a_sustainable_future [Accessed 09 September 2017].

Transparency International (2015a) *Corruption on Your Doorstep. How Corrupt Capital Is Used to Buy Capital in the UK*. [pdf] Available at: http://www.transparency.org.uk/publications/corruption-on-your-doorstep/#.Wg3G1LacZsY [Accessed 10 September 2017].

Transparency International (2016*) New Asset Recovery Powers for Law Enforcement* [pdf] Available at: http://www.transparency.org.uk/publications/new-asset-recovery-powers-for-law-enforcement/#.Wg3D7bacZsY [Accessed 16 November 2017].

Transparency International (2017) *Transparency International UK*. Available at: http://www.transparency.org.uk [Accessed 25 April 2017].

Transparency International (2017a) *Corruption Perceptions Index 2017*. Available at: https://www.transparency.org/news/feature/corruption_perceptions_index_2017 [Accessed 24 May 2018].

Transparency International (2017b) *Anti-Money Laundering. G20 Position Paper*. [pdf] Available at: https://www.transparency.org/whatwedo/publication/g20_position_paper_open_data_and_corruption_2017 [Accessed 18 June 2018].

Transparency International (2017c) *Faulty Towers. Understanding the Impact of Overseas Corruption on the London Property Market*. [pdf] Available at: http://www.transparency.org.uk/publications/faulty-towers-understanding-the-impact-of-overseas-corruption-on-the-london-property-market/#.WzM2yiDTVjE [Accessed 27 June 2018].

Transparency International (2017d) *HM Treasury's Consultation on Money Laundering Regulations 2017*. Available at: https//www.transparency.org.uk [Accessed 28 June 2018].

Transparency International (2018) *Unexplained Wealth Orders in Use: Here's at Least 5 Cases the Police Should Consider Today!* Available at: http://www.transparency.org.uk/uwo-consider-today/#.WznSfbjTVjE [Accessed 02 July 2018].

Traversals (2024) *Surface Web Is Only the Tip of the Iceberg*. Available at: https://traversals.com/blog/surface-web/ [Accessed 29 April 2024].

UK Parliament (2009) *Memorandum by the Association of Chief Police Officers of England, Wales and Northern Ireland (ACPO) – Enquiry into Money Laundering and the Financing of Terrorism.* Available at: https://publications.parliament.uk/pa/ld200809/ldselect/ldeucom/132/132we02.htm [Accessed 24 May 2018].

United Nations (1988) *Convention Against Illicit Traffic in Narcotic Drugs and Psychotropic Substances* [pdf] Available at: www.unodc.org/pdf/convention_1988_en.pdf [Accessed 06 September 2016].

United Nations (2016) *Organised Crime.* Available at: https://www.unodc.org/unodc/ar/organized-crime/index.html [Accessed 18 June 2017].

United Nations Office on Drugs and Crime (1999) International Convention for the Suppression of the Financing of Terrorism. Available at: https://www.unodc.org/documents/treaties/Special/1999%20International%20Convention%20for%20the%20Suppression%20of%20the%20Financing%20of%20Terrorism.pdf [Accessed 29 October 2024].

United Nations Office on Drugs and Crime (2002) *International Convention for the Suppression of the Financing of Terrorism.* Available at: https://www.unodc.org/documents/treaties/Special/1999%20International%20Convention%20for%20the%20Suppression%20of%20the%20Financing%20of%20Terrorism.pdf [Accessed 12 August 2017].

United Nations Office on Drugs and Crime (2004) *United Nations Convention Against Corruption.* [pdf]. Available at: https://www.unodc.org/documents/brussels/UN_Convention_Against_Corruption.pdf [Accessed 15 July 2017].

United Nations Office on Drugs and Crime (2004a) *UN Convention against Transnational Organised Crime and the Protocols Thereto.* [pdf] Available at: https://www.unodc.org/unodc/en/treaties/CTOC/ [Accessed 17 July 2017].

United Nations Office on Drugs and Crime (2011) *Estimating Illicit Financial Flows Resulting from Drug Trafficking and other Transnational Organised Crimes.* [pdf] Available at: https://www.unodc.org/documents/data-and analysis/Studies/Illicit_financial_flows_2011_web.pdf [Accessed 02 February 2014].

United Nations Office on Drugs and Crime (2012) *Monitoring the Impact of Economic Crisis on Crime.* [pdf] Available at: https://www.unodc.org/documents/data-and-analysis/statistics/crime/GIVAS_Final_Report.pdf [Accessed 08 May 2018].

United Nations Office on Drugs and Crime (2018) *United Nations Convention on Transnational Organized Crime and the Protocols Thereto.* [pdf] Available at: https://www.unodc.org/unodc/en/organized-crime/intro/UNTOC.html#Fulltext [Accessed 13 April 2018].

United Nations Office on Drugs and Crime (2023) *Use of the Dark Web and Social Media for Drug Supply.* Available at: https://www.unodc.org/res/WDR-2023/WDR23_B3_CH7_darkweb.pdf [Accessed 30 April 2024].

United States White House (2011) *Strategy to Combat Transnational Organised Crime.* [pdf] Available at: https://obamawhitehouse.archives.gov/sites/default/files/Strategy_to_Combat_Transnational_Organized_Crime_July_2011.pdf [Accessed 24 April 2018].

University of Portsmouth, Experian and PKF Litteljohn LLP (2016) *'Annual Fraud Indicator 2016'.* [pdf] Available at: http://www.experian.co.uk/assets/identity-and-fraud/pkfexperian-fraud-indicator-report.pdf [Accessed 13 March 2017].

van Duyne, P. C., and Levi, M. (1999) Criminal Financial Investigation: A Strategic and Tactical Approach at a European Level. *Transnational Organized Crime,* Vol. 5, No. 1, Spring, pp. 37–66. London: Frank Cass.

van Duyne, P. C., and Nelemans, M. D. H. (2012) Transnational Organised Crime. Thinking in and out of Plato's cave. In: F. Allum and S. Gilmour, eds. *Routledge Handbook of Transnational Organised Crime*. London: Routledge, pp. 36–51.

van Duyne, P. C., Pheijffer, M., Kuijl, H. G., van Dijk, A. Th. H., and Bakker, G. J. C. M. (2003) *Financial Investigation of Crime*. Wolf Legal Publishers: Nijmegen.

van Duyne, P. C., and Van Dijck, M. (2007) Assessing Organised Crime: The Sad State of the Impossible Art. In: F. Bovenkerk and M. Levi, eds. *The Organised Crime Economy Essays in Honour of Alan Block*. New York: Springer, pp. 101–124.

von Lampe, K. (2012) *Definitions of Organised Crime*. [pdf] Government of Quebec. Available at: https://www.ceic.gouv.qc.ca/fileadmin/Fichiers_client/centre_documentaire/CEIC-R-3538.pdf [Accessed 27 April 2018].

Warner, M. (2002) *Wanted- A Definition of "Intelligence"*. Studies in Intelligence 46/3. [pdf] Washington: CIA. Available at: https://www.cia.gov/library/center-for-the-study-of-intelligence/csi-publications/csi-studies/studies/vol46no3/article02.html [Accessed 12 November 2017].

Wall, D. S. (2008). Cybercrime, Media and Insecurity: The Shaping of Public Perceptions of Cybercrime1. *International Review of Law, Computers & Technology*, Vol. 22, No. 1–2, pp. 45–63. Available at: https://doi.org/10.1080/13600860801924907 [Accessed 26 April 2024].

Wood, H. (2016) *Enforcing Criminal Confiscation Orders. From Policy to Practice.* [pdf] London: Royal United Services Institute. Available at: https://rusi.org/sites/default/files/201602_op_enforcing_criminal_confiscation_orders.pdf [Accessed 16 September 2017].

Wood, H. (2017) *Every Transaction Leaves a Trace. The Role of Financial Investigation in Serious and Organised Crime Policing*. [pdf] London: Royal United Services Institute. Available at: https://rusi.org/sites/default/files/201709_rusi_everytransactionleavesatrace_wood_web.pdf [Accessed 18 April 2018].

Woodiwiss, M. (2001) *Organised Crime and American Power: A History*. Toronto: Toronto University Press.

Woodiwiss, M. (2003) Transnational Organised Crime: The Strange Career of an American Concept. In: M. E. Beare, ed. *Critical Reflections on Transnational Organised Crime, Money Laundering and Corruption*, pp. 1–34. Toronto: University of Toronto.

Woodiwiss, M., and Hobbs, D. (2008) Organised Evil and the Atlantic Alliance: Moral Panics and the Rhetoric of Organised Crime Policing in America and Britain. [pdf] *The British Journal of Criminology*, Vol. 49, No. 1, pp. 106–128. Available at: https://academic.oup.com/bjc/article/49/1/106/374864 [Accessed 26 April 2018].

Wright, A. (2013) *Organised Crime*. Oxon: Routledge.

Yar, M. (2013) *Cybercrime and Society*. 2nd edition. London: Sage Publishing.

Zavrsnik, A. (2014) Cybercrime-Definitional Challenges and Criminological Particularities. [pdf] *Masaryk University Journal of Law and Technology*, pp. 1–29. Available at: https://journals.muni.cz/mujlt/article/view/2506 [Accessed 10 May 2018].

United Kingdom Statutes

Anti-Terrorism, Crime and Security Act 2001, c. 24. London: The Stationery Office.

Computer Misuse Act 1990, c. 18. London: The Stationery Office.

Coroners and Justice Act 2009, c. 25. London: The Stationery Office.
Crime and Courts Act 2013, c. 22. London: The Stationery Office.
Criminal Finances Act 2017, c. 22. London: The Stationery Office.
Criminal Justice Act 1988, c. 33. London: The Stationery Office.
Criminal Justice Act 1993, c. 36. London: The Stationery Office.
Criminal Justice (International Co-operation) Act 1990, c. 5. London: The Stationery Office.
Data Protection Act 1998, c. 29. London: The Stationery Office.
Data Protection Act 2018, c. 12. London: The Stationery Office
Drug Trafficking Act 1994, c. 37. London: The Stationery Office.
Drug Trafficking Offences Act 1986, c. 32. London: The Stationery Office.
Enterprise Act 2002, c. 40. London: The Stationery Office.
Financial Services and Markets Act 2000, c. 8. London: The Stationery Office.
Fraud Act 2006, c. 35. London: The Stationery Office.
General Data Protection Regulations 2018, Regulation (EU) 2016/679. Brussels: European Union.
Human Rights Act 1998, c. 42. London: The Stationery Office.
Misuse of Drugs Act 1971, c. 38. London: The Stationery Office.
Modern Slavery Act 2015, c. 30. London: The Stationery Office.
Money Laundering and Terrorist Financing (Amendment) Regulations 2019, No1511. London: The Stationery Office.
Police and Criminal Evidence Act 1984, c. 60. London: The Stationery Office.
Police Reform and Social Responsibility Act 2011, c. 13. London: The Stationery Office.
Proceeds of Crime Act 2002, c. 29. London: The Stationery Office.
Serious Crime Act 2007, c. 27. London: The Stationery Office.
Serious Crime Act 2015, c. 9. London: The Stationery Office.
Theft Act 1968, c. 60. London: The Stationery Office.

United States of America Statutes

Annunzio-Wylie Anti-Money Laundering Act of 1992, ss U.S.C. 102–550 (1992)
Anti-Drug Abuse Act of 1988, ss U.S.C.100–690 (1988)
Bank Secrecy Act of 1970, Titles I and II of Public Law 91–508 (1970)
Money Laundering Control Act 1986, ss U.S.C. 1956/1957 (1986)
Racketeer Influenced and Corrupt Organisations Act of 1970, 18, ss U.S.C. 91–452 (1961)
Uniting and Strengthening America by Providing Appropriate Tools Required to Intercept and Obstruct Terrorism (USA PATRIOT) Act of 2001, ss U.S.C. 107–156 (2001)

United Kingdom Cases

Fletcher v Chief Constable of Leicestershire: [2013] EWHC 3357 (Admin)
Iqbal (R on the application of) v Luton &South Bedfordshire Magistrates Court [2011] EWHC 705 (Admin)
R v Cuthbertson [1981] AC 470;2 All ER. 401

United Kingdom Statutory Instruments

Proceeds of Crime Act 2002 (Recovery of Cash in Summary Proceedings: Minimum Amount) Order (S.I. 2004/420). London: The Stationery Office.

Proceeds of Crime Act 2002 (Recovery of Cash in Summary Proceedings: Minimum Amount) Order 2006 (S.I. 2006/1699). London: The Stationery Office.
The Money Laundering Regulations 2007 (S.I. 2007/2157). London: The Stationery Office.
The Money Laundering, Terrorist Financing and Transfer of Funds (Information on the Payer) Regulations 2017 (S.I. 2017/692). London: The Stationery Office.

Legislation

NB: for ease of reference this list is in alphabetical order rather than chronological.

Code of Practice issued under section 377 of the Proceeds of Crime Act 2002. Investigations (March 2016)
Codes of Practice issued under section 47S of the Proceeds of Crime Act 2002 (Search, seizure and detention of property in England and Wales) (March 2016)
Codes of Practice issued under section 292 of the Proceeds of Crime Act 2002. Recovery of cash: Search Powers (March 2016)
Companies Act 2006
Counter Terrorism and Security Act 2015
Crime and Courts Act 2013
Crime (International Co-operation) Act 2003
Crime and Police Act 2000
Criminal Finances Act 2017
Criminal Justice Act 1987
Criminal Justice Act 1988
Criminal Justice and Police Act 2001
Criminal Procedure and Investigations Act 1996
Criminal Justice and Public Order Act 1994
Customs and Excise Management Act 1979
Data Protection Act 1998
Data Protection Act 2003
Drug Trafficking Act 1994, c. 37. London: The Stationery Office
Drug Trafficking Offences Act 1986
Enterprise Act 2002
Financial Services and Markets Act 2000
Fraud Act 2006
General Data Protection Regulations 2018
Human Rights Act 1998
Law Enforcement Directive 2018
Legislation.gov.uk (2009) The Proceeds of Crime Act 2002 (References to Financial Investigation (Amendment) Order 2009: UK statutory instrument 2009 No 2707 Article 1).
Misuse of Drugs Act 1971
Police and Criminal Evidence Act 1984
Police Property Act 1987
Police (Property) Act 1997
Proceeds of Crime Act 1995
Proceeds of Crime Act 2002
Serious Crime Act 2007
Serious Crime Act 2015

Terrorism Act 2000
The Criminal Law Act 1977
The Money Laundering (Amendment) Regulations 2012
The Money Laundering (Amendment) Regulations 2015
The Money Laundering Regulations 2007. Statutory Instrument 2007/2157.
The Money Laundering, Terrorist Financing and Transfer of Funds (Information on the Payer) Regulations 2017. Statutory Instrument 2017/692.
The Proceeds of Crime Act 2002 (Recovery of Cash in Summary Proceedings: Minimum Amount) Order 2004 SI 2004/420.
The Proceeds of Crime Act 2002 (Recovery of Cash in Summary Proceedings: Minimum Amount) Order 2006 SI 2006/1699.
The Proceeds of Crime Act 2002 (References to Financial Investigators) (Amendment) Order 2009 SI 2009/2707.
The Theft Act 1968

United Kingdom Case Law

Montila [2004] UKHL 50; [2005] 1 Cr. App. R. 26
R v Cuthbertson [1981] AC 470;2 All ER. 401
R v Layode 1993
R v May [2008] UKHL 28
R (on a prosecution by Mirchandani) v Somaia [2017] EWCA Crim 741, [2017] All *ER (D)* 66 (Jun)
R v Vernon 1993
R v Waya [2010] EWCA Crim 412

Appendix 1

Table of proceeds of Crime Court Orders

POCA investigation orders and powers	*Description*
Restraint order. Section 41 POCA. Only confiscation trained AFI to obtain.	Court order issued at any time in an investigation to restrain assets of a suspect and prevent dissipation before sentence.
Civil recovery powers. Part 5 POCA, sections 240 to 288.	Civil recovery applications are made in the High Court and only by Director of Public Prosecutions, Director of Serious Fraud Office and Director of NCA. All POCA orders can be used for investigation.
Cash detention powers. Section 289 POCA.	Powers which allow seizure of cash suspected to be in excess of £1,000 and may be dealt with by way of civil hearing at magistrate's court separately to any other proceedings.
Account freezing order. Section 303Z3 POCA as amended by Criminal Finances Act (2017)	Order granted if satisfied that money in account is suspected of being recoverable property or intended for use in criminal conduct. Minimum account is £1,000.
Revenue functions: taxation powers. Part 6 POCA sections 317 to 326.	Allows a tax assessment to be made where source of income is identified and suspected to be of criminal origin. Includes provenance of assets. Powers only exercisable by NCA.
Production order. Section 345 POCA.	Order granted by a Crown Court and served on the holder of required information which otherwise could not be obtained.
Order to grant entry. Section 347 POCA	Order granting entry (such as to a block of flats) where a production order is to be served.
Search and seizure warrant. Section 352 POCA.	A search warrant to gain entry and search a premises for material specified in the warrant.
Disclosure order. Section 357 POCA, amended by Criminal Finances Act (2017).	Order granted by a High Court which may require a person to answer questions at a specified time and place or to provide information as specified in the order by a specified time or at a specified place. Can now be used for money laundering investigations.

POCA investigation orders and powers	*Description*
Customer information order. Section 363 POCA.	Order granted by a Crown Court to determine whether unidentified accounts exist and request core details of individuals or companies.
Unexplained wealth order. Section 362A POCA amended by Criminal Finances Act 2017 and Part1 Serious Crime Act 2007 (test for serious crime).	Granted by the High Court, an order served on an individual or company if identified funds are suspected of being criminal property usually from abroad involving "politically exposed persons". It is a civil power and investigation tool.
Account monitoring order. Section 370 POCA.	Order granted by a Crown Court allowing the holder of information or expected information to liaise "real-time" with the investigating officer for a period of up to 90 days from the data of the order.
Section 55 production order. Preserved power under Drug Trafficking Act 1994.	Order granted by a Crown Court for drug trafficking investigations only.

Appendix 2

"Culture of control" (Garland, 1996, 2001) considerations

Proceeds of crime	*Sovereign state strategy*	*Adaptive/denial strategy*
POCA 2002 was the watershed which drew previous legislation under one Act, created for money laundering offences and cash detention. Civil recovery was introduced for the first time.	Assets Recovery Agency formed as a political statement. Negatively affected by target driven environment which led to its demise in 2008.	Alongside the adaptations there is a recurring attempt to evade its terms altogether particularly on the part of elected officials who play an increasingly prominent role in criminal justice policy making. This politicised reaction takes two recurring forms. Either it wilfully denies the predicament and re-asserts the old myth of the sovereign state and its plenary powers to punish. Or else it abandons reasoned, instrumental action and retreats into an expressive mode that can be described as acting out – a mode that is concerned not so much with controlling crime as with expressing the anger and outrage that crime provokes (Garland, 2001:110).
Money laundering regulations.	Devised as a reaction to a money laundering problem which has recently been acknowledged to be in excess of £100 billion per annum in London alone despite the regulations.	Constant denial of the problem as there is no realistic estimate of the size of the problem. Nor is there a combative stance to affect it although now the portfolio of the new NECC is in NCA.

Proceeds of crime	*Sovereign state strategy*	*Adaptive/denial strategy*
Suspicious activity reports (SARs).	The financial sector has no option other than to comply. Any suspicious activity (undefined) MUST be reported by way of a SAR.	The number of SARs outweighs their probative value. There are too many of them, now in excess of 600,000 per year and largely not dealt with by law enforcement. Arguably moved into realm of denial strategy because of adverse publicity about excess numbers and poor uptake by law enforcement. Triage system now in place to manage SAR numbers. Relatively ineffective except to act as a library of information which can be checked for any investigation. Rarely used proactively.
Confiscation provisions (POCA).	Recognised as draconian legislation. Targets benefit from criminality (not profit), originating with drug trafficking offences as a result of Hodgson Report in 1984. Legislation arguably a politicised reaction to publicity of drugs epidemic in late 1970s and early 1980s. Makes a big political statement that crime will not pay and has a toolbox to penetrate privacy legislation.	Parliamentary Accounts Committee (PAC) in 2013 completed an assessment of the confiscation regime and found it to be wholly ineffective. 26 pence recovered in every £100.
Money laundering offences under POCA 2002.		Can be considered an adaptive response to the problem of criminal property. Handling was not working and money laundering applies to all property.

Proceeds of crime	*Sovereign state strategy*	*Adaptive/denial strategy*
Default sentence after confiscation hearing (POCA).	Offenders can receive up to 12 years imprisonment to run consecutive to their main sentence if they do not pay a confiscation order within a time allocated by the court. However, default sentences are notorious for not being followed up on (Wood, 2017).	Section 22 re-visits under POCA have been largely ignored until recently when it has been realised that if there is an outstanding confiscation order and the defendant has acquired new assets then they can be seized/ restrained for the original debt which remains for life. This is arguably a way to deny the impotency of the default sentence and publicise results as part of Garland's denial theory.
Unexplained wealth orders (Criminal Justice Act).	New orders in response to highly publicised money laundering from abroad into and through London primarily.	Arguably adaptive response to publicised problem of property being bought in London by foreign persons, the source of funds unexplained. In truth money laundering provisions were adequate but the push for UWOs may have been political to deflect from the problem (denial) and the fact that the UK does not have a national money laundering unit (denial).
Cash detention provisions (POCA).		Strategy to deal with the politicised message that the government was attempting to take the cash out of crime. Overall the average seizure rate has remained around £45 million. It is not prioritised by law enforcement who are still commodity based. Intelligence is not geared to cash, not supported by strategic layer. Yet it is incentivised and apparently under-used (Home Office, 2018e). Information difficult to ascertain due to NCA having responsibility for Joint Asset Recovery Database and immunity from Freedom of Information requests.

Proceeds of crime	*Sovereign state strategy*	*Adaptive/denial strategy*
Regional Asset Recovery Teams (RARTs).	First one set up in 2004 to focus solely upon asset recovery in line with government targets. In theory were the link between police forces and cross border criminals with asset bases to attack (HMIC, HMCPSI, HMMCI, 2004).	Could be argued to have detracted from the ability of the ARA to succeed and choice of name was confusing to law enforcement, even financial investigators.
Regional Organised Crime Units (ROCUs).		Arguably a strategy to focus attention on the fact that mutli-agency co-operation has been achieved to focus on regional cross border criminals. Empirical evidence is still required to demonstrate the effect ROCUs are having. Cases are reportedly difficult for forces to pass to ROCUs and RARTs (now mainly joined) so whether rank and file investigators 'buy in' to the idea is not proven.
Cyber offending.	The sovereign state appears to be at a loss to deal with the problem.	Denial strategy appears to be counting offences in a way which seems to suggest that crime has not increased (in fact the opposite) and computer-based frauds and similar have only started being recorded since 2017 by the National Audit Office (NAO, 2017).

Index

accredited financial investigators (AFI) 1–2, 16, 20–23, 27–28, 33–38, 40, 49, 60, 70–74, 98–99
ACPO *see* Association of Chief Police Officers
acquisitive crime 24, 41, 69, 84–86, 100, 125
Action Fraud 25, 106, 111–112
adaptive strategies *see* culture of control
AFI *see* accredited financial investigators
asset recovery 27–39, 49, 52–54, 68–79, 86–89, 103–105; *see also* confiscation
Assets Recovery Agency 39, 70
Asset Recovery Bulletin 52
asset recovery targets 52; *see also* confiscation
Association of Chief Police Officers 29, 91

Bank Secrecy Act 1970 57–58, 86
Basel Institute 84
Blair, Tony 39, 100
British Banker's Association 43
bullying online 107

capable guardian *see* routine activity theory
cash detention 62–65
City of London Police 20–21
civil recovery 52, 95, 105
College of Policing 31–32, 36, 49–50, 93
Computer Misuse Act (1990) 24–25
concept of financial investigation 7–8, 24, 42, 75, 86, 120–121
confiscation 27–33, 35–48, 50–56, 67, 69–79, 88, 100, 120, 122
consent SAR *see* defence against money laundering
Council of Europe 32
crime survey for England and Wales 22, 25, 41, 59
Criminal Finances Act 2017 55, 88, 95, 98, 102
criminal investigation process 29–33
Criminal Justice Act 1988 57, 79, 85, 94
Criminal Justice Act 1993 85
culture of control 99, 116, 120–122
cyber choices 107
cybercrime 11, 18, 20–26, 106–108, 110–114
cybercrime units 23–25, 107–110, 112
cyber-dependent crime 107
cyber-enabled crime 21, 107

dark web 108–110
data gaps 37–38
deep web 108–109, 111
defence against money laundering page 97
digital environment 106–114
digital footprint 108–109
drug profit confiscation officers 85
drug trafficking 55–57
Drug Trafficking Act 1994 85–86
Drug trafficking Offences Act 1986 49, 78–79, 85
DTA *see* Drug Trafficking Act 1994

economic crime 15–17
Economic Crime (Anti-Money Laundering) Levy 23
Economic Crime Command 17
economic crime units 16
EFIS *see* Enhanced Financial Investigation Skills
Electronic Line Management Enterprise Recording (ELMER) 94

ELMER *see* Electronic Line Management Enterprise Recording
enforcement 53–55
Enhanced Financial Investigation Skills (EFIS) 42
essential characteristics of financial investigation 65–66, 117–126

FATF *see* Financial Action Task Force
Federal Bureau of Investigation 12, 18–19
Financial Action Task Force (FATF) 34–36, 80–84, 99
financial crime 17–19
financial footprint 2–3, 6, 64, 104, 113, 122, 124
financial intelligence 3, 90–105, 110–112, 118–119
financial investigation 28–57, 60–62, 65–67, 71–76, 86–89, 101–105, 113–114, 116–126
financial investigation: integration with the NIM 123
financial investigation: specialists 19
financial investigation: synonym for confiscation 50–52
Financial Investigation Support System 49
financial investigation units 17, 21, 107
Financial Services and Markets Act 2000 18
Financial Services Authority 18
FISS *see* Financial Investigation Support System
forfeiture *see* confiscation
forty recommendations 34, 81–82
fraud 10–11, 15–21, 24–26, 41, 69, 110–112
funding 23, 47, 70–71, 84

Gale, E. 33
Garland, D. *see* culture of control
general investigators 33, 38, 40, 42, 49–50, 63, 67, 103
generic philosophy of financial investigation 124–125
government reports 68–76

Her Majesty's Courts and Tribunals Service 51
Her Majesty's Revenue and Customs 62
HMIC report 2016 48–49
Hodgson Report 79
Home Affairs Committee Review 2016 73–75
hunters and gatherers 104

ICAR *see* Basel Institute
incentivisation scheme 68–72
independent influences 8, 73, 77, 84–89
information technology 48, 94
intelligence 64–65, 90–93, 113, 123
international standards 77–89
internet 11, 21–25, 106–114
internet jurisdiction 112–113

Joint Money Laundering Intelligence Task Force 99

Kelly, J. 33

Law Commission 52–54
Law Commission recommendations *see* Law Commission
limitations 37, 100

Misuse of Drugs Act 1971 77–78
money laundering 11, 13, 16, 25, 34–36, 40–42, 49–50, 55, 57–62, 78–83, 88–89, 94–97, 112
Money Laundering Control Act 1986 13, 58, 87

National Crime Agency (NCA) 22–24, 38, 41, 44, 48, 55, 61, 70, 73–74, 93–98, 107
National Cyber Security Strategy 24
National Economic Crime Centre 70, 82
National Financial Investigation Working Group 91
National Fraud Intelligence Bureau 25
National Intelligence Model 8, 23, 90–93, 118
National Police Improvement Agency 29, 35; *see also* College of Policing
National Policing Curriculum *see* training
National Policing Plan 39
NCA *see* National Crime Agency
NIM *see* National Intelligence Model

Office for National Statistics 21–22, 59, 69
Onion Router (TOR) 109
open-source intelligence *see* OSINT
organised crime 10–15, 22, 37, 83–84, 87
organised crime group (OCG) 12–15

organised crime group mapping 14
OSINT 111–112

Palermo Convention 12–14, 83
Paris 81
Payback Report 40, 71
perceptions 7–26, 33–37, 57, 101–105, 114
phraseology 9–10
PIU Report 87
POCA *see* Proceeds of Crime Act (2002)
Police and Crime Commissioners 46
police authorities 39, 46
policing the internet 110–113
policy 28–33, 66, 81, 83–89
political hinterland 68–70
predicate offence 13, 16, 34, 57, 87, 94
private prosecution 47–48
private sector 17, 47–48
Proceeds of Crime Act (2002) (POCA) 11, 25, 28–29, 35–36, 39–43, 49–50, 52, 54, 57, 61, 68–69, 71, 87–88
proposed definition financial intelligence 103–104
proposed definition financial investigation 103–104

R *v* Cuthbertson 77–78
Racketeer Influenced and Corrupt Organisations Act (RICO) 12–13, 86–87
RAIF *see* incentivisation
RART *see* Regional Assets Recovery Team
recommendations 118–126
Recovered Asset Incentivisation Fund *see* incentivisation
reduction of crime 52, 68–69, 87, 100
Regional Assets Recovery Team (RART) 40
Regional Organised Crime Unit (ROCU) 14, 28, 108
RICO *see* Racketeer Influenced and Corrupt Organisations
ROCU *see* Regional Organised Crime Unit
routine activity theory 112–113
Rudner *see* hunters and gatherers
R *v* Zinga 47

SARs *see* suspicious activity reports
Senior Appropriate Officer 44
serious and organised crime 22–23, 96; *see also* organised crime
Serious and Organised Crime Agency 70
Serious and Organised Crime Strategy 2013 22–23
Serious Crime Act, 2015 2, 101
Serious Fraud Office 51, 73
sovereign state strategy *see* culture of control
surface web 108–110
suspicious activity reports (SARs) 64, 93–99, 102, 118–123
Sutherland, E. 19

Talbot, K. 43
tax evasion 16, 19, 86
terminology 7–26
terrorist financing 61, 81, 83; *see also* money laundering
theoretical considerations *see* culture of control
tin box 40, 68–70, 75; *see also* incentivisation
TOR *see* Onion Router
training 20–21, 36–50, 63–67, 70–75, 83, 93, 110, 115, 118–126
Transparency International 84
typologies 9, 27, 117

UK Financial Intelligence Unit (UKFIU) 97–98
unexplained wealth orders (UWO) 55, 88, 95–96, 102, 122
United Nations Conference Against Corruption 83
United Nations Convention Against Illicit Traffic in Narcotic Drugs and Psychotropic Substances *see* Vienna Convention
United Nations Office for Drugs and Crime (UNODC) 11–12, 81–83
United States (USA) 12–13, 57–58, 82, 86
UNODC *see* United Nations Office on Drugs and Crime
USA *see* United States
UWO *see* unexplained wealth orders

Vienna Convention 58, 79–80
volatile data 111

white collar crime 19–21

Kolibri 360 GmbH
Ferdinand-Jühlke-Straße 7
99095 Erfurt, Deutschland
produktsicherheit@kolibri360.de